Our Voices Matter:
A Community-Based Social Justice Art Exhibition

by

Lakeshore Intergenerational School

Printed in the United States of America

EDITOR: *Christa Boske*

PAGE DESIGNER: *Ashley Mae Pancho*

COVER DESIGNER: *Ashley Mae Pancho*

CONTRIBUTIONS: *ElevatedWaves Publishing Corp.*

PUBLISHER: Arts for Resistance Through Change (A.R.T.-C.)

ISBN (Paperback): ISBN: 979-8-9894744-1-7

Library of Congress Control Number: 2024902352

ART FOR RESISTANCE THROUGH CHANGE

(A.R.T.-C.)

This book is an authentic collaboration among teachers, school leaders, community organizations, K-8 students, families, and Art for Resistance Through Change (ART-C). This artmaking examines the lived experiences of young people. Each student reflected on their sense of self, their lived experiences, and most importantly, what matters to them as young people. The role of emotions throughout this artmaking process inspired young people to utilize their voices, art, and writing to promote social justice-oriented work throughout communities and schools.

Kindergarteners through second graders researched the power of people's names. Each of them learned about what their names meant. Afterward, they wrote poems about their names and experiences that shaped how they understood the world. They translated these understandings into phenomenal self-portraits. Youth reflected on the power they possess, how they make a difference in the world, and the strengths they bring to every community.

Fifth through eighth graders explored topics such as identity, systems thinking, holistic views, marginalization, and the power of voice. Each of them researched topics that interested them. Some of these areas of interest ranged from Black Lives Matter to the use of the "n" word to police brutality to their desire to see more people who look like them in schools (e.g., teachers and school leaders). They researched their justice-oriented topics and translated those interests into written narratives. Next, they planned out their artmaking. Youth identified what each piece of their art symbolized. They supported all of their claims made and provided their audiences with a myriad of resources to engage in this work. Their artmaking involved a plethora of materials and styles.

We hope their artmaking moves you in unexpected ways. Make a difference and join them in their community social justice-oriented work.

ART-C would like to thank *NeighborUp* and the *St. Luke's Foundation* for supporting this significant work.

CONNECT WITH US

on Instagram

@ArtCart4ResistanceThruChange

@ARTCART4RESISTANCETHRUCHANGE

SCAN QR with your smartphone

LISTEN TO OUR

"Voices Matter Young Adults Educational Community Podcast"
(Two Seasons Available)

Spotify

YouTube

Social Justice Issues Tackled by Students in an Art Exhibit
at Akron's Summit Artspace

Ideastream

SCAN QR with your smartphone

TABLE OF CONTENTS

The Very Beginning 01

K-3rd Graders 03

I am a Fighter! I am Strong! - *Madison*

I Like Dinosaurs - *Dinozzo*

I am the Only Me - *Kylon*

I am Dark Beauty - *Laila* 04

My Best Friend Bumblebee - *Avin*

Me - *Morgan*

I Come From Greatness - *Wisdom* 05

I am Beautiful - *McKenzie*

I am Earth Mother - *Demi*

I Light Up a Room and Sparkle - *Jamez*

I am King and Powerful - *King* 06

I Must Be Famous or Something - *Jordyn*

We Fly to the Sky - *Corey*

I Run Fast - *Rayce*

My Name Means "The Light" - *Zaria* 07

I Want to Be the Tooth Fairy When I Grow Up - *Nevaeh*

I am a Green Valley - *Denver*

I Wish I Had More Friends - *Demetrius* 08

The Life of Jaiden - *Jaiden*

All About Me - *Diamond*

I Love Me - *Noah* 09

My Brother and My Best Friend - *Kayden*

This is Me! - *Adam* 10

5-6th Graders 11

Slavery - *Octavia Unique Allen*

Someone in my family told me, "Even though you are Black and other people are White, we all bleed the same color." - *Breylon Amankwah*

TABLE OF CONTENTS

Black Girls Get in More Trouble Than White Girls - *Addison Allen* 12
The Black Hockey Player - *Vincent Nixon*
Black Women are Powerful - *Dominque Watson*
All White Eyes Are On Black Girls: We Should Be Celebrated - *Kamayah Hunter & Kylie Cromity* 13
The History of Slavery - *London Marie D*
Nature Now: The Earth is on Fire - *Caleb Davis*
Mama, Please Save Me! - *Lorenzo Bryant* 14
This is Me - *Colin Floyd*
Black Lives Matters - *Aalayah Brown* 15
"N" Joes - *Donald Chatmon Jr*
Bad Cop - *Jayson Johnson*
Police Brutality. The "N" Word - *Santanah Morton* 16
Can't Afford It - *Mya Gaston*
Black Girls Get in More Trouble Than White Girls - *Camella McDougall*
The Loss of the Young - *Khylia Goldwin* 17
George Floyd Racist Cops - *Tyrell Stovall*
Why Many People Can't Say the "N" Word - *Zahkai Hussein-Be* 18
PJ's Project: Am I Next? - *Paige Ferguson*
Men in White - *Aden Hardy*
Why Can't Girls Play Football? - *MJ Lavalais*
Black Knowledge - *Korden Laborn-Walker* 19
Sexism - *Jace Zeigler*
Black People Should Not Be Killed - *Kyree Harden*
Colorism - *Shaundre'a Jones* 20
Black Girl Magic - *Zanyh Hicks*
Harriet Tubman and Fredrick Douglas - *Marcus Anderson Wilkerson Jr*
SOS - *Raphael Smith Jr* 21
Colorism: Black is Magic - *Nyja Walker*
Boys Need More Elementary Teachers - *Makenzie Williams*

TABLE OF CONTENTS

The Story of 13th - *William Cornelius Jr* 22
He Means A Lot To Me - *Cayden Jackson*
When I Was Cyber Bullied - *Douglas Byers Baldwin*
Racism - *Damiya Tucker* 23
I Only Feel Safe in Certain Places - *Kevin St. Clair* 24
Stop the Police! - *Brian Robinson Jr*

7th Graders 25

You Can't Stop Me From Reading - *Jaylon Chatmon*
Bullied - *Kamayah Hunter* 26
White Man Dollar - *Deandre' Chapman*
Let Us Read About Our Culture - *Marlon Duncan* 27
Lost It All - *Kayla Jackson*
The Pain of Gender Inequality - *Aaryn Walker* 28
All Black Lives Matter - *Duane Lumpkin* 29
The Lack of Black Teachers - *Aryana Major*
Draymond Green; Black History Month - *Brooklynn Johnson* 30
Why Black History Month Should Last Longer - *Casey Goldwin*
Employment Discrimination - *Kennis Talton* 31
Women's Rights - *E'Laysia Rucker*
The New Norm; Broken American Schools - *Angel Cunningham* 32
Emmett Till Tragedy - *Jayden Garrett* 33
Differences Are Driven By Society - *Marquel Darby*
Gun Violence - *Stephen Goldwind* 34
Black Lives Matter - *Autumn Allen*

8th Graders 35

Injustice - *Sebastian Montiel*
The School-to-Prison-Pipeline - *Xayden Harrell* 36
Toxic Masculinity - *Bria Johnson*
On Fire-Book Banning! - *James*

TABLE OF CONTENTS

It Should Not Be a Secret! - *Hailey* 37
The Causes of HB 327 - *Christopher Salary Jr*
A Refugee Problem - *Azaryah Paulk* 38
Differences vs. Disabilities - *Eric Calhoun*
Why We Need More Black Teachers - *Taron Bell* 39
Money Talks - *Ce Ce* 40
Black Wall Street - *Sincere Davis*
Harlem Cultural Festival Unity Art Piece - *Zion Hicks*
Black Lives Do Matter - *Jayden Pollard*
Body Shaming - *Samiya Hughes* 41
Women's Rights - *Madison Cox*
Time - *Jayden Johnson* 42
Black Dolls v. White Dolls: Children Choose the White Dolls - *Diamond Watson* 43
Fighting for Rights - *Beautiful Walker* 44
Injustice to Boys - *Kelvontae Hardaway* 45
The Mind of a Child - *Richard Treadwell* 46
Blue-Eyed Project - *Chinja Scott* 47
The Problem and Solution to Gun Violence - *Jaidyn Wise* 48
Reality - *Laquoia Patterson* 49
Dream Popper - *Phillip A Lane*
Equal (Neighbor) Hoods - *Marquis Hicks* 50

Akron Art Museum Exhibition 51
Our Voices Matter: A Community-Based Social Justice Art Exhibition 54
Speakezie Art Exhibition 57
Human Heart Studios Art Exhibition 61
WOVU 95.9 FM 65

Testimonials 68

The Very Beginning

KINDERGARTEN THRU 3RD GRADE

K-3 students began their artmaking process by identifying their strengths. Children shared their talents and joys. Next, we explored the meaning behind their names. For example, Jaquana may learn her/his/their name means brilliant, honest, inventive, and courageous. After learning about the power of names and sharing their strengths, students reflected on their new understandings. They wrote about themselves, and what they discovered. Next, students translated their new understandings to painting/drawing and shared the symbolism behind their art. Photos below capture their excitement and artmaking process.

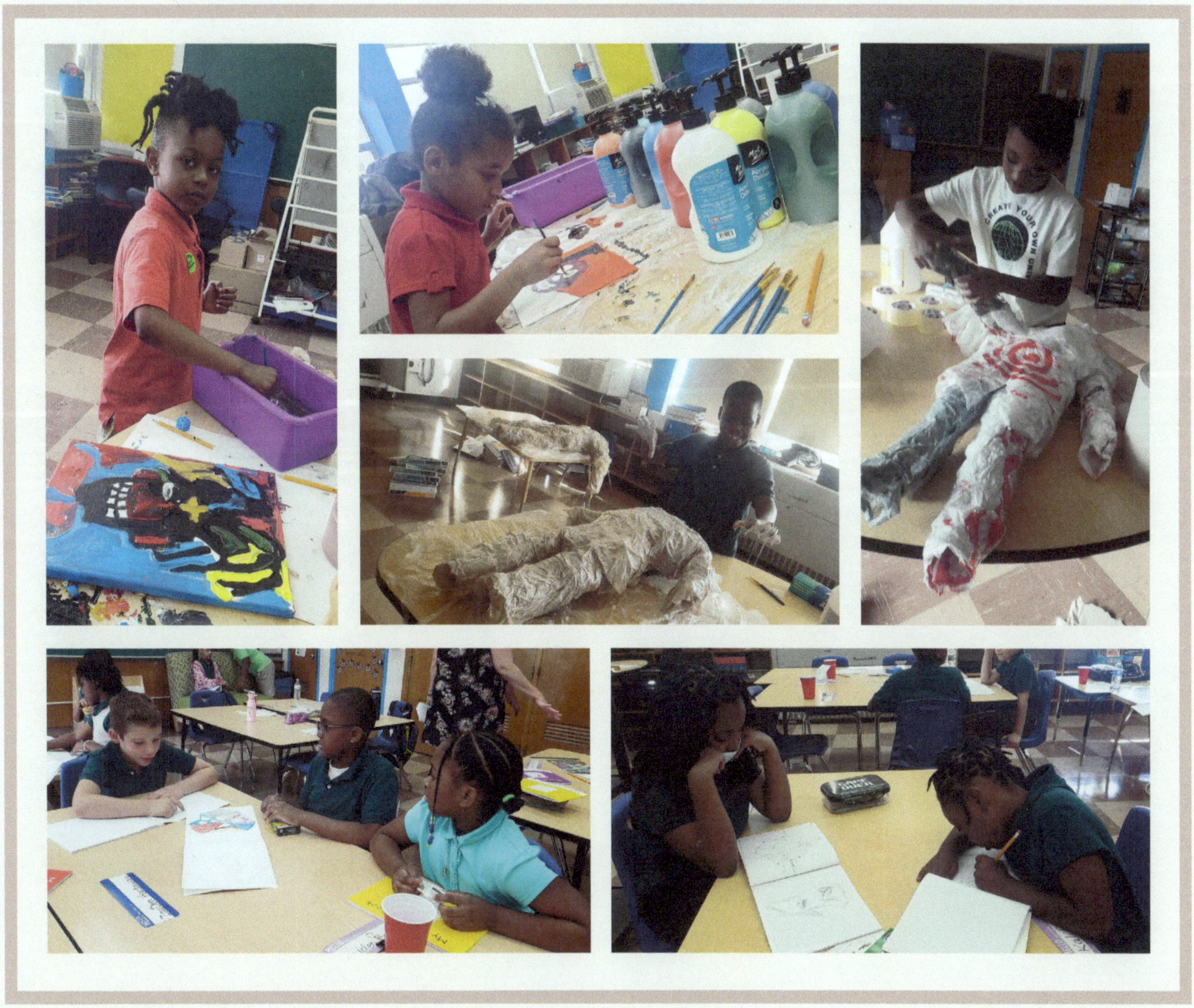

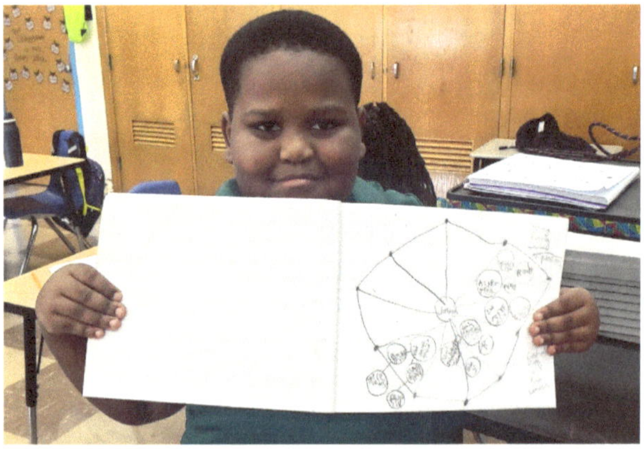

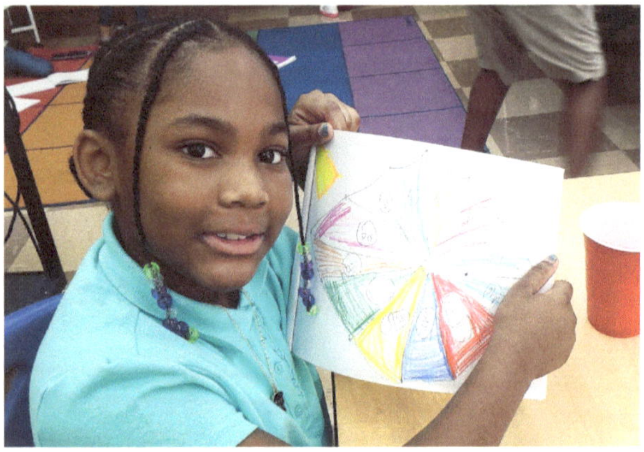

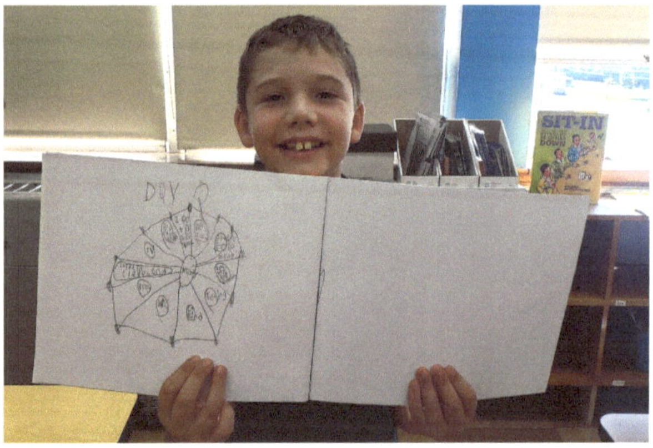

Meaning through art.

Strength through art.

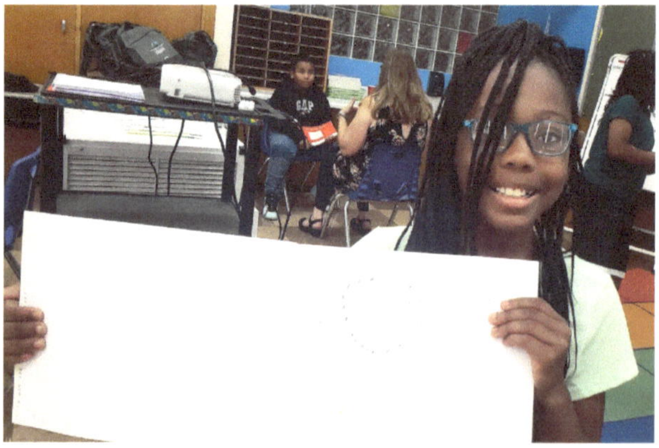

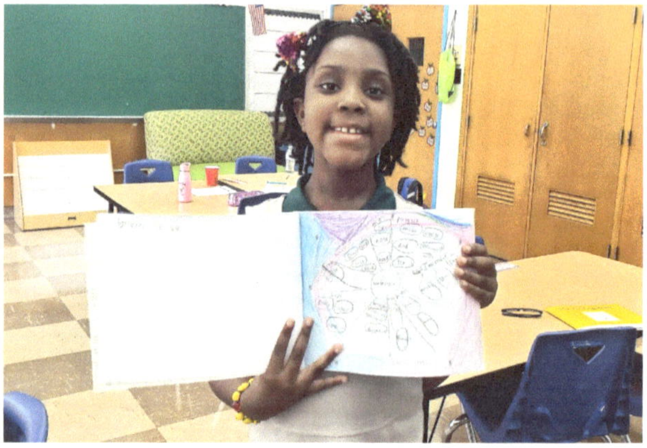

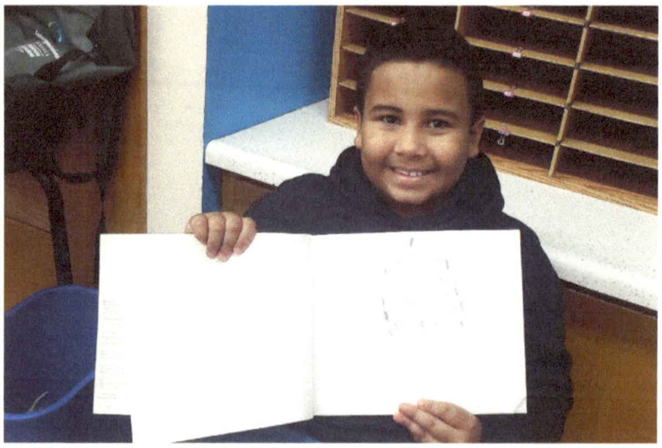

K-3RD GRADERS

I AM A FIGHTER! I AM STRONG!

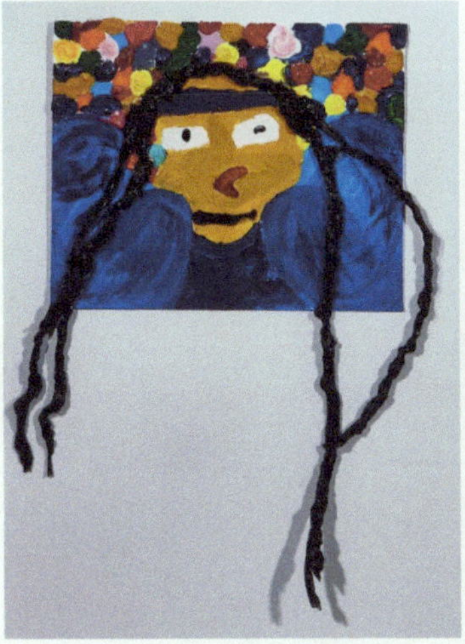

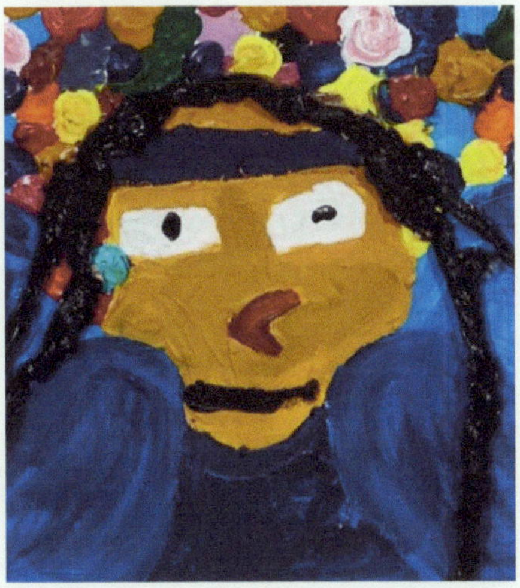

My name is a name of strength. It means I am a strong person. It is an old German name and people were fighters in battle.

- Madison

I LIKE DINOSAURS

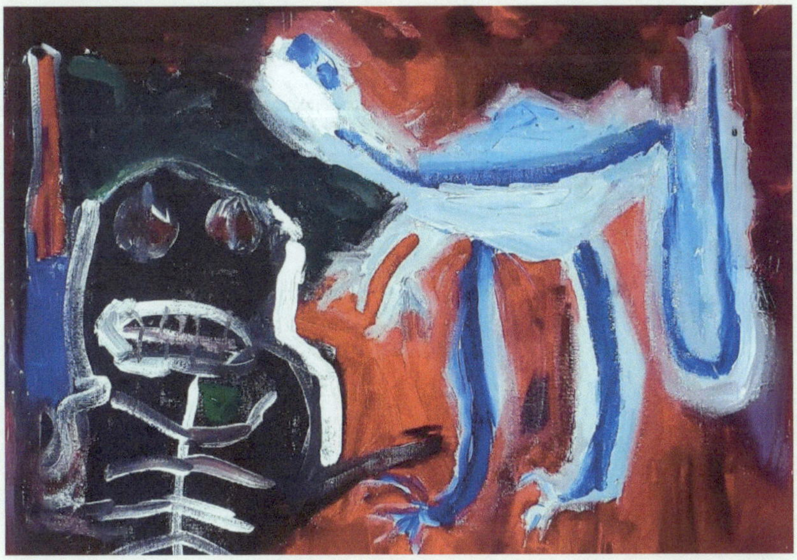

My name means I am a diamond. I am brilliant. I shine. I love dinosaurs.

- Dinozzo

I AM THE ONLY ME - Kylon

My name means I am handsome, I am love, I am adventurous, I am fun, I am loving. There is only one me, Kylon.

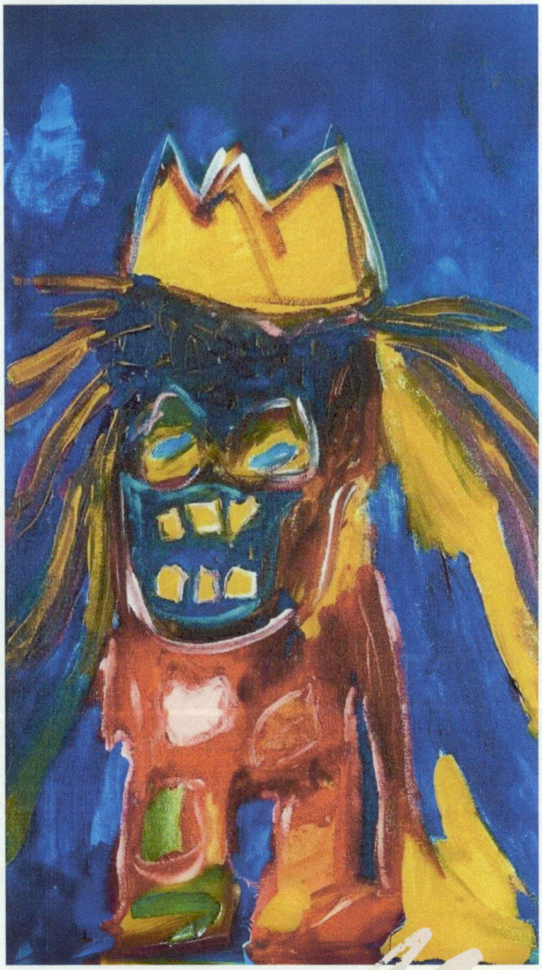

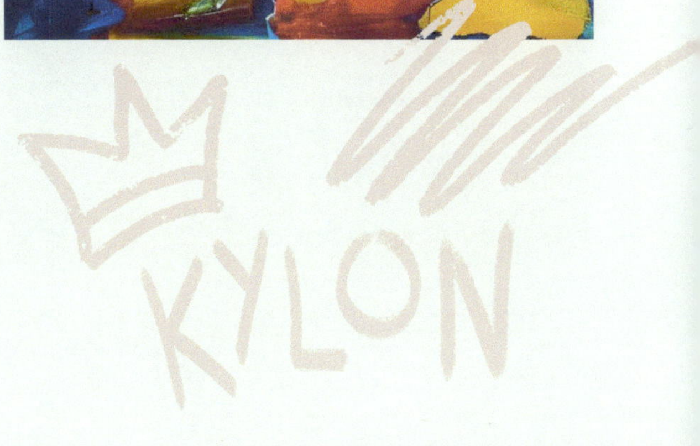

I AM DARK BEAUTY

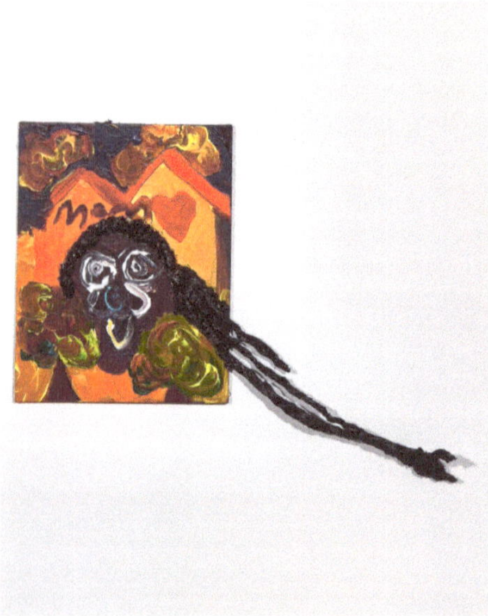

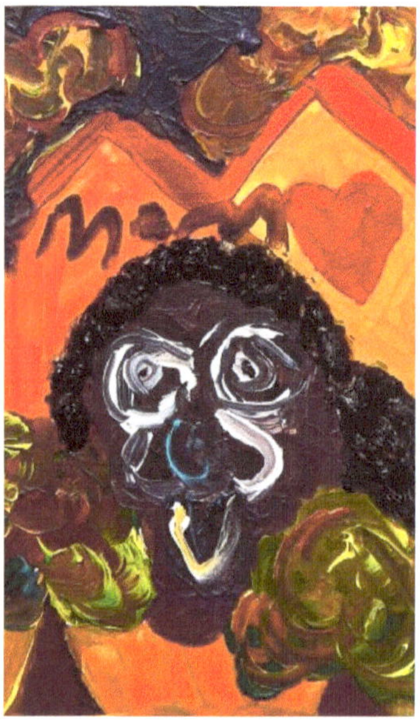

My name means darkness and night. I am a dark beauty. I love who I am. I am celebrated for being a dark beauty. This means I was born at night.

- Laila

MY BEST FRIEND BUMBLEBEE

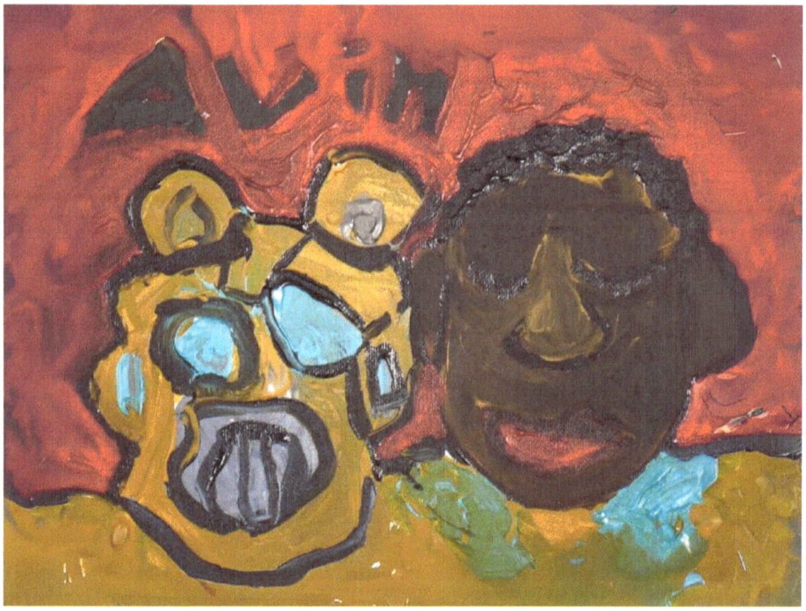

My name means I am a beautiful person. I am handsome. I am a beautiful person inside and outside. My best friend is Bumblebee.

- Avin

ME

- Morgan

My name means I am from the sea. It means circle. I have power. I give joy to the world. My name means I am strong. I can be bossy sometimes. I can be stubborn sometimes cuz I want things my way. I am me.

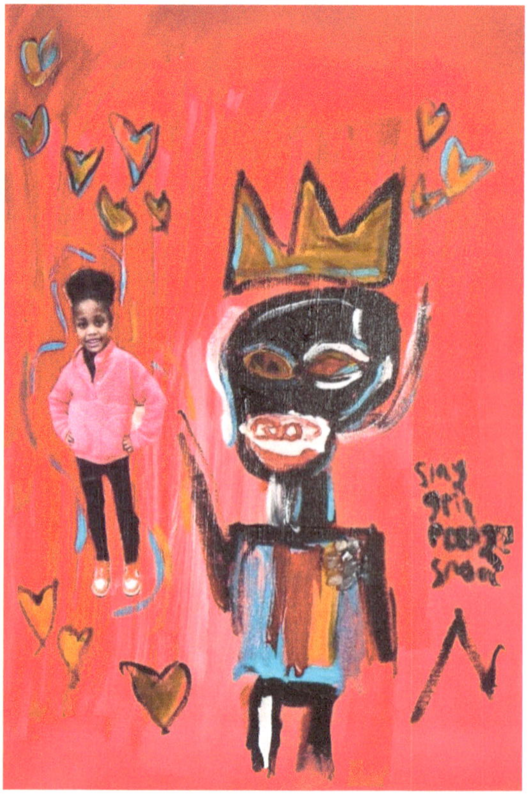

I COME FROM GREATNESS - Wisdom

I am smart. My name means I have knowledge. I love to learn. I am wise. I make good choices. I go with life.

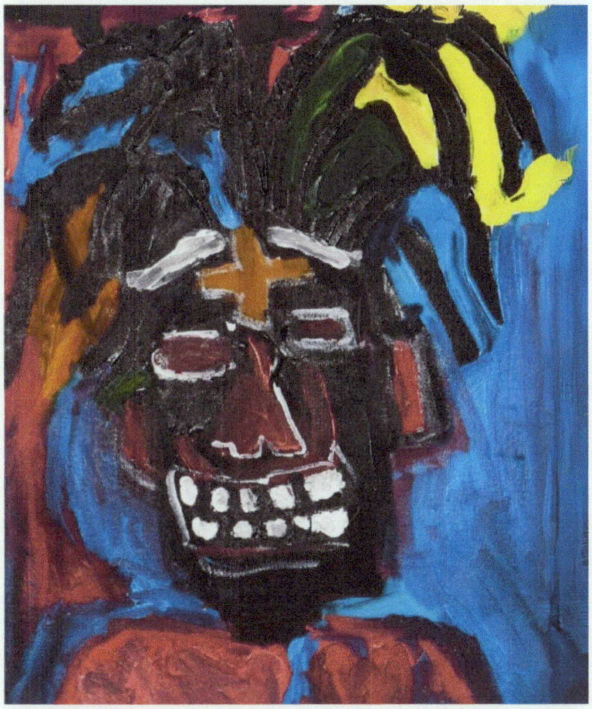

I AM BEAUTIFUL - McKenzie

My name means to be pretty. To be beautiful. To be smart. To be born of fire. I am beautiful standing next to the bird. I am playful.

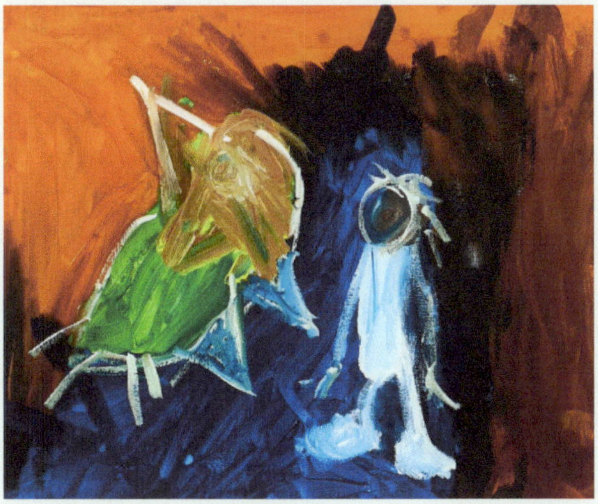

I AM EARTH MOTHER

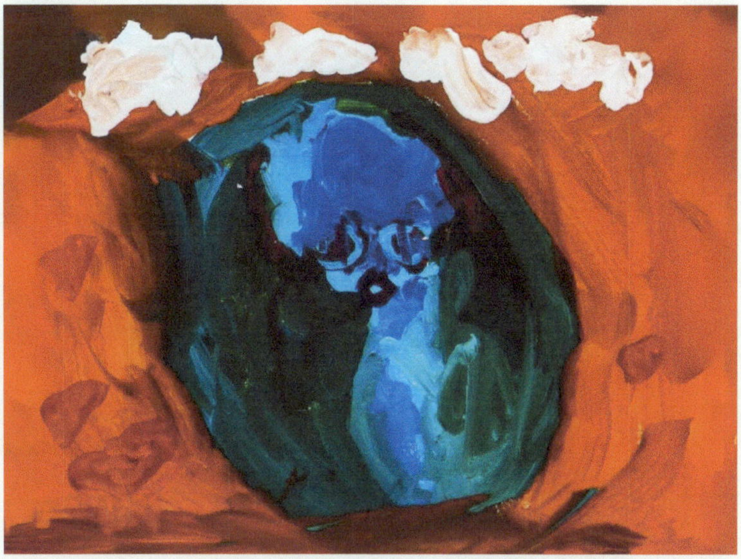

My name is the name of the earth mother. Demeter was a Greek goddess. She made sure there was a lot of food for people. I have a strong name.

- Demi

I LIGHT UP A ROOM AND SPARKLE

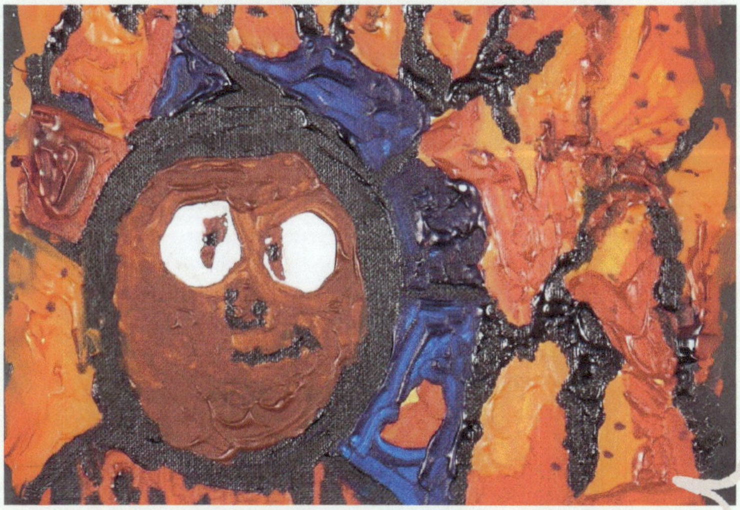

My name means to bring light to a room. I am a protector.

- Jamez

I AM KING AND POWERFUL - King

My name is powerful. I am a ruler. I can help people by being a king.

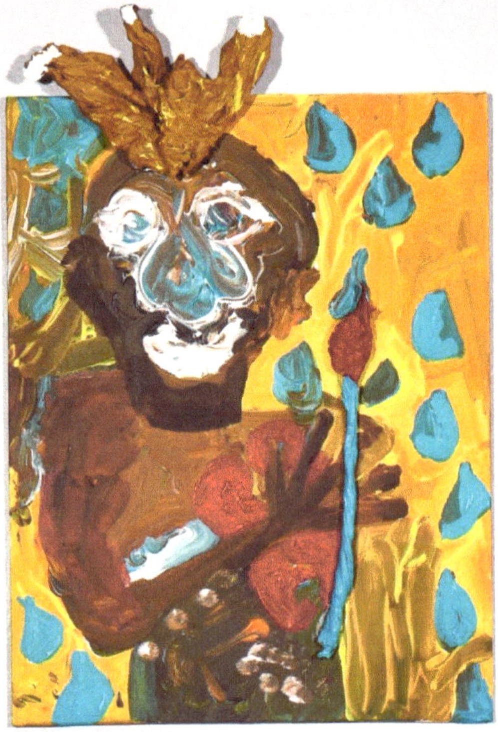

I MUST BE FAMOUS OR SOMETHING - Jordyn

My name means flowing like a river. I made a river with flowers and I am floating in the river. I didn't realize my name was so famous cuz I am putting this art in a museum.

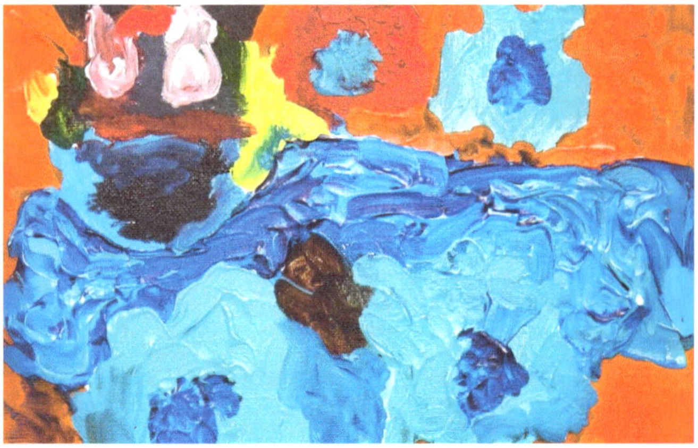

WE FLY TO THE SKY

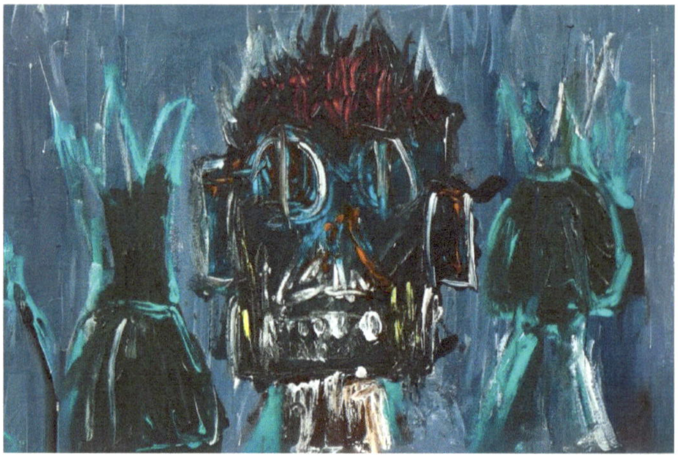

My name means I have a heart. I have courage. I am strong. I am not afraid. I can do things by myself. I want to fly to the sky and help save people. This is my power-courage.

- Corey

I RUN FAST

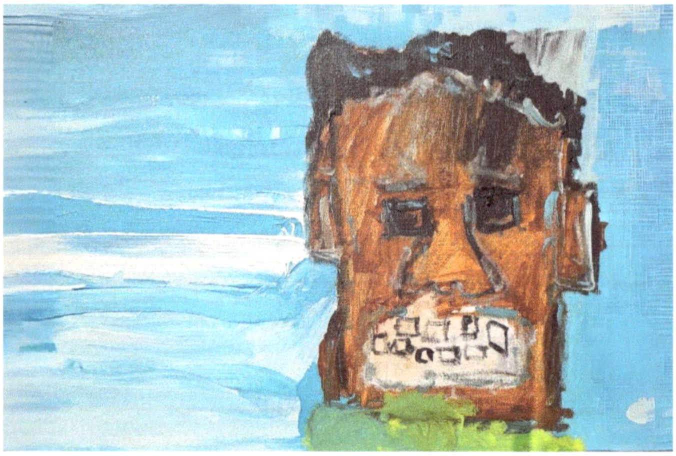

I am a protector. My name means I have protective hands. I have super powers to run fast. I look out for my family...friends. I will protect them through their life.

- Rayce

MY NAME MEANS ' THE LIGHT '

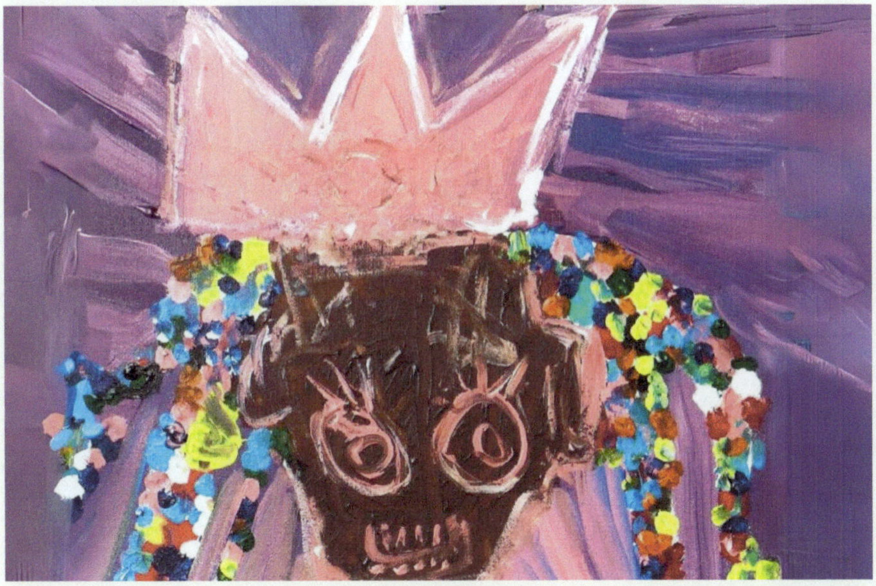

My name means I am the light. I am the sunrise. I bring happiness and light to people. I like starting over again. I give people chances.

- Zaria

I WANT TO BE THE TOOTH FAIRY WHEN I GROW UP

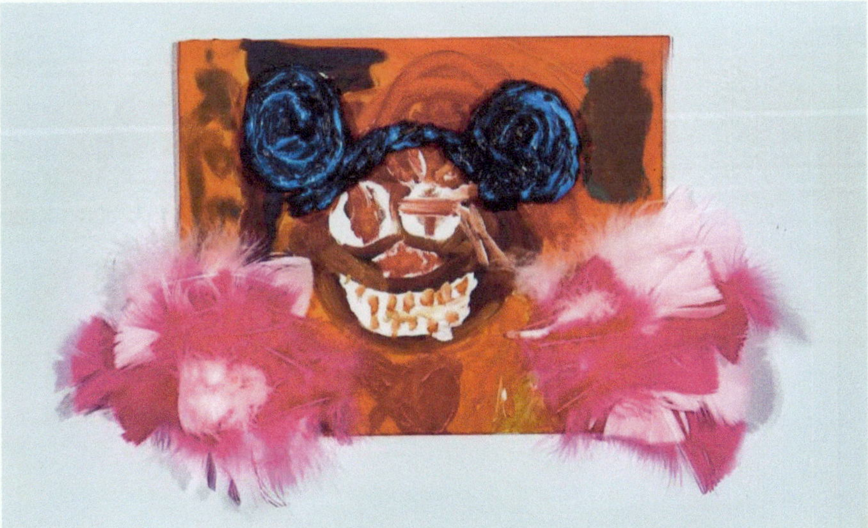

My name means heaven. I bring peace to the world. I want to be the tooth fairy when I grow up. I want to make kids happy when I come as the tooth fairy from the clouds. My name backwards is heaven.

- Nevaeh

I AM A GREEN VALLEY

- Denver

My name means green valley. I keep the valleys and fields alive with rivers running through me. I bring life to the mountains. I am a green valley. I have nutrients to give the animals and the plants and the trees.

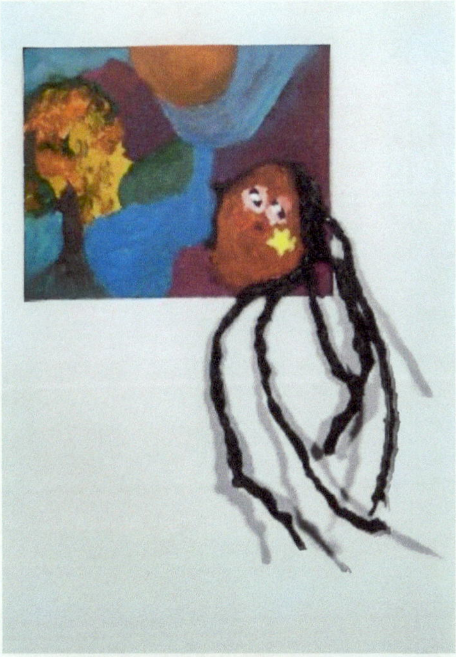

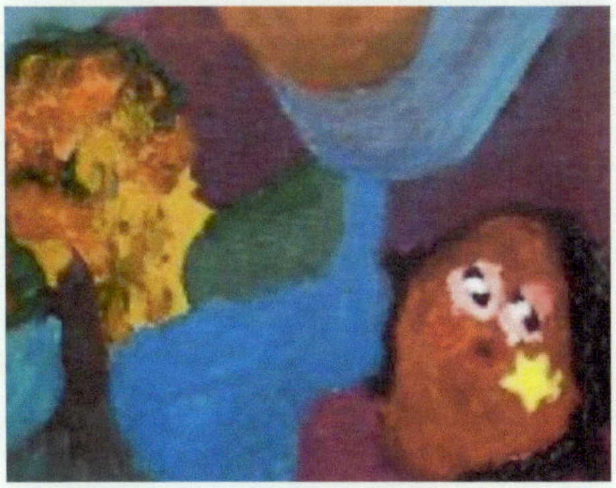

I WISH I HAD MORE FRIENDS - Demetrius

My name means I look over the food that is growing. I am the harvest and watch over corn. My name also means I bring life to the world. I wish I had more friends. I would share my light.

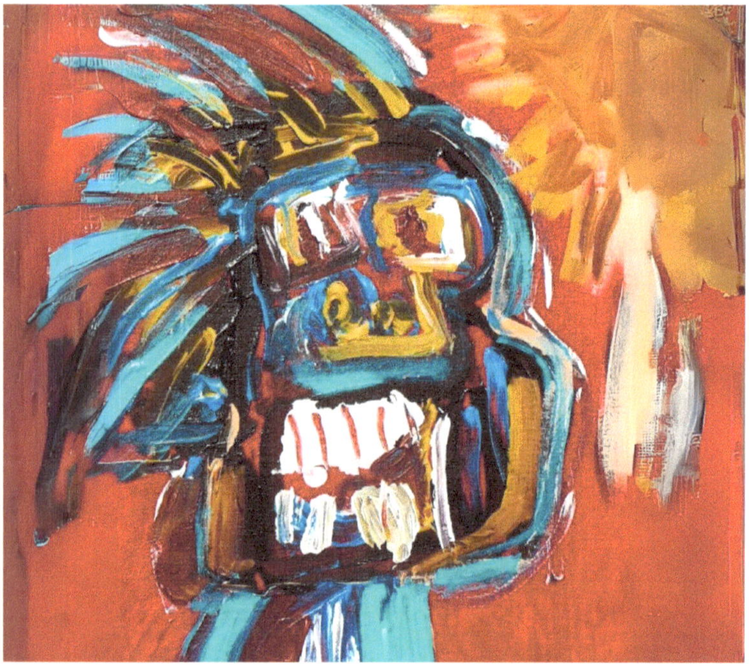

THE LIFE OF JAIDEN - Jaiden

My name means I am thankful. I am thankful. I love my teacher. I love my family. I love my friends. I love me.

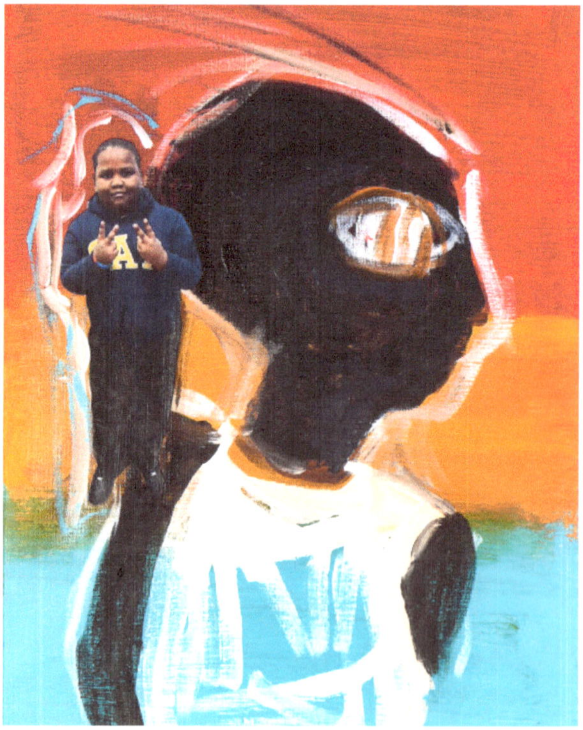

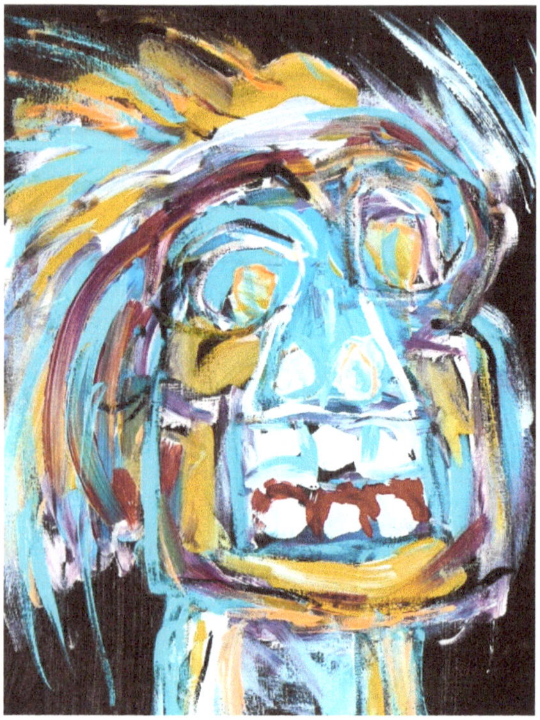

ALL ABOUT ME

My name means I am precious. I am perfect being me. I share about me. I am a precious child.

- Diamond

I LOVE ME

- Noah

I made my body. This is me, and I love me. I have friends. I like to do things. My name means to rest. I like me. I bring comfort to people. I mod-podged all of my favorite things about me on my art. I painted it red and black because those are my favorite colors.

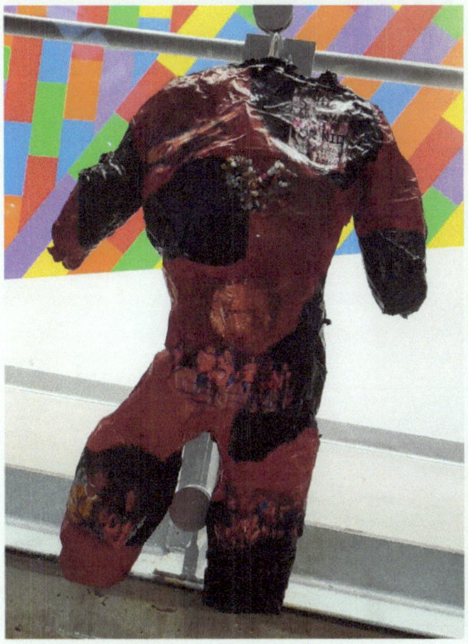
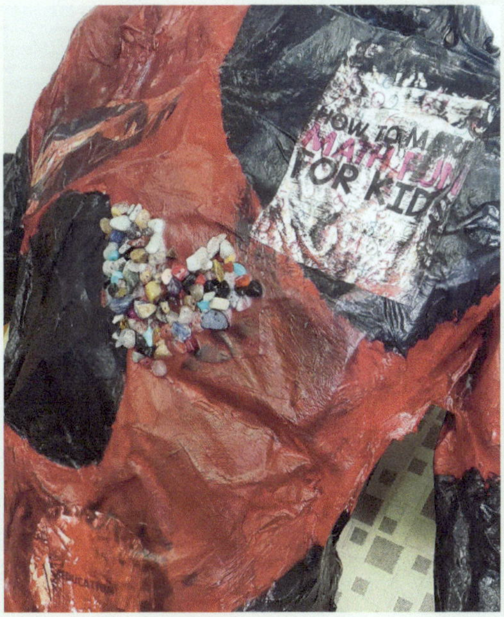
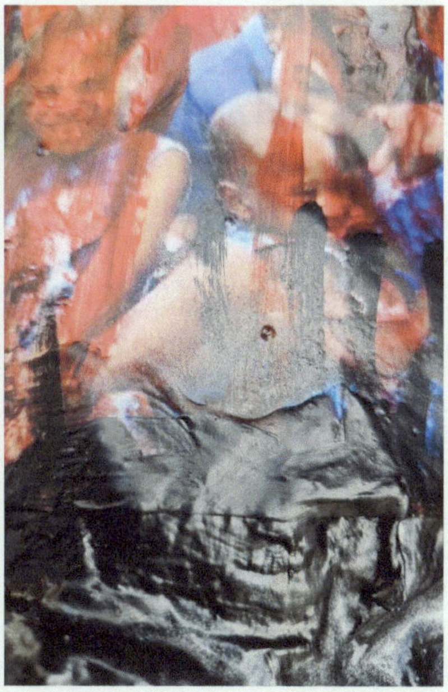

MY BROTHER AND MY BEST FRIEND

- Kayden

I am gentle. I am a good friend. I am someone you would like. I made my body. I called him my brother. He is my best friend. I tell him everything. I put all the things I want. I want friends. I want a brother. I am a good person.

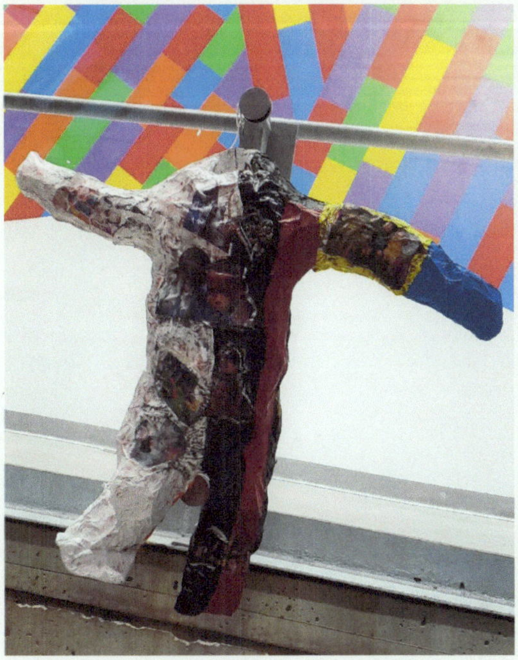
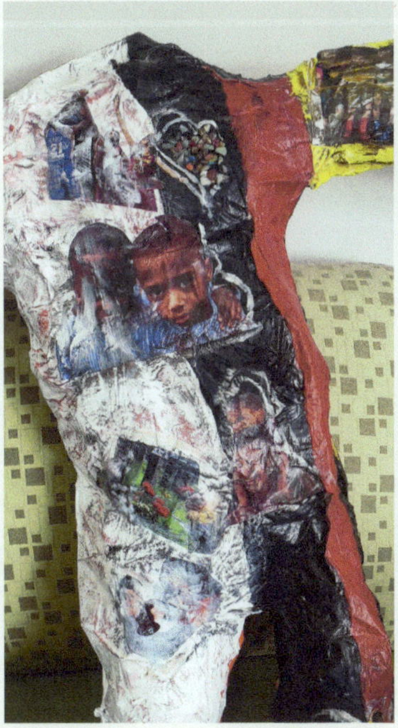
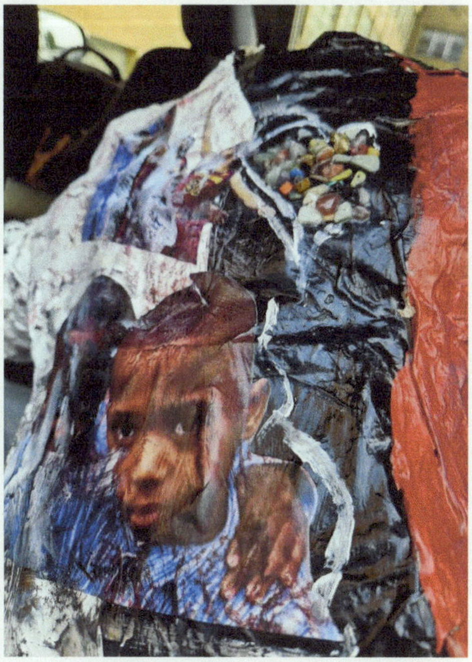

THIS IS ME ! - Adam

My name means I am the son of the red earth. This is how the earth was made. I made my body. I painted it black and blue because those are my favorite colors. I fight for good.

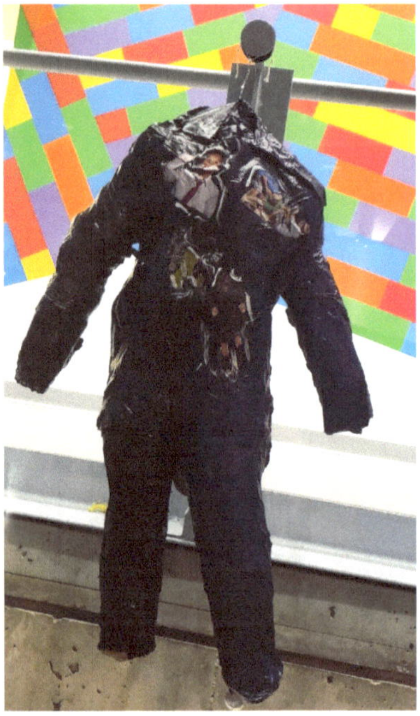

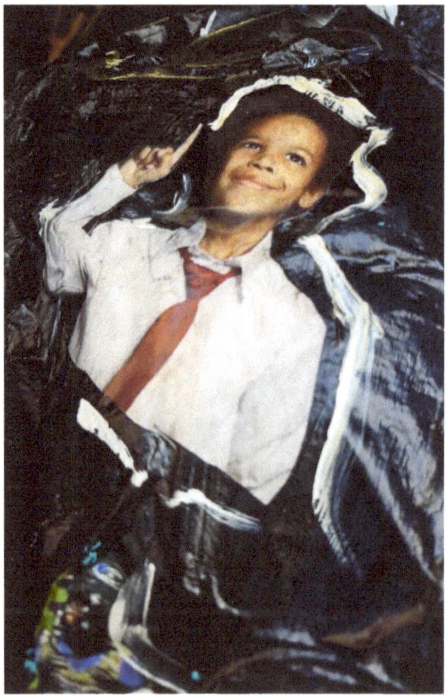

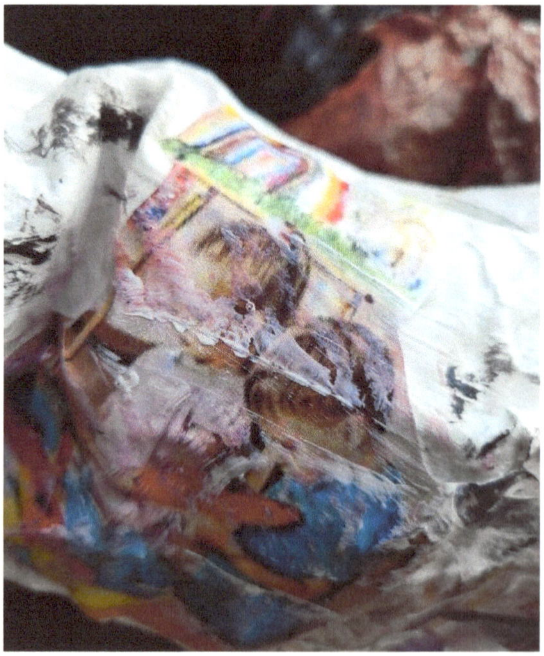

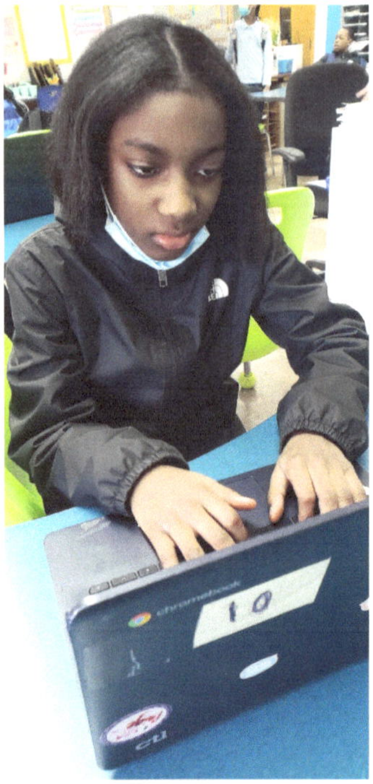

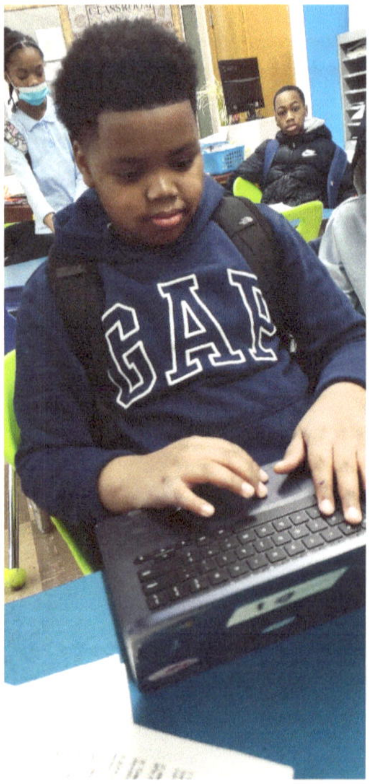

Middle School Scholars
WORKING ON THEIR RESEARCH

FIFTH & SIXTH GRADERS

Slavery

My social justice was about slavery. I never even heard about slavery until I was in this art project. I wanted to learn more. I made a slave ship. I found branches outside to make the slave ship out of wood. My painting is a slave ship. It has seven canvases connected to each other. I thought they were metal, but I learned they were made out of wood back in the day. I also learned how many slaves died when they were put on these ships. They were piled on top of each other. They starved them. They went to the bathroom on each other. That racism hasn't stopped. I crossed out the blue bodies with red paint to show how many people died on a slave ship. Racism is wrong. It still happens today.

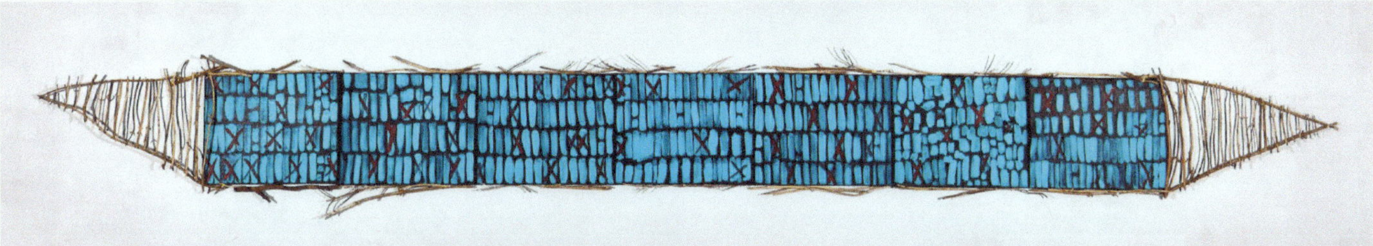

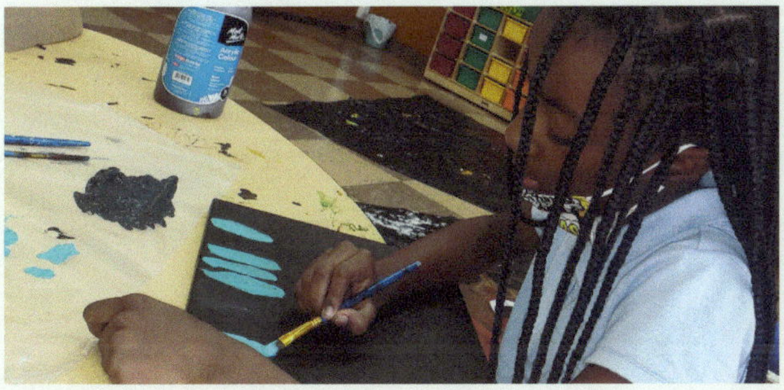

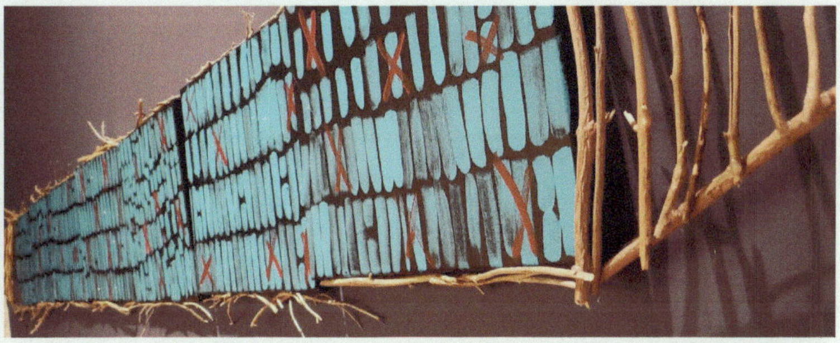

- Octavia Unique Allen

Someone in my family told me, "Even though you are Black and other people are White, we all bleed the same color."

Why did they split White people and Black people? The government is "they" and after the Civil war, the government passed Jim Crow laws. The purpose of my art is how we can improve as a nation, society, and people to not be separated and to stick together because we are all the same, no matter what.

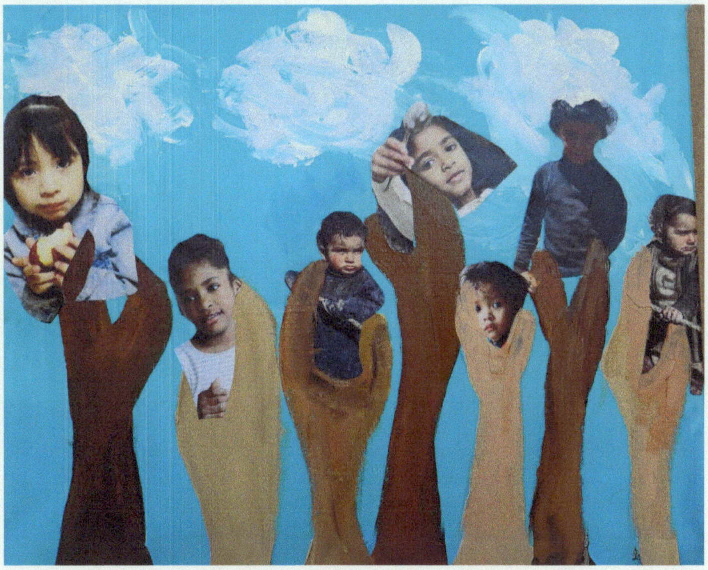

- Breylon Amankwah

Black Girls Get in More Trouble Than White Girls

Did you know that Black girls get punished more than White girls in schools? I know it might not seem like it, but it's in plain sight. Some kids might not notice this is actually happening.

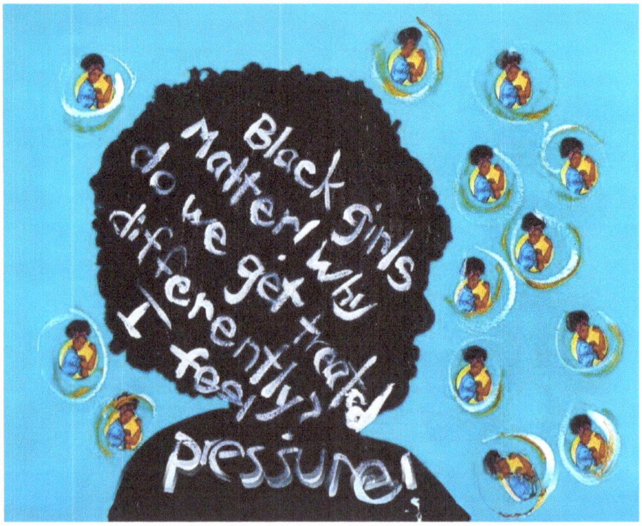

- Addison Allen

The Black Hockey Player

I was discriminated against last year. Why? I was just a different color. That's it. The purpose of my art is to make history and show you I am another good Black hockey player. Remember, Black Hockey Players Matter.

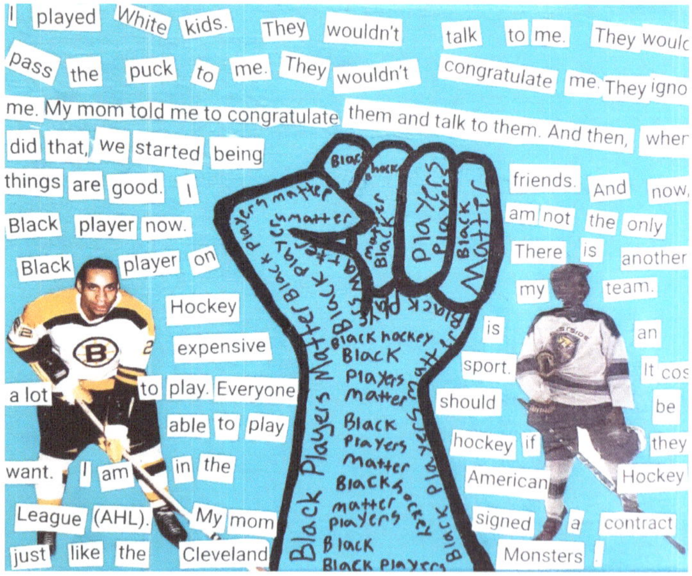

- Vincent Nixon

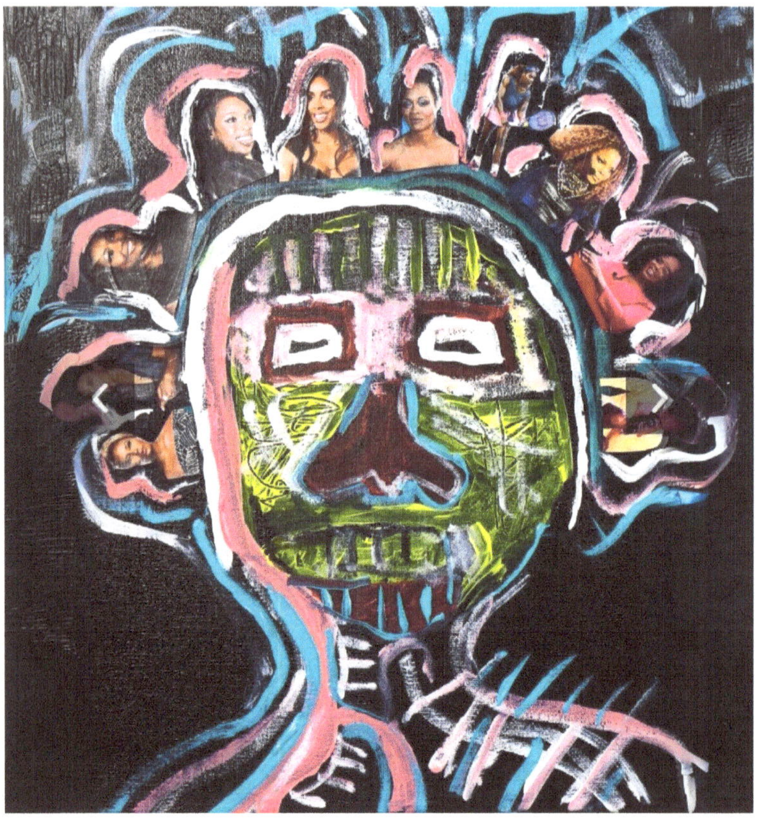

Black Women Are Powerful

My art is about all the Black women I never even heard of. I never learned about Black women in school until this art. I made myself and put these famous Black women in my hair. It's like they are a part of me and in my brain now. I wish schools would do more of this.

- Dominque Watson

All White Eyes Are On Black Girls: We Should Be Celebrated

Our art is about knowing that Black girls are disciplined more in schools than White girls. It's like all eyes are on them in school. Instead of being punished, Black girls should be celebrated. It's not right to know Black girls are the most at risk for being disciplined in schools.

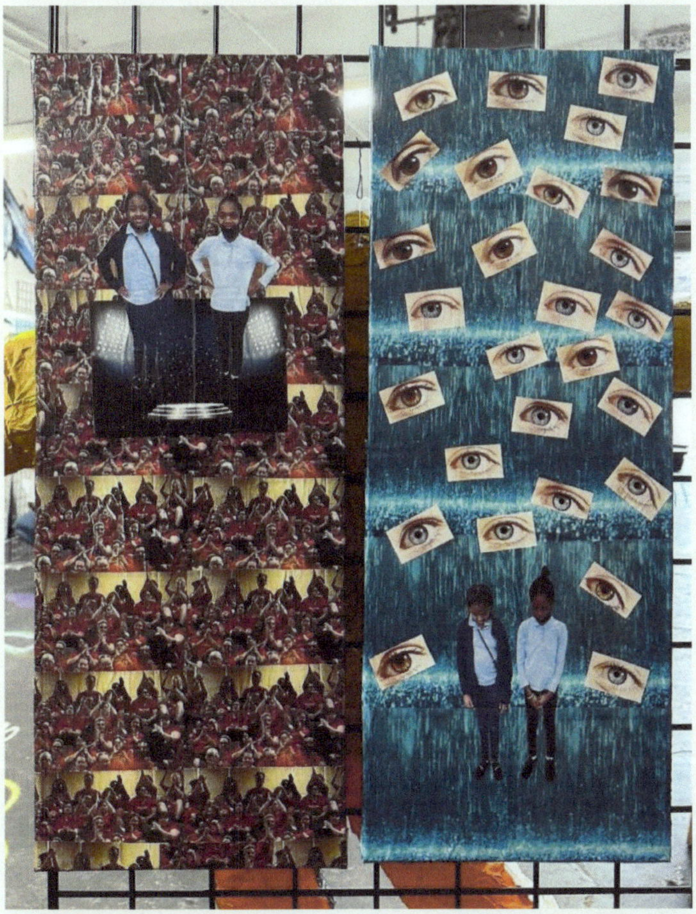

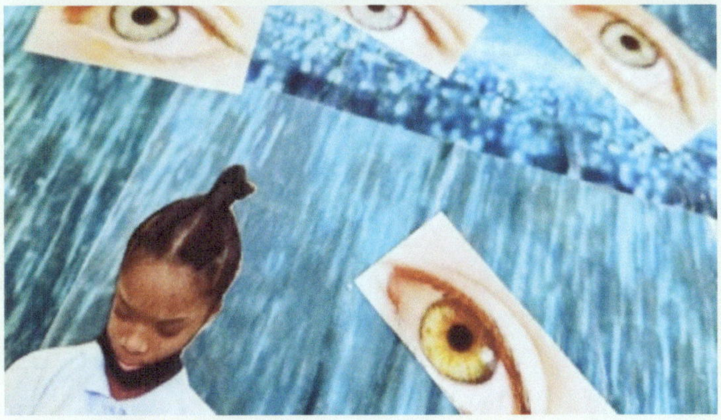

- Kamayah Hunter & Kylie Cromity

The History of Slavery

The purpose of my art is to tell you how Black people were being treated back when there was slavery. I want people to read this so they can start treating people better and learn that just because people are different doesn't mean you need to treat them like animals.

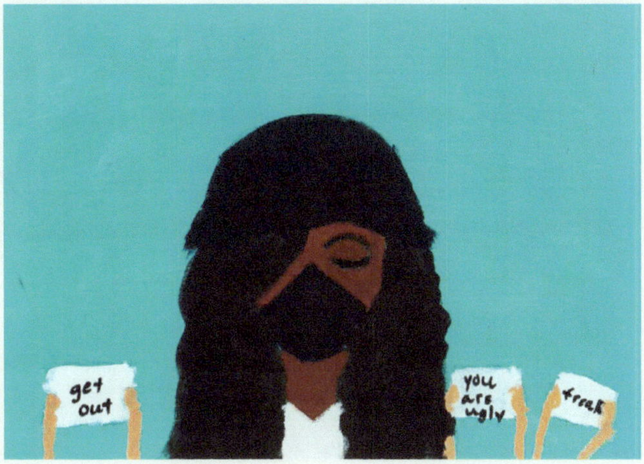

- London Marie D

Nature Now: The Earth is on Fire

I did my art on the health of the earth. Our earth is on fire! I am putting the fire out. All of us need to do our part to keep our earth. If we don't do something now, we will lose our earth.

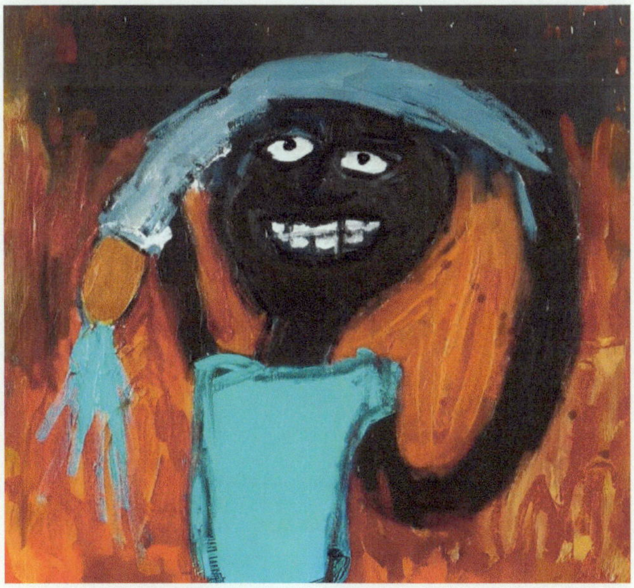

- Caleb Davis

Mama, Please Save Me!

I wanted to learn about Emmet Till. He was about my age when he was tortured. I made my art about him. I made a casket out of paper towels. I painted it red and orange because the red is for blood and the orange is to make it stand out because Emmett Till's mother wanted everyone to see what the White men did to her son. I took a photo of Emmett Till and cut it up to show he was deformed. His mother couldn't recognize him. This hatred to Black people can't keep happening.

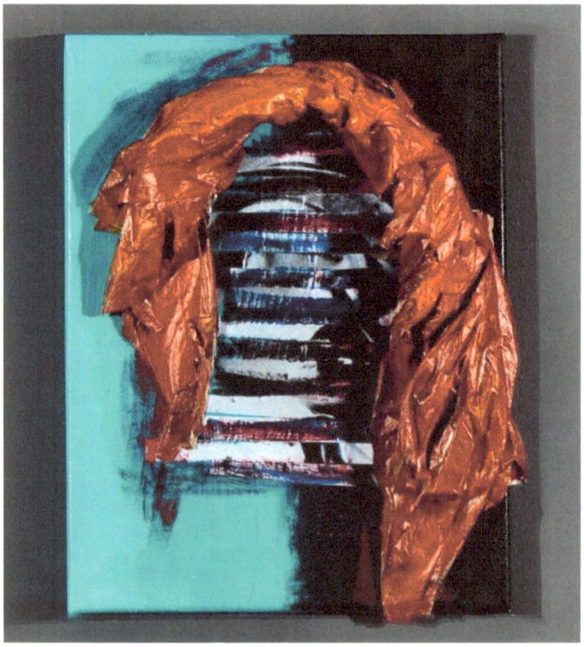

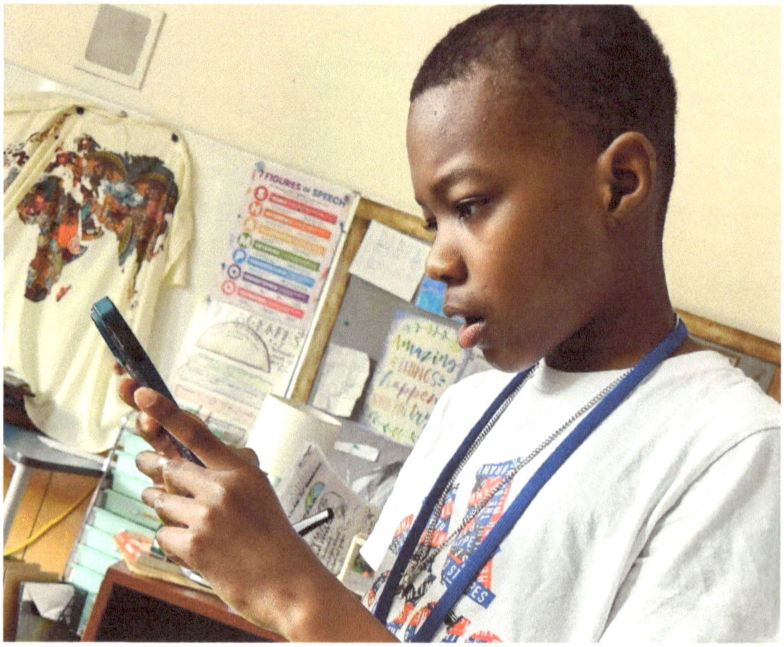

- Lorenzo Bryant

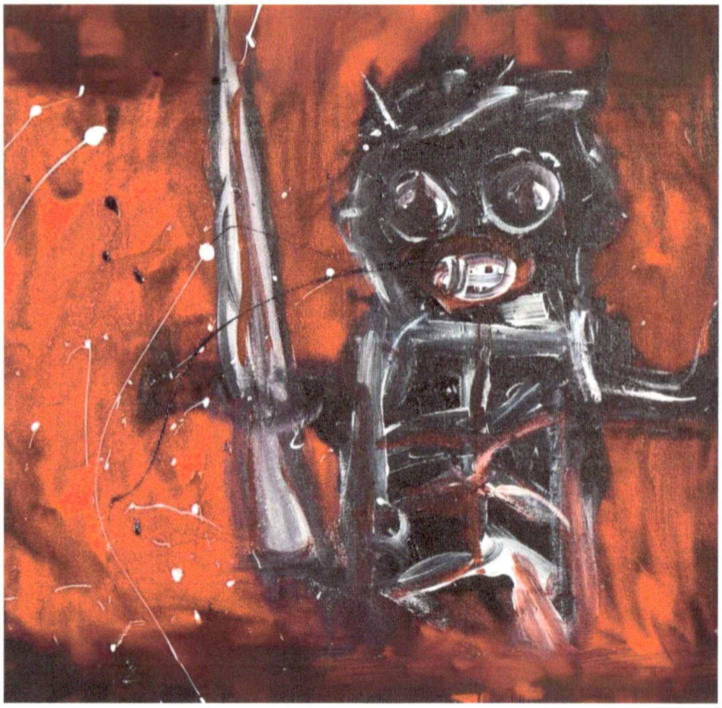

This is Me

I want to tell you what it is like to be a young Black man. I show this in my art. I want everyone to know it's important to support each other and understand each other. A grown up needs an older family member to talk to and help them out with stuff. So it's like, say if a grown up has to deal with a lot of stuff and it's super painful and they want to do something themselves... like kill themself... they need someone to talk to... like a therapist. Kids should have grownups to talk to. Not everybody has someone to talk to about their problems. It makes me feel horrible for people who don't have anybody to talk to about their problems. My mama and all my family members can help me talk about my problems. That's helpful because I can be feeling sad for a very long time.

- Colin Floyd

Black Lives Matters

I made my art into four pieces. This is me screaming. I am making sure people hear what I have to say. It doesn't seem like to many people care about Black people. They need to. We matter. And just because I am a kid, that doesn't mean my voice doesn't matter. It does!

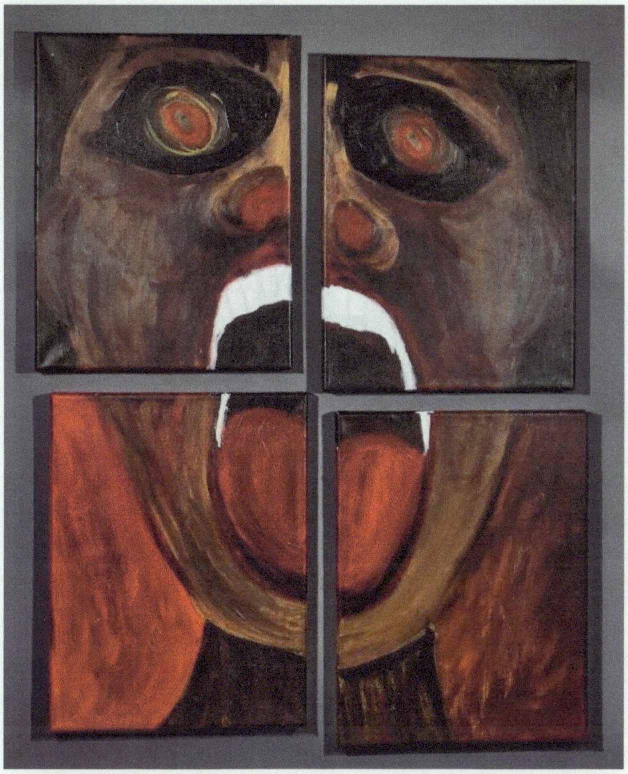

- Aalayah Brown

"N" Joes

I learned about the "N" word. I hear people using it. I used it. I didn't know that it was a word people didn't want to be used. When it is used, it's about hate. We need to stop the violence toward Black people

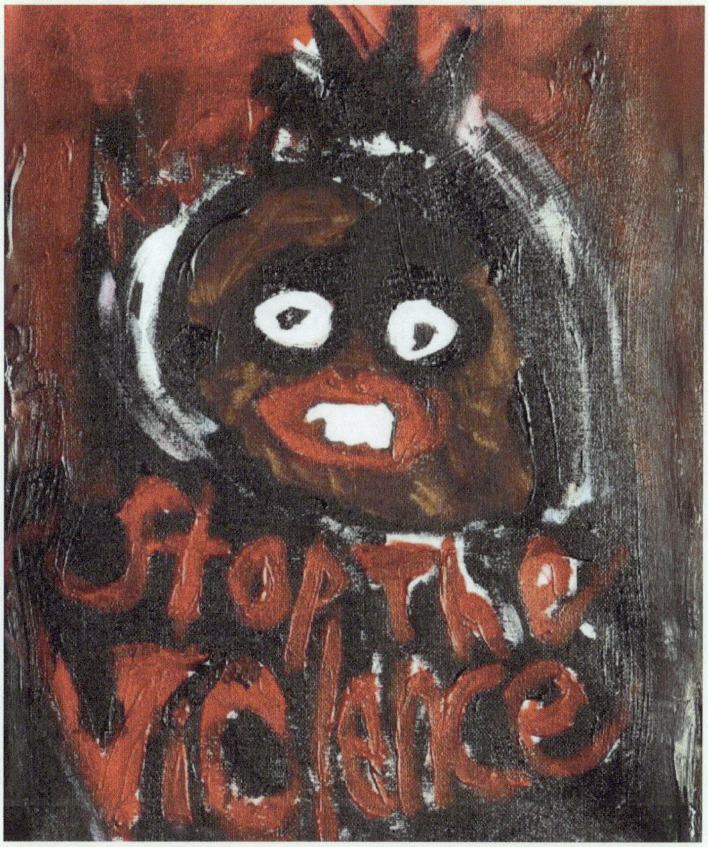

- Donald Chatmon Jr.

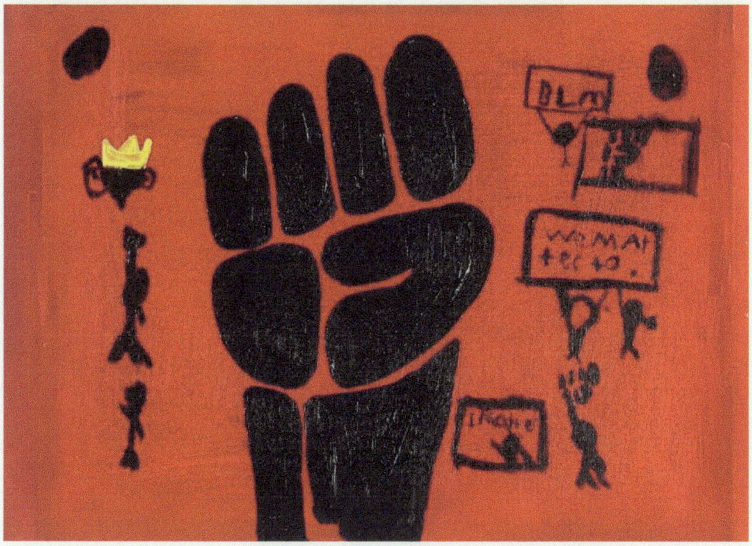

Bad Cop

My art is about police brutality against Black people. Black lives do matter. We can't keep having bad cops kill Black people. Over the past few years police officers have failed in their duty to protect and serve everyone, especially innocent Black men and women. The purpose of my art is to help you understand police brutality needs to stop.

- Jayson Johnson

Police Brutality. The "N" Word

Do you know what the "N" word is? It has lots of history. People used to use it to call a Black man. The purpose of my art is to show people that the "N" word is wrong. I researched how many Black people are called the "N" word and how many police hurt Black people. I crossed off their faces with red to show blood and anger because these Black people died from police brutality.

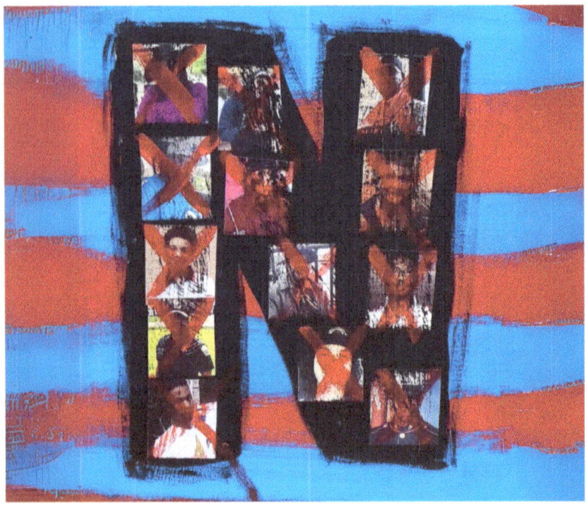

- Santanah Morton

Can't Afford It

My art is about the need for universal preschool. I didn't know it cost more to have your child in daycare than it does to send someone to college! That is not right. We need universal preschool so everyone can be at the same level. There are so many people who don't have that kind of money. We should help the kids.

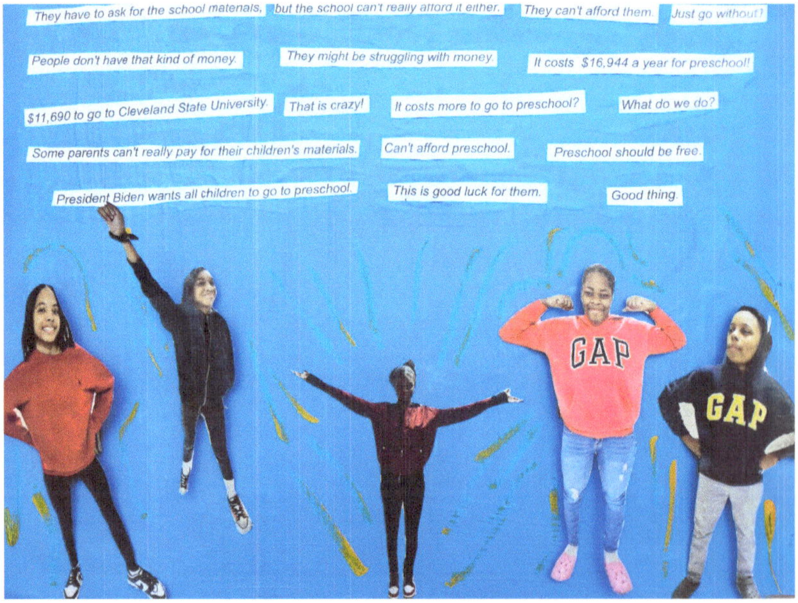

- Mya Gaston

Black Girls Get in More Trouble Than White Girls

Pushed out. On the news, I learned how Black girls get in more trouble than White girls. The purpose of my art is to encourage people to stop punishing Black girls for being themselves. I painted the background blue. I painted it to look like a sky. I painted a dark sky. I am mad and angry. I painted my feelings about how Black girls are treated in school. I chose to put my words from my poem on my canvas because this is how I am feeling. I mod podged a Black girl on my canvas because they went with my poem. She is at the center and at the bottom so we can see the words and the words lead to her. This might be how she feels. This is how I feel.

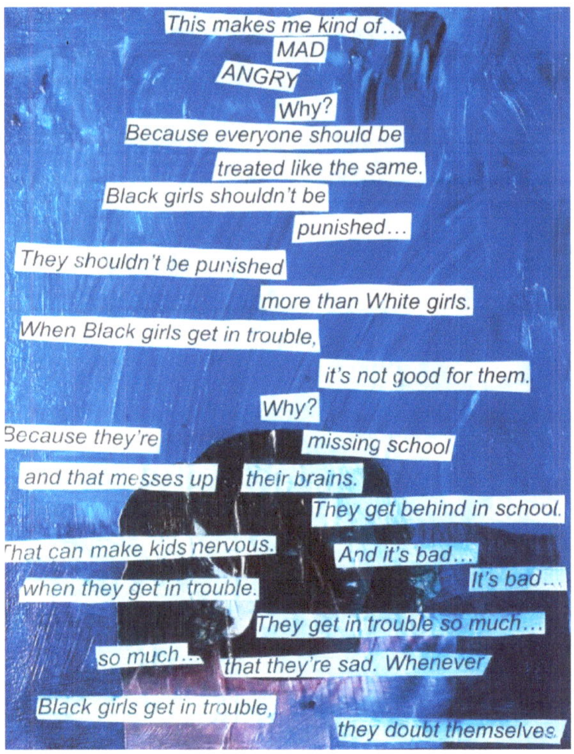

- Camella McDougall

The Loss of the Young

My art is about making sure everyone knows how important it is to protect animals and kids. I made a box on my canvas. This box represents the letters I wrote to my mom who died when I was little. This is the first time I ever talked about this. I used my art to express myself. I made a chain around the box and made my heart. We have to protect animals and children from all of the pain in the world.

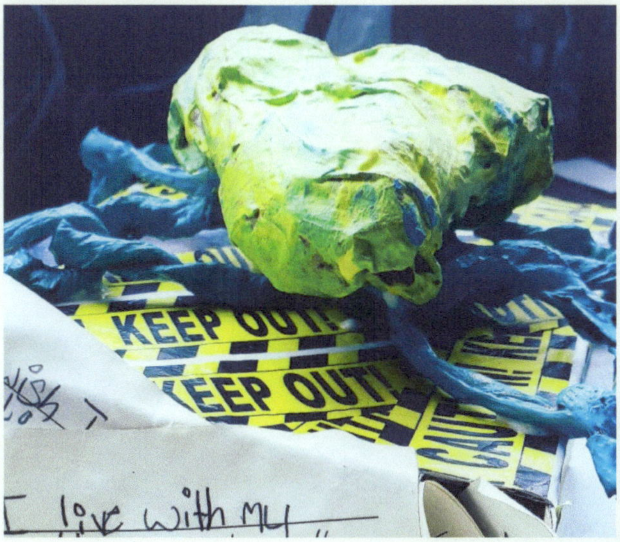

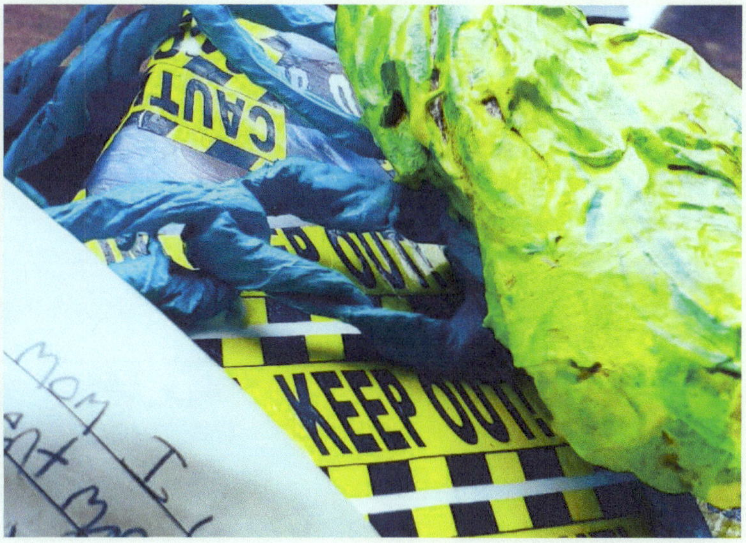

- Khylia Goldwin

George Floyd Racist Cops

I chose racist cops because it meant something to me. There was no reason to pull over this Black man just because he is Black. This is called "driving while Black." This phrase started in 1967. Why? There were 130 witnesses across 150 cities who recognized that Black people were being pulled over just because they were Black. My art is about George Floyd. I didn't know who he was until I started doing my research. I learned about racist cops and that we can't have that. Racist cops don't belong on the police force. I was very sad to learn what happened to George Floyd. I put rocks on his heart to show how sad I am.

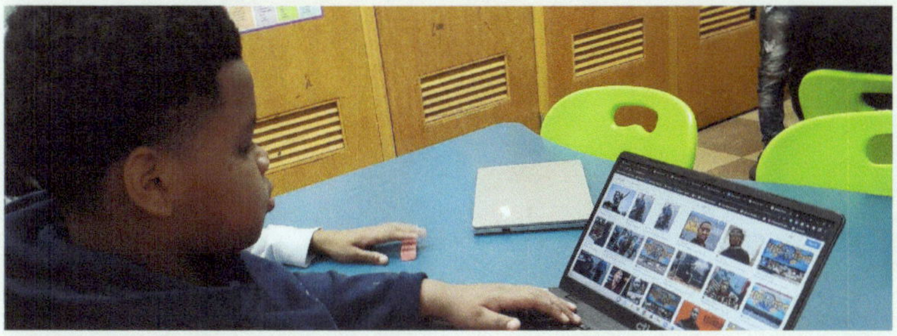

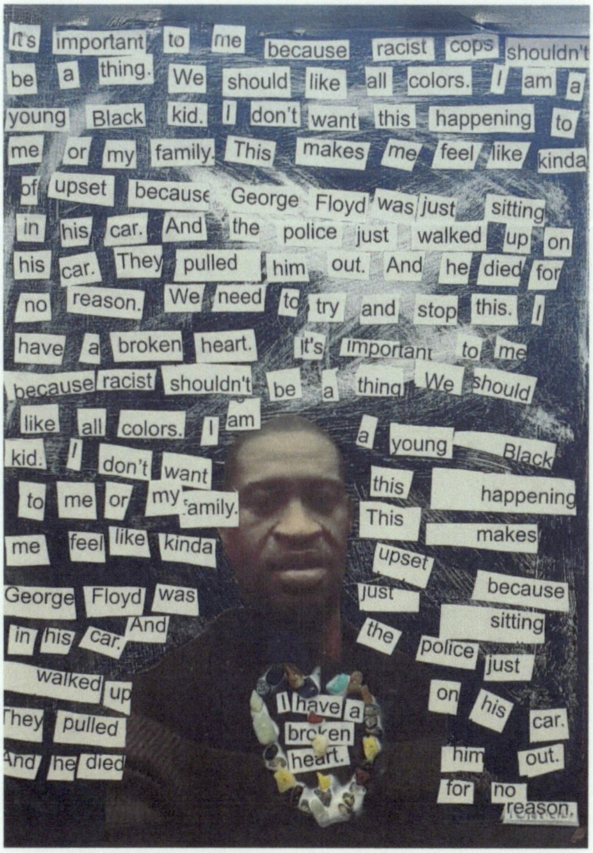

- Tyrell Stovall

Why Many People Can't Say the "N" Word

The N word Is offensive. Often used as a slur toward my ancestors and people of my demographic. The purpose of my art is to express why the N word is offensive to me and other people of my color.

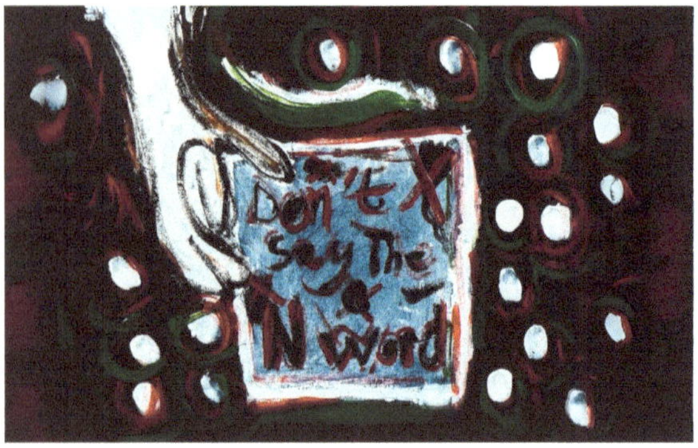

- Zahkai Hussein-Be

PJ's Project: Am I Next?

Black Lives Matter. Those words can change the world if people would believe in these words. First, I talk about Black Lives Matter. Second, I tell you how I feel about Black Lives Matter. Third, I tell you about my art and what everything means. Finally, I tell people that I don't want them to be racist. BLACK LIVES MATTER!!!!!!!!!!!

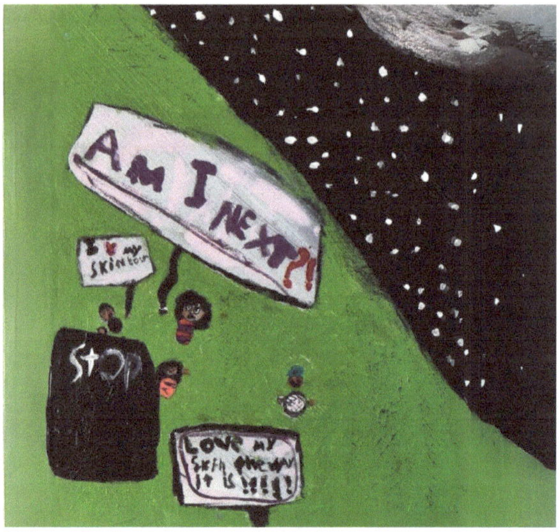

- Paige Ferguson

Men in White

My art is about the Klu Klux Klan. I didn't know anything about any of this. I wanted to research this. I found out about the KKK and all the horrible things that they still do. I made a boot and painted it the colors of the African American flag. We are kicking the KKK person, like getting rid of the hate in the world. There is blood on the hood of the KKK person. This is because we need hate to go away.

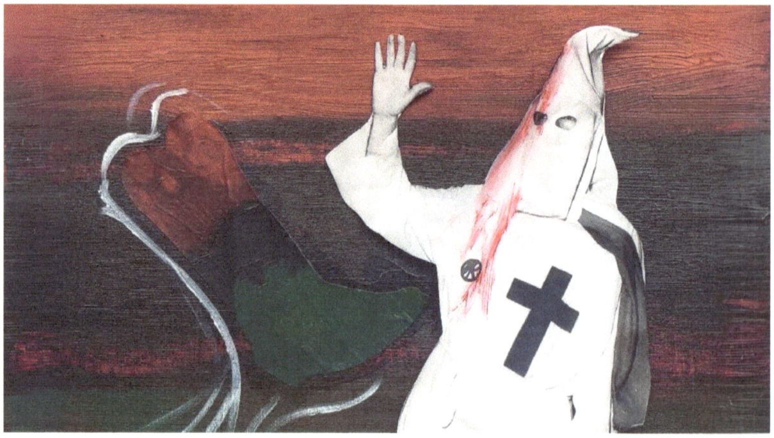

- Aden Hardy

Why Can't Girls Play Football?

My art is about girls and boys playing football together. Girls should be allowed to play football. I had a girl on my team. I liked to play football with her. Then, we couldn't be on the same team anymore just because I am a boy and she is a girl. That's just not right. I did my research on girls who are playing football in high school and in college and in the NFL.

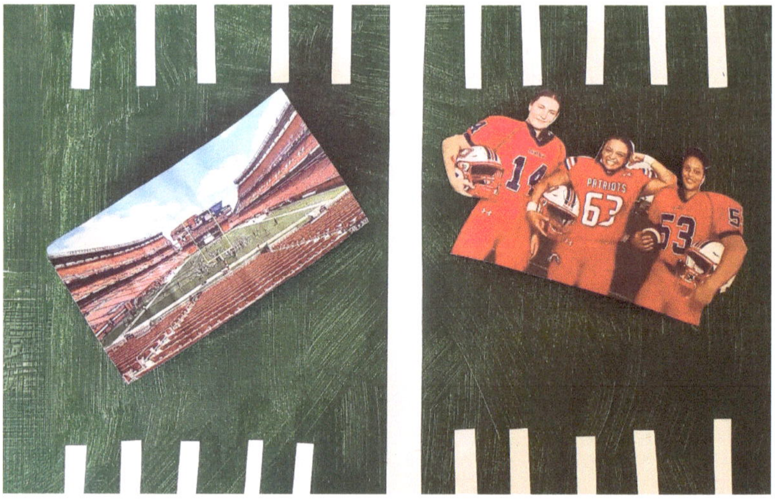

- MJ Lavalais

Black Knowledge

My art is about the research I did on a bill that is trying to get passed in Ohio. It's a bill that is trying to make sure we don't learn about Black people or other cultures. It's wrong. I don't get to learn about this in school. I learned about this in my art and research. We have Black Knowledge. No one can take that away from us. We should be learning about Black people in school. I cut up my poem and put it in my mind. This is what I am thinking about. The colors are the colors of the African-American flag. Each color has a purpose.

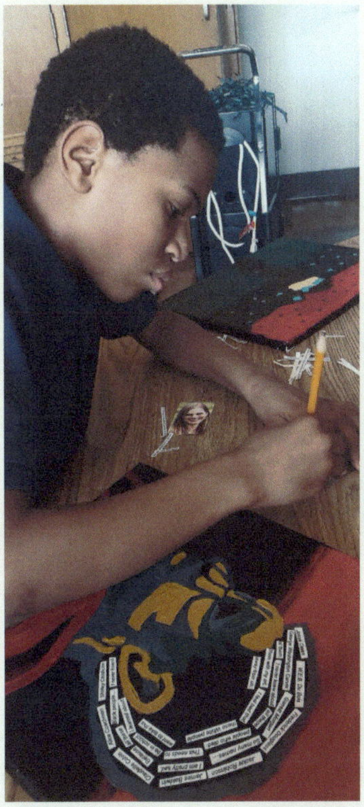

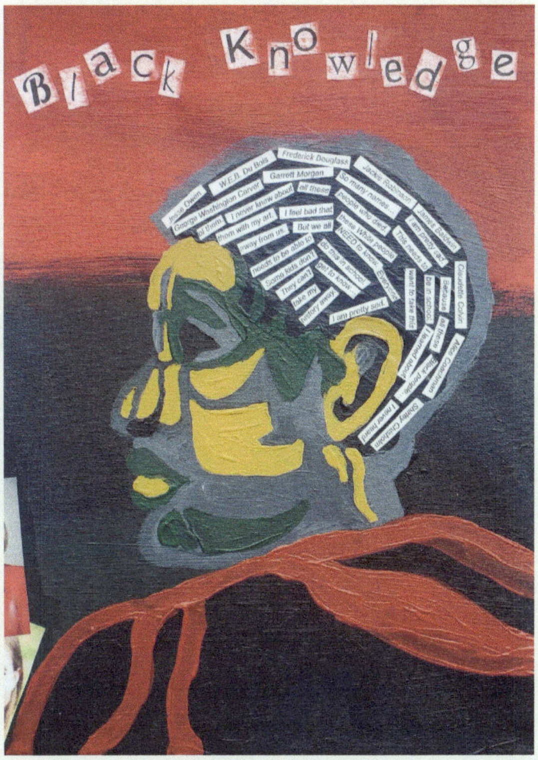

- Korden Laborn-Walker

Sexism

Boys should be able to wear whatever they want to wear. Schools should not tell people boys can't wear skirts or girls can't wear pants or a tie. Clothes are a way to express yourself. They are just clothes. You should be able to wear whatever you want!

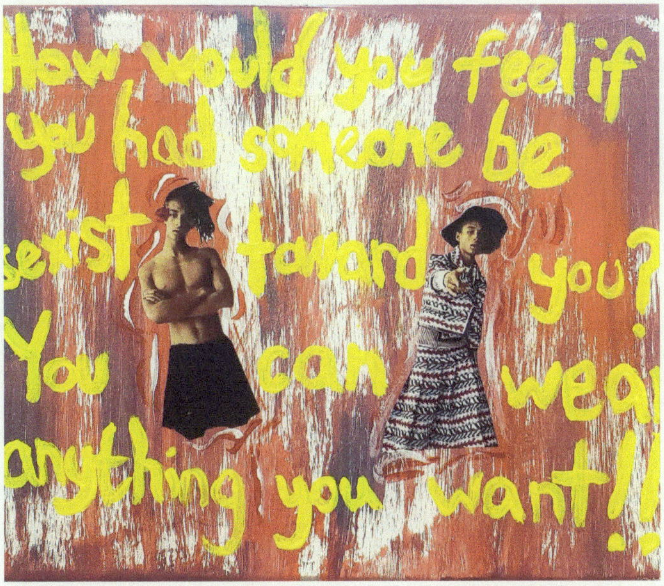

- Jace Zeigler

Black People Should Not Be Killed

My art is about the way Black athletes are treated by White people. There are White people who threw trash at the players. They yelled names. They threatened them. This needs to stop.

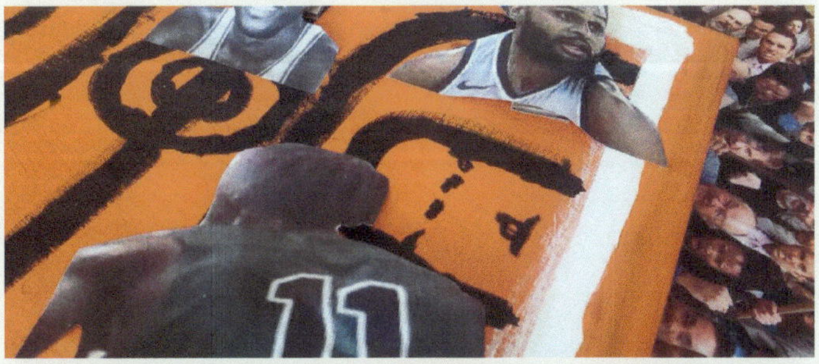

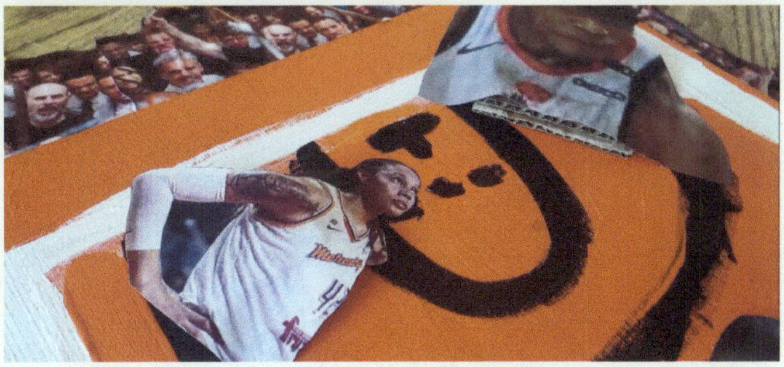

- Kyree Harden

Colorism

We all need to love each other and not judge someone because of the color of their skin. This started in the United States during slavery. Slaves who worked in the field had Black skin or darker skin than the lighter skinned slaves. Lighter skinned slaves worked in the slave master's house. The purpose of my art is to say colorism is wrong.

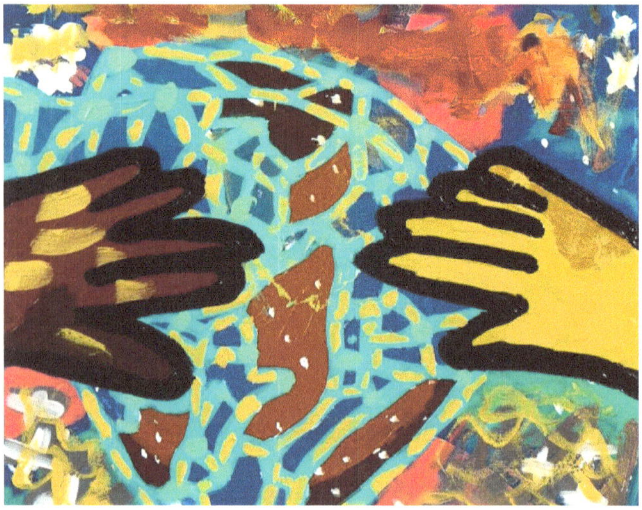

- Shaundre'a Jones

Black Girl Magic

I think Black girls are powerful. This art is about being a Black girl. We are magic. These are my friends. We are magic.

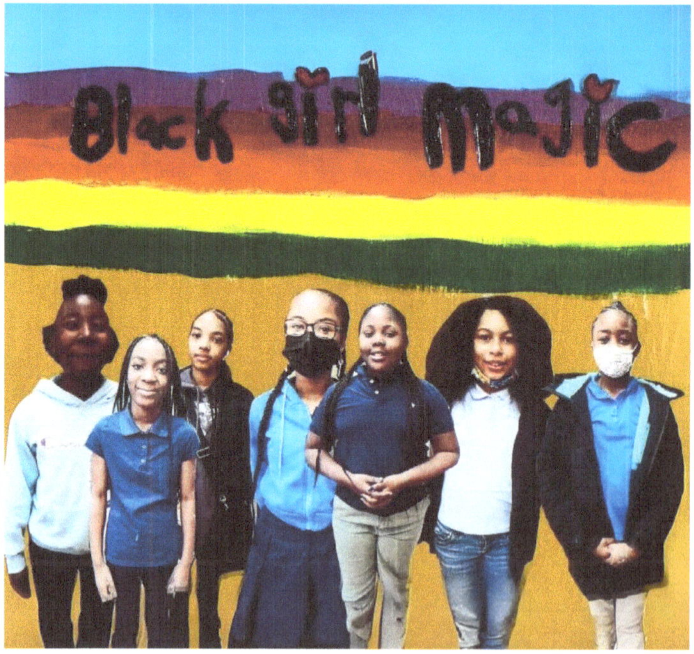

- Zanyh Hicks

Harriet Tubman and Fredrick Douglas

My art is about famous Black people I didn't learn about in school. I researched a lot of famous Black people. I put them on the stage I made in my art. Black lives should matter. We should be learning about famous Black people in school. We should be learning about Black people in school. We should be in the spotlight.

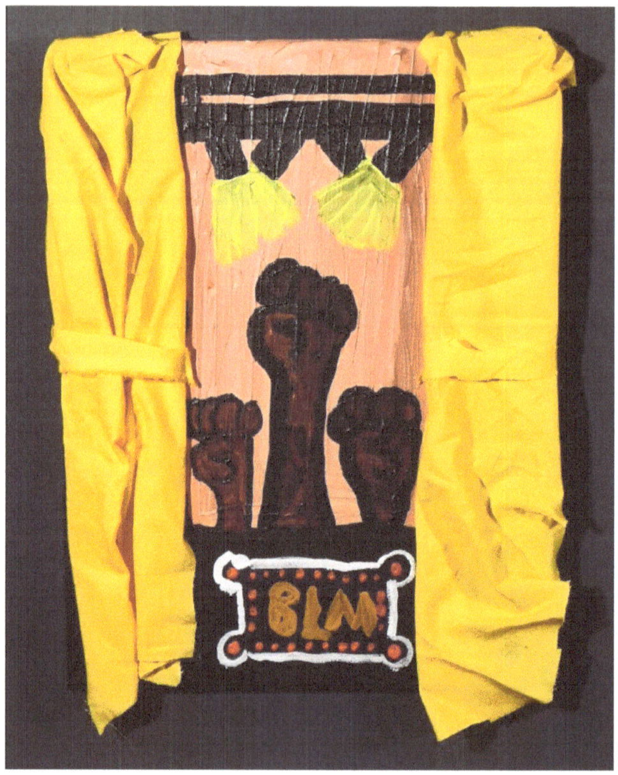

- Marcus Anderson Wilkerson Jr

SOS

The purpose of my art is to discuss animal cruelty because I hate to see animals fighting each other and I really hate people hunting animals for sport, greed and the fun of it. Animals are equal to us, not less than.

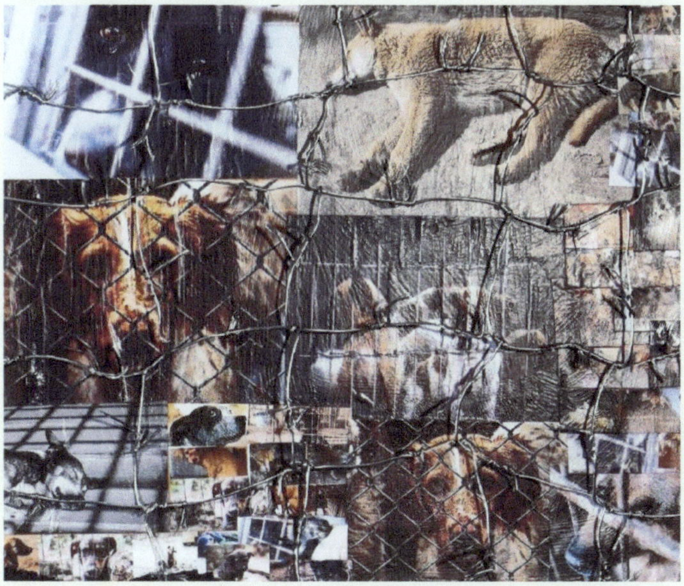

- Raphael Smith Jr

Boys Need More Elementary Teachers

My art is about the need for more Black teachers in school. I didn't have Black teachers in school. I like when there are Black teachers. I feel like they understand me.

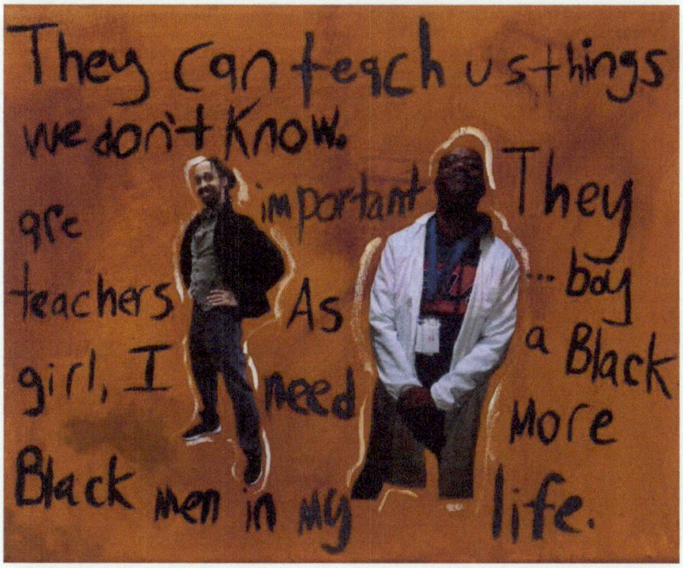

- Makenzie Williams

Colorism: Black is Magic

My art is about colorism. Colorism is when people judge you because of how dark or light-skinned you are. I learned about colorism and where it came from-slavery. I am trying to show how we are all colors and colorism is wrong. We are all beautiful.

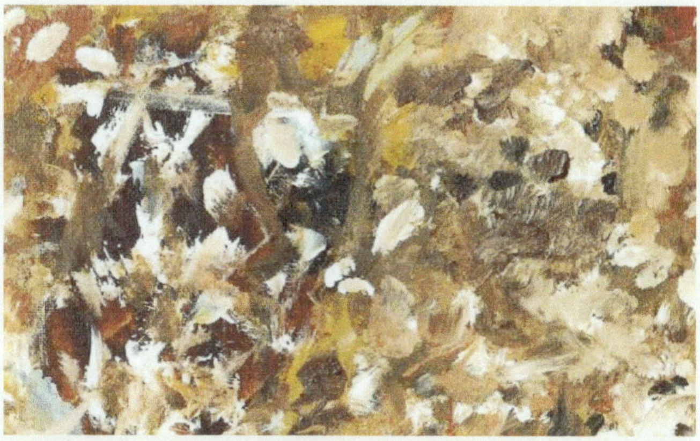

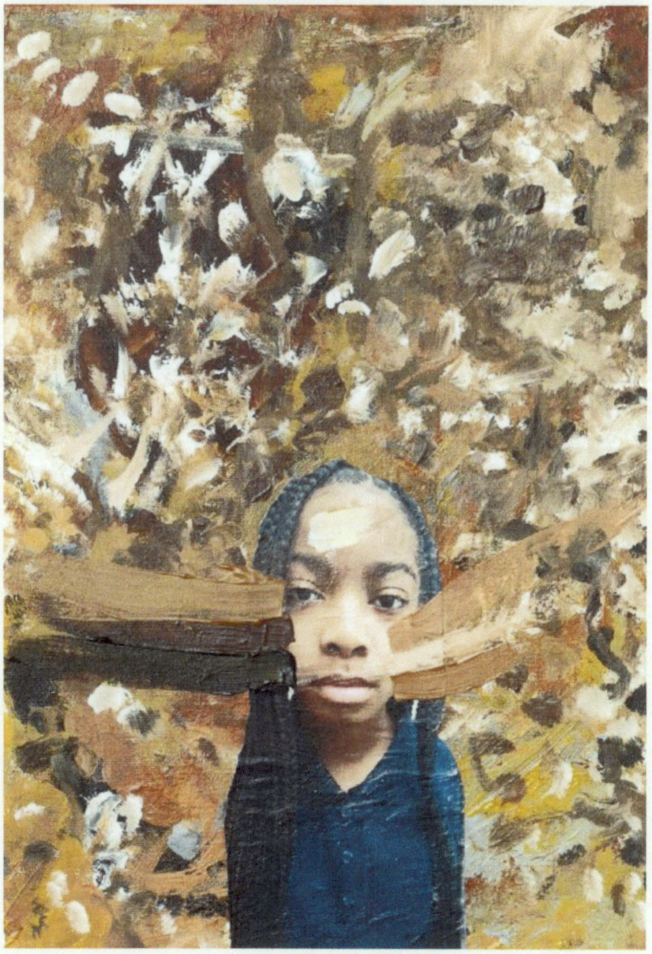

- Nyja Walker

The Story of 13th

I didn't know anything about racism and jails before doing this. Police were taking a lot of people to jail and White people forced them to go to jail because they were Black. The purpose of my art is to stop racism and lower the percentage of Black people going to jail.

- William Cornelius Jr

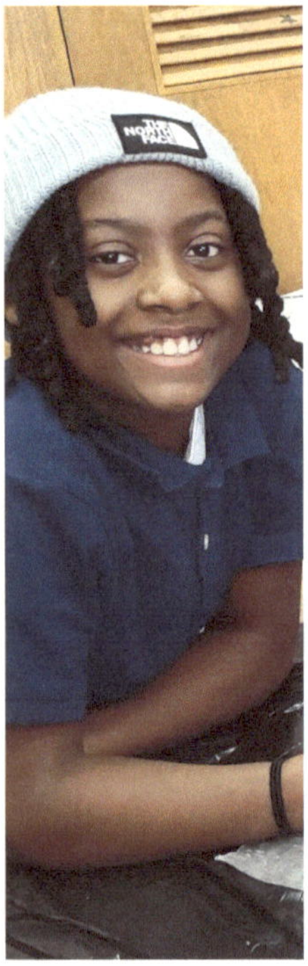

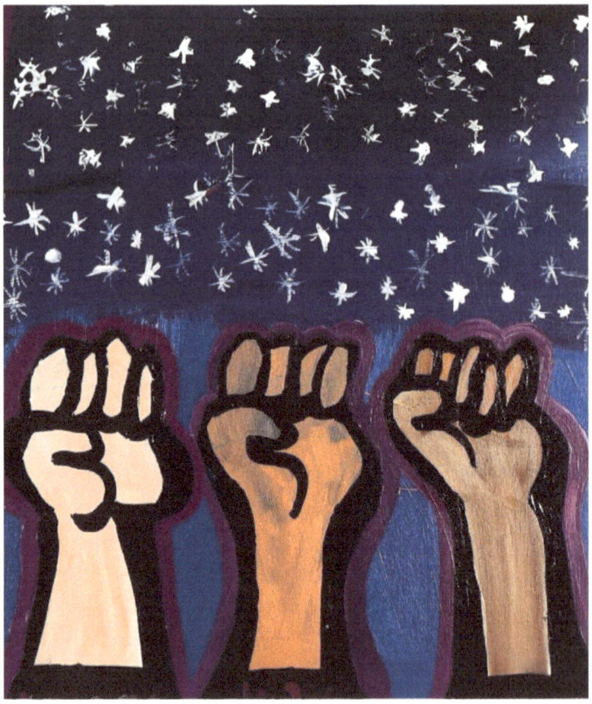

He Means A Lot To Me

This is my second year having a male teacher since preschool and I am 11 years old. I think that we should have way more male teachers because I want to be able to talk to a male teacher about my problems. The purpose of my art is to make sure you all know we need more male elementary teachers in school.

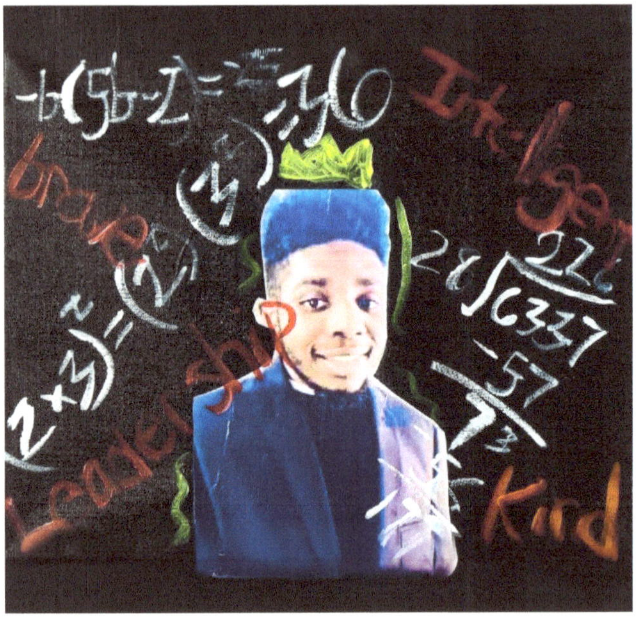

- Cayden Jackson

When I Was Cyber Bullied

I was cyber bullied. Did you know that? The purpose of my art is to talk about not getting bullied.

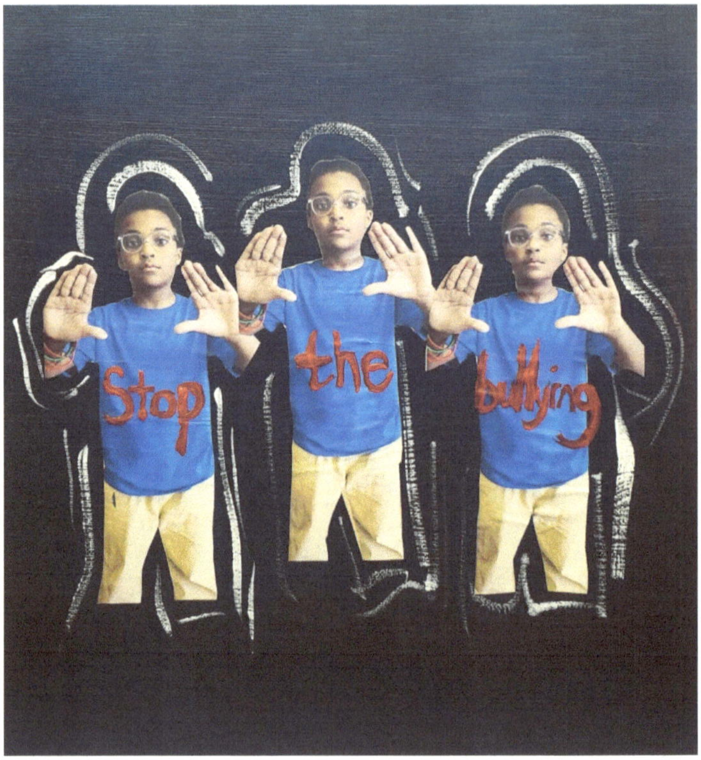

- Douglas Byers Baldwin

Racism

My art is about the racism Black people face in the world. These are pictures of my friends. There are four canvases. I wrote a poem about being Black. I cut the poem in strips because people don't see who we really are. They see that we are Black. I showed some of the people, but just some of them. You need to really understand who we are to know us.

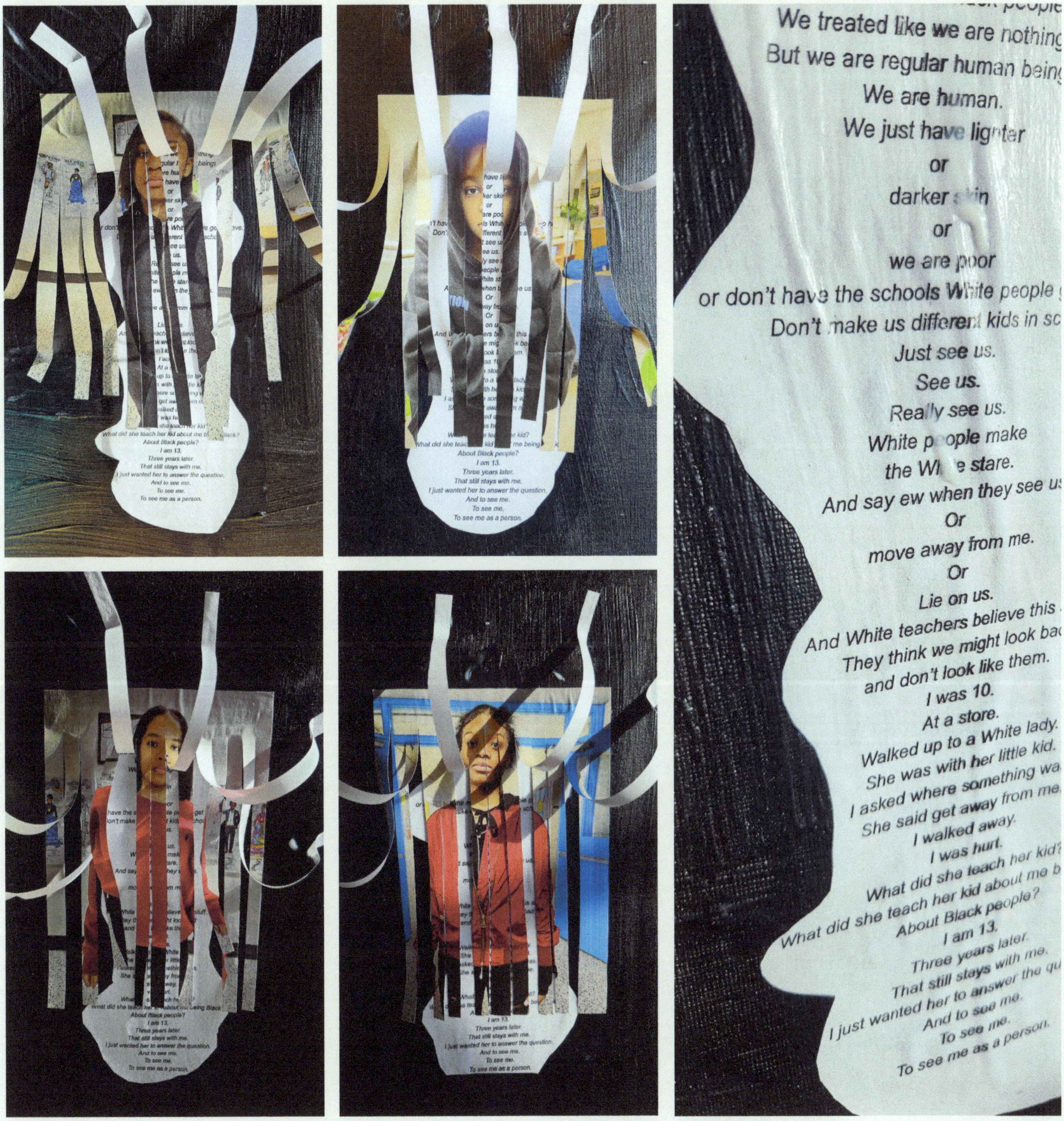

- Damiya Tucker

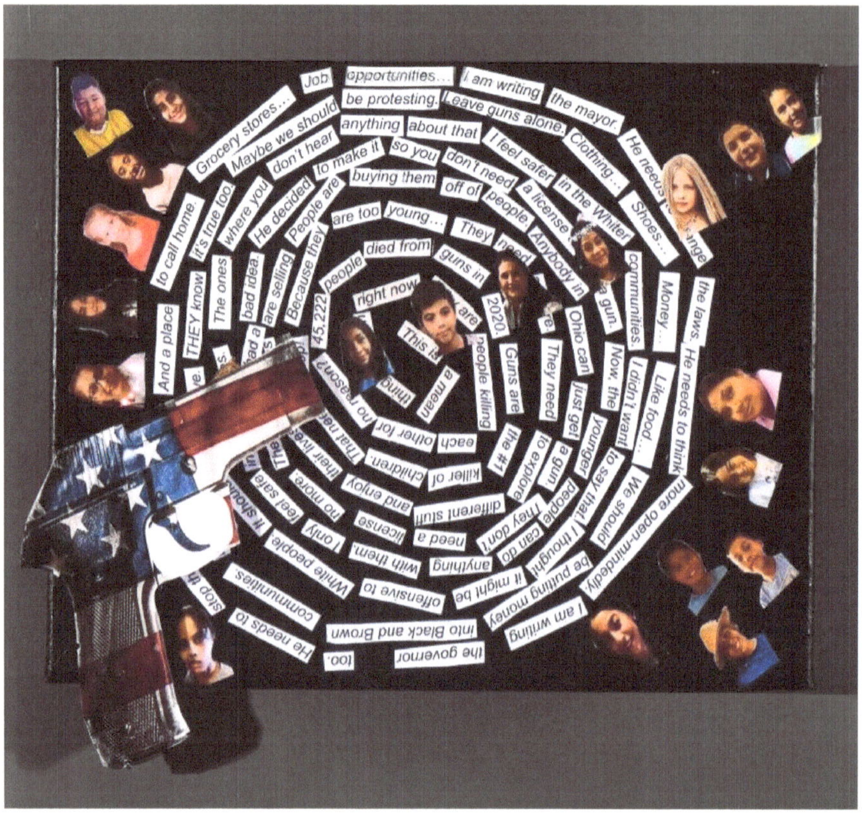

I Only Feel Safe in Certain Places

My art is about gun control. There are too many people getting shot and killed. I researched and learned Ohio doesn't have a real gun law. You can get a gun now even if you don't have a permit. I wrote to the mayor of Cleveland. I told him I wanted him to make sure anyone in Cleveland needed a permit for a gun. I even scheduled a meeting with him. I didn't hear back.

- Kevin St. Clair

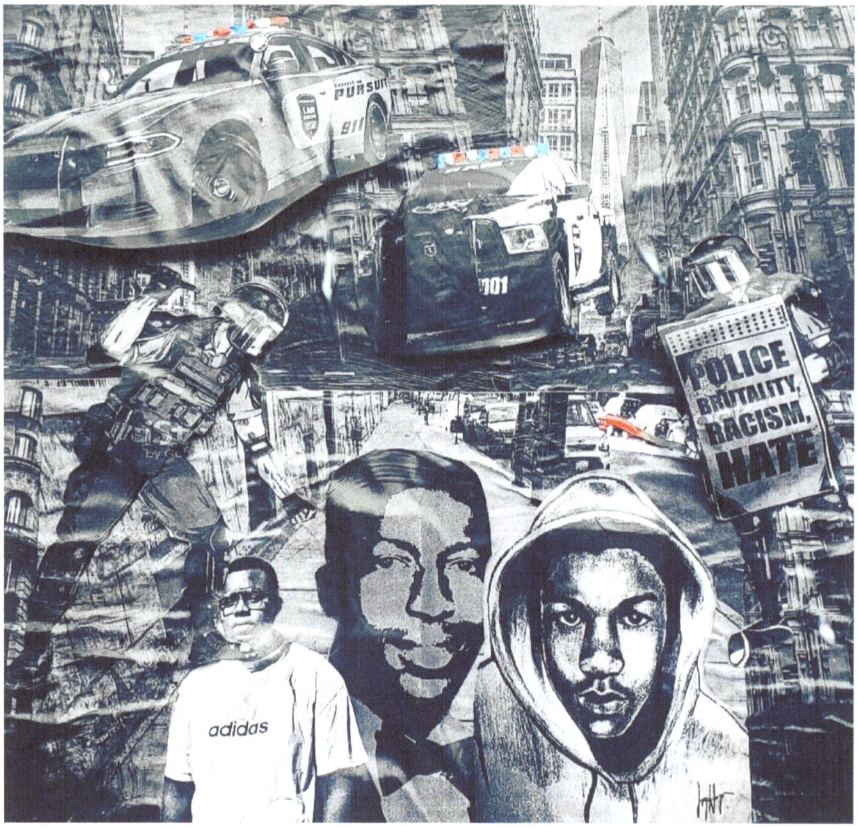

Stop the Police!

I didn't know what to do for my art. I decided to do police brutality. I made a collage of police cars and a police officer beating the three Black men and kids who were killed for being Black. I mod-podged everything and made the police cars pop out with the police. I also painted the baton red to show the blood from beating them.

- Brian Robinson Jr

SEVENTH GRADERS

YOU CAN'T STOP ME FROM READING

- Jaylon Chatmon

The purpose of my art is to let people know schools should not ban books. We should be able to read what we want to read. It's wrong. I want to learn about Black people and my culture. I researched and learned there are people trying to pass a law so schools keep books out about people like me. It's wrong. I made a chain over the books to show they are being kept from us.

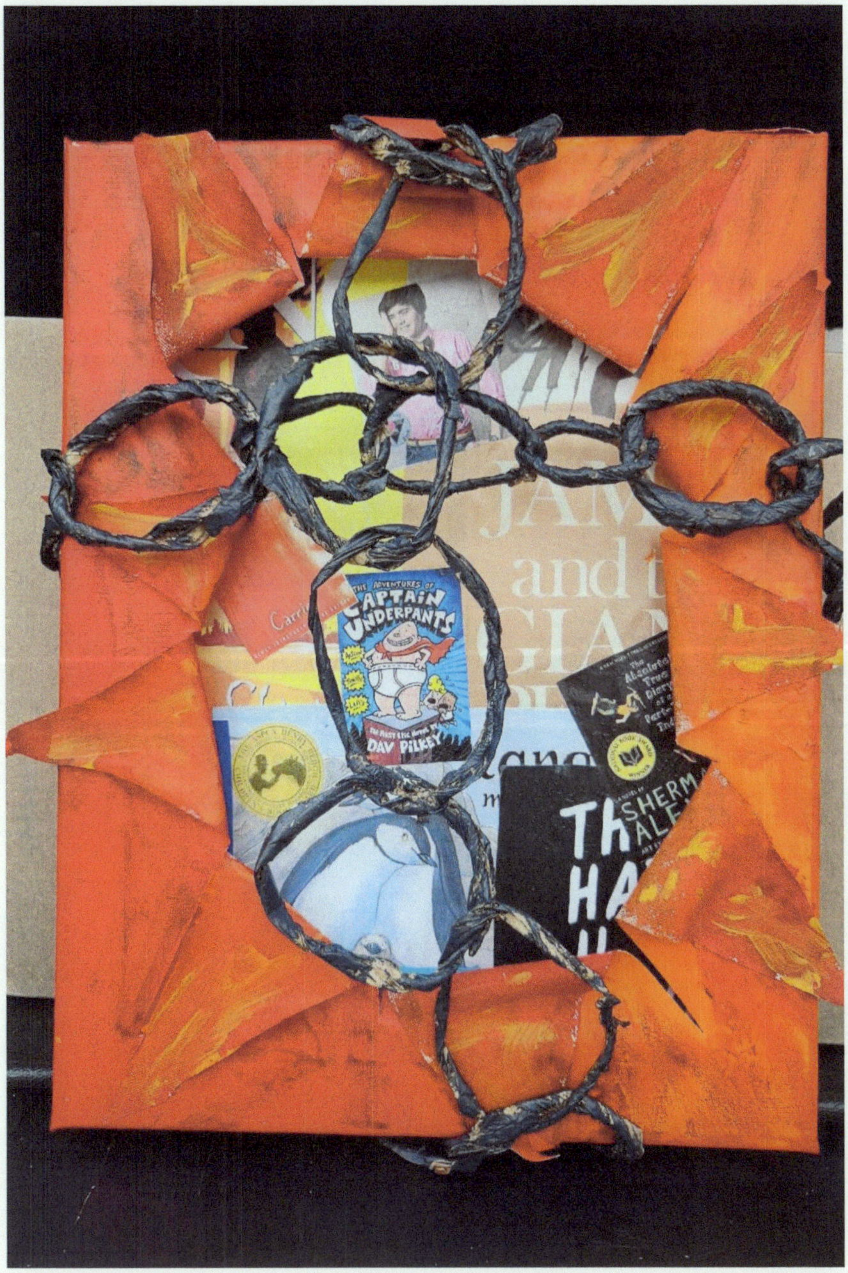

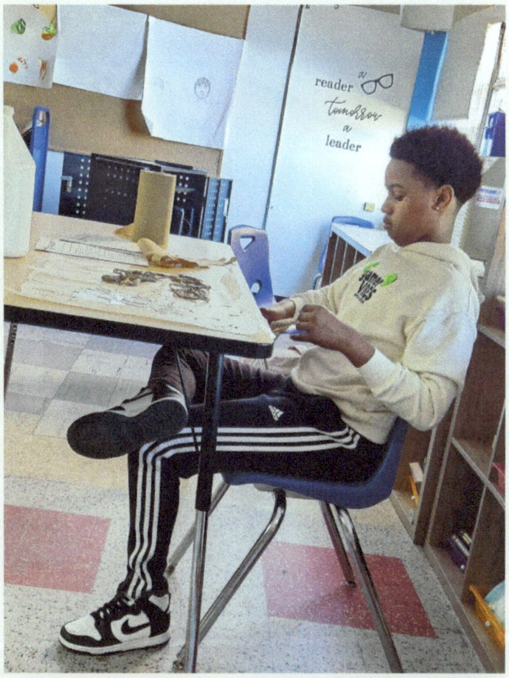

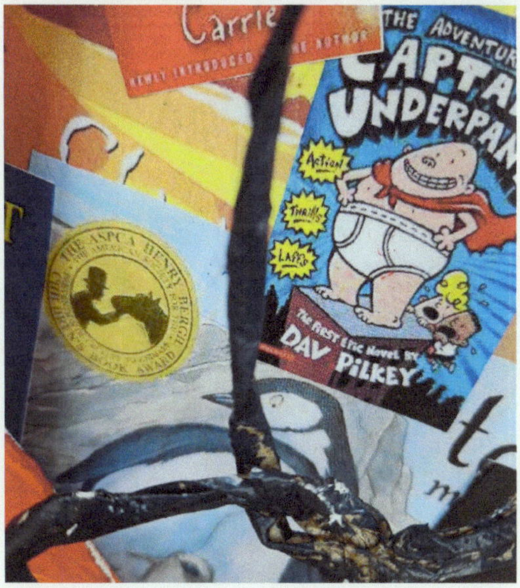

BULLIED

My art is personal. It is about what can happen if someone keeps getting bullied. I wrote a poem and mod-podged it on my art. The rocks represents the bullying. They are bringing the person down.

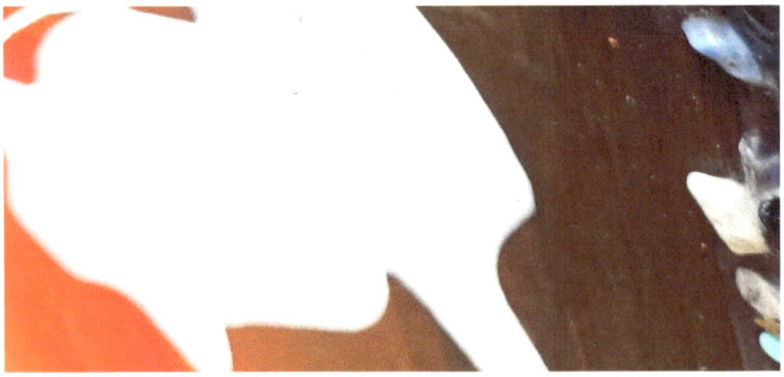

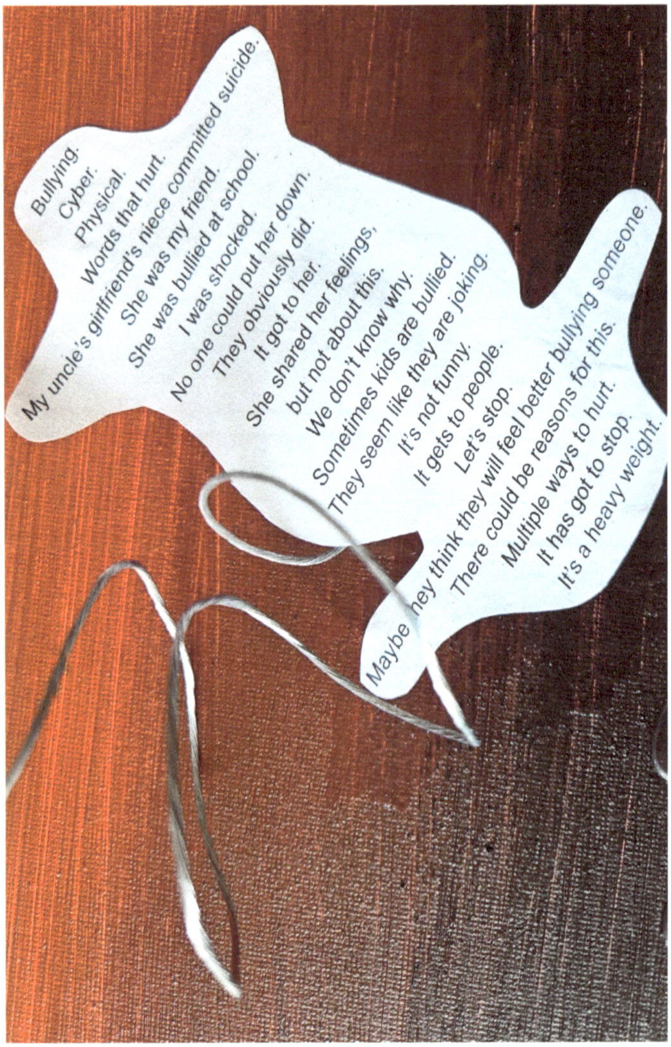

- Kamayah Hunter

WHITE MAN DOLLAR

My art is about knowing women make 80 cents to a man's dollar and Black women make 60 cents to a White man's dollar. This is not right.

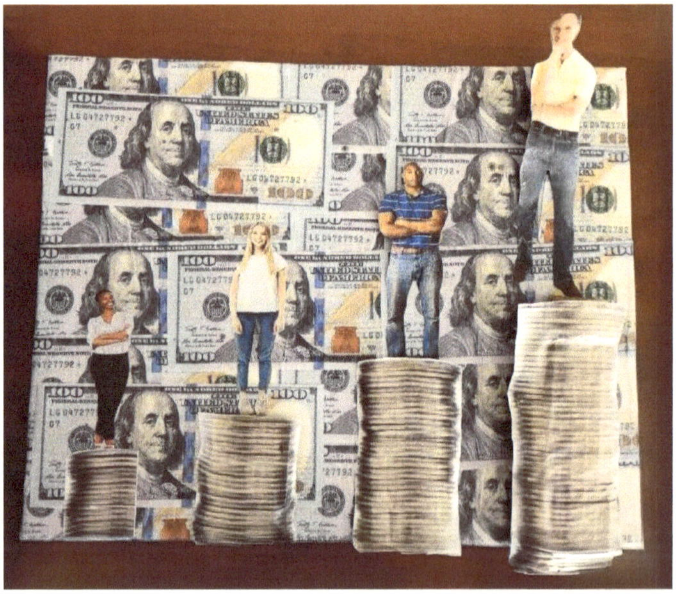

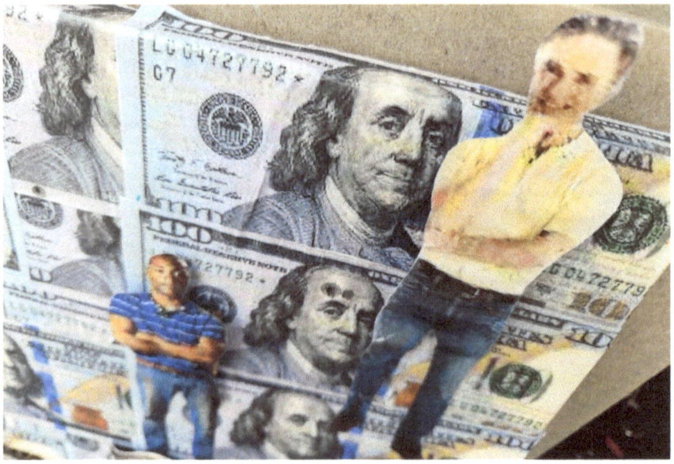

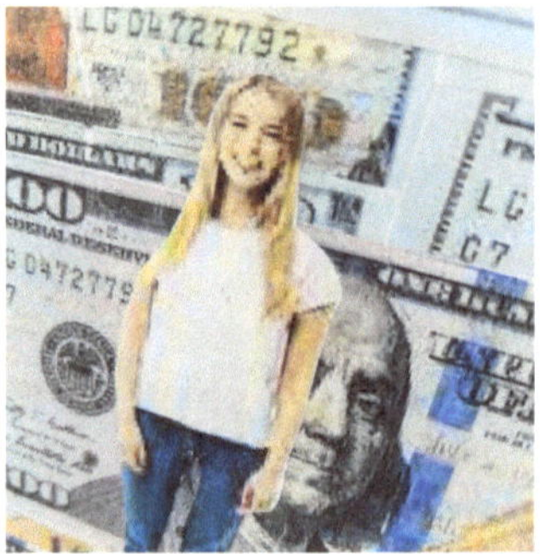

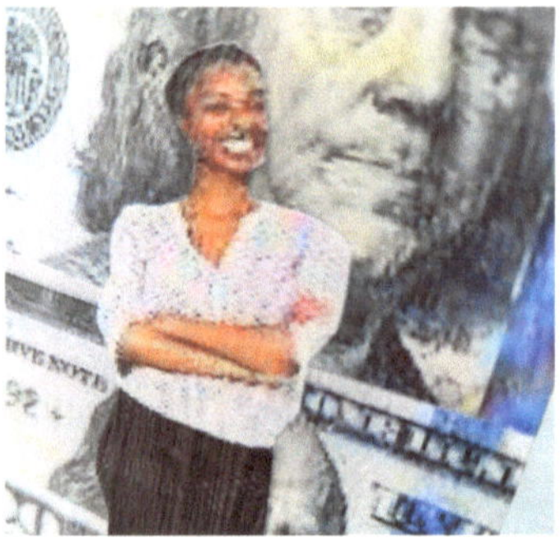

- Deandre' Chapman

LET US READ ABOUT OUR CULTURE

I didn't know this before. There are all these books being banned. We aren't allowed to read them because there are people changing laws. There are laws out there telling kids they can't read about their culture. I can't read about Black people in some schools. That's wrong.

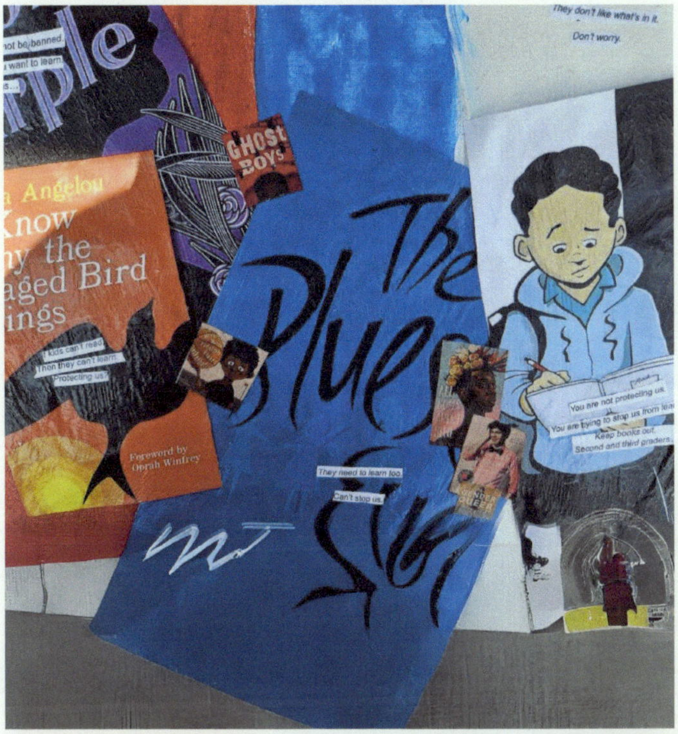

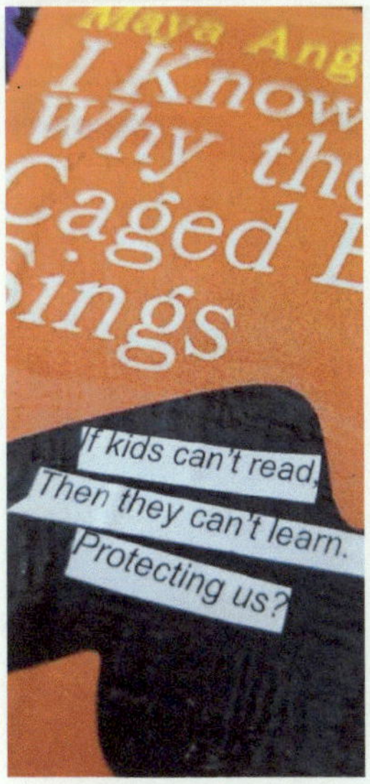

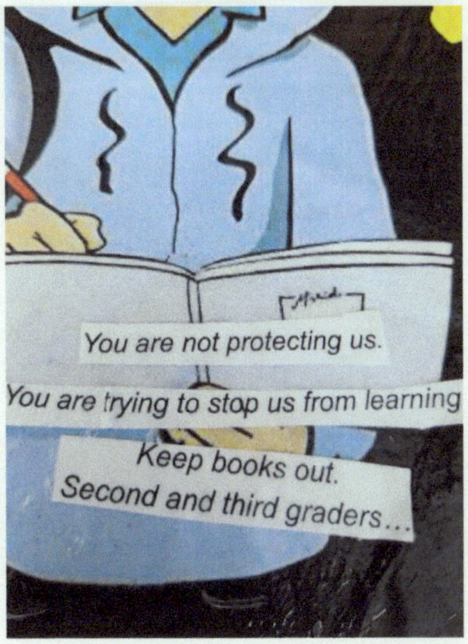

- Marlon Duncan

LOST IT ALL

My art is about the Tulsa Massacre. I didn't learn about this in school. I researched this and learned about what happened. The red line was painted because it shows how their neighborhood was turned upside down. Hundreds of lives were lost. Everything was destroyed by angry White people.

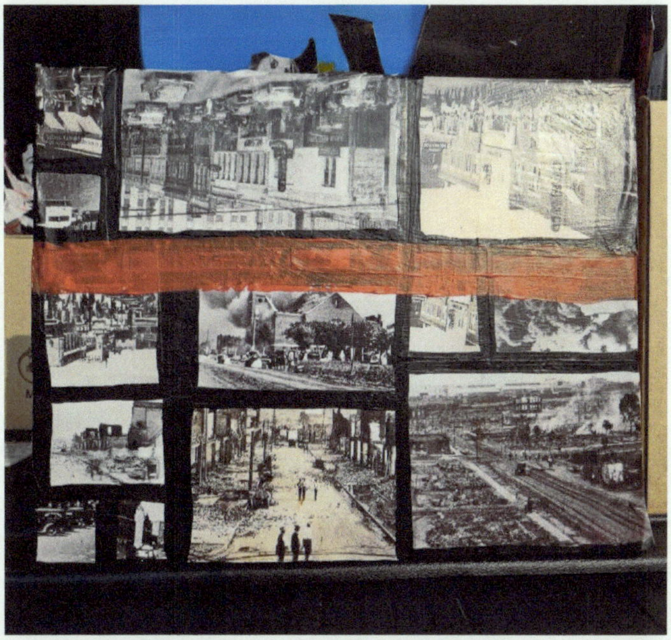

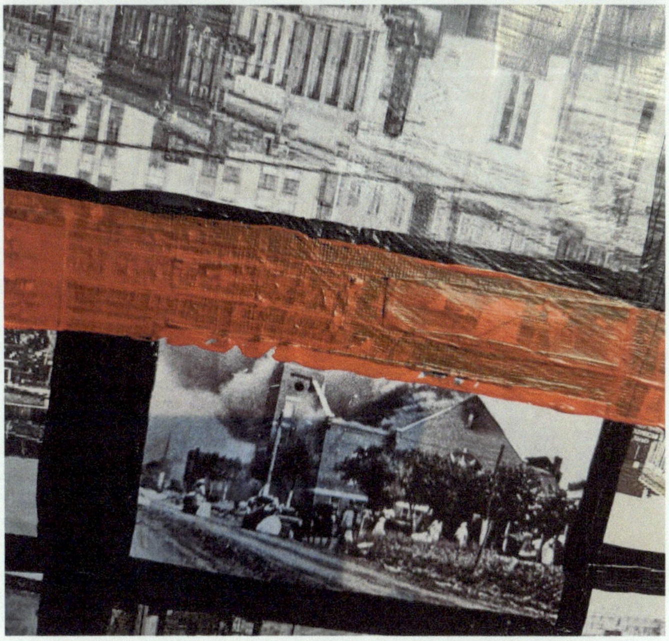

- Kayla Jackson

THE PAIN OF GENDER INEQUALITY

- Aaryn Walker

My name is Aaryn. I'm doing my project on gender because it's a really big problem in the U.S. Gender inequality is when, for example, a woman works way more than a man, but the man is paid way more than the hard-working woman. This is VERY wrong. Another example of gender inequality is when a husband expects his wife to work, cook, clean, and even take care of their child just because he's "the man". This belief goes back centuries! In the days of the first humans, men were expected to hunt and do the dirty "manly jobs", while the woman had to watch the children, cook, and clean! So that belief and way of life has evolved all the way into how we live right now. Even though some people are more aware of it now and try to stop it, some other people want women to do all the hard stuff anyway. So, I KNOW and claim that gender inequality needs to end!!!

I made a piece of art that shows how unfair gender inequality can be jobwise. I cut out and glued sad women's faces onto a canvas in the form of steps that lead up to a male boss looking down the "steps" to men who are coming to meet the boss for a job interview. This art piece shows how men can get a job from another man more easily than a woman. The steps represent women working as hard as they can, but men still get a HUGE advantage, which is why the man is walking up the steps with ease. I want people to know about how unfair this world usually is towards women through the artwork. To summarize this all up, I just want to encourage you to treat all people fairly. No matter what the gender, all people should have the same opportunities. There shouldn't be "manly" and "womanly" things! There should just be human things.

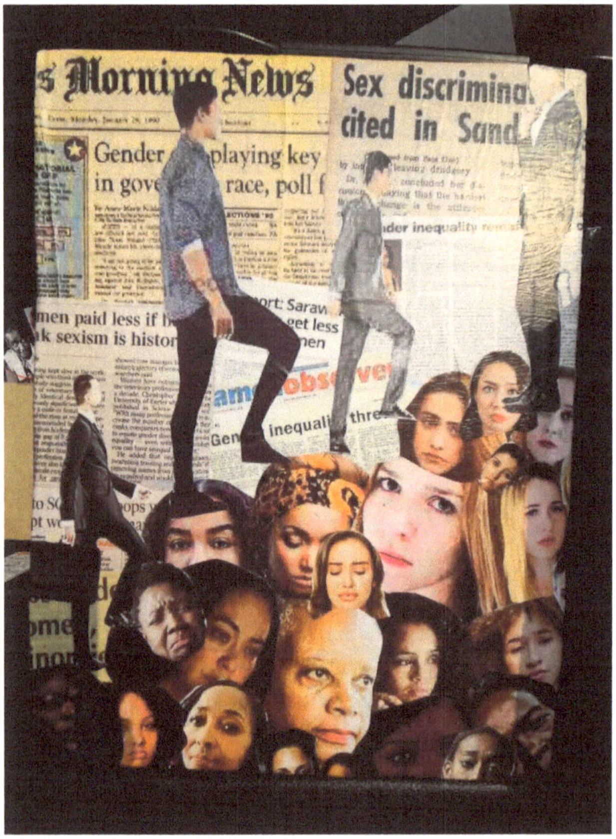

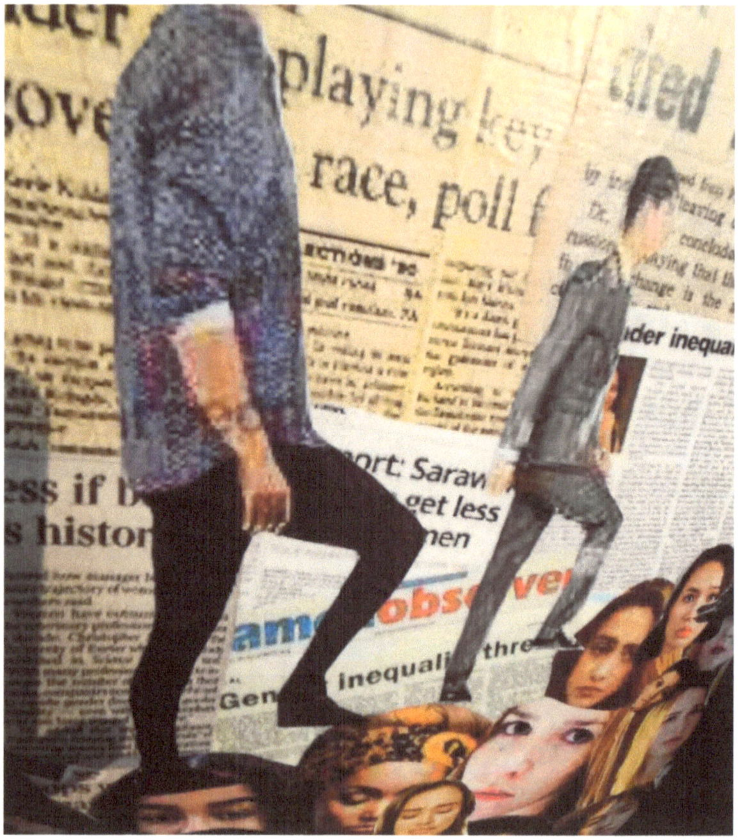

ALL BLACK LIVES MATTER

My art is about Black Lives Matter. I wrote my first poem and put it in my art. I tell you what it is like to be a young Black man.

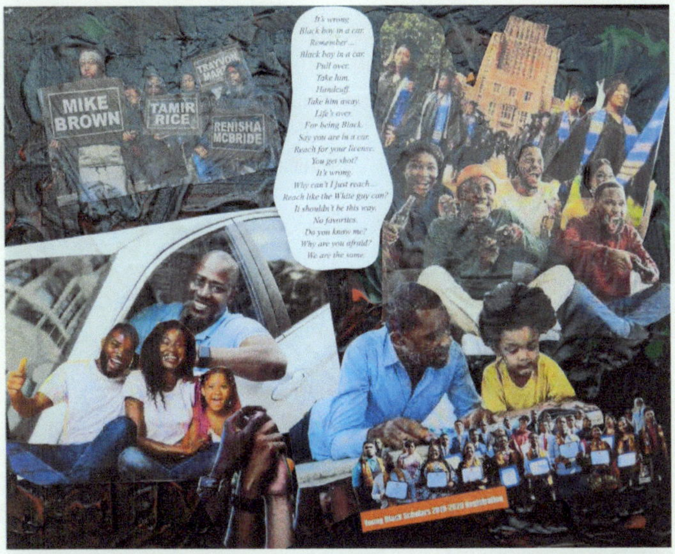

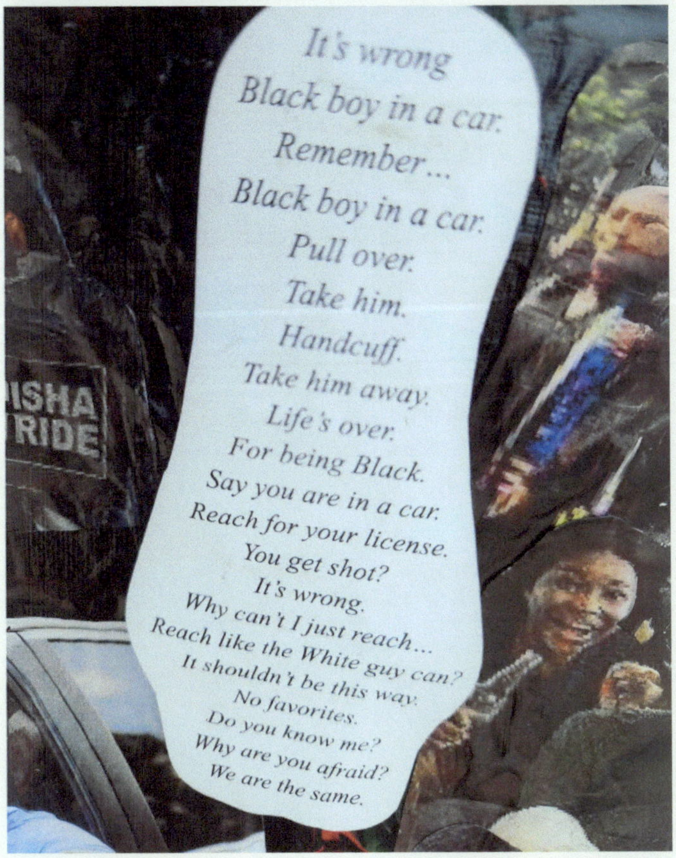

- Duane Lumpkin

THE LACK OF BLACK TEACHERS

My art is about the need for more Black teachers in schools. Over 90% of teachers are White, but schools have Black students. We need Black teachers in schools because they understand us and we can learn about our culture.

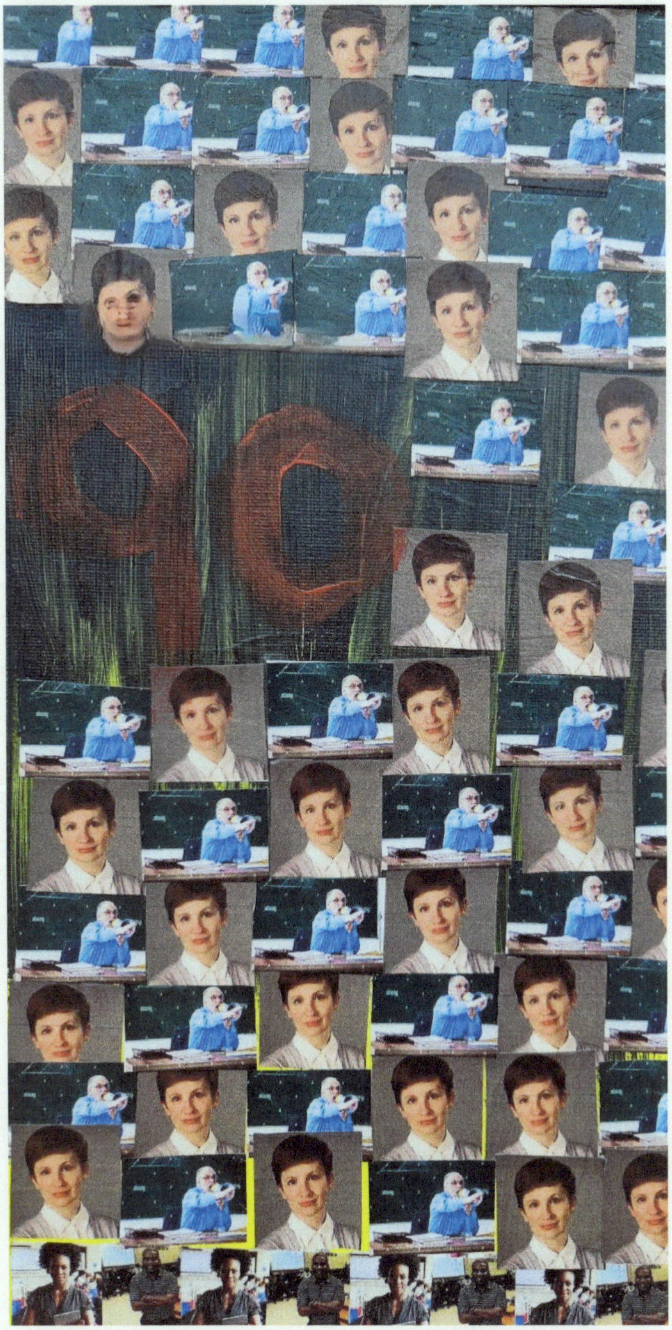

- Aryana Major

DRAYMOND GREEN; BLACK HISTORY MONTH

My art is about Black power. Black history should not be just 28 days in one month. This needs to be something we learn all year long. Let's go!

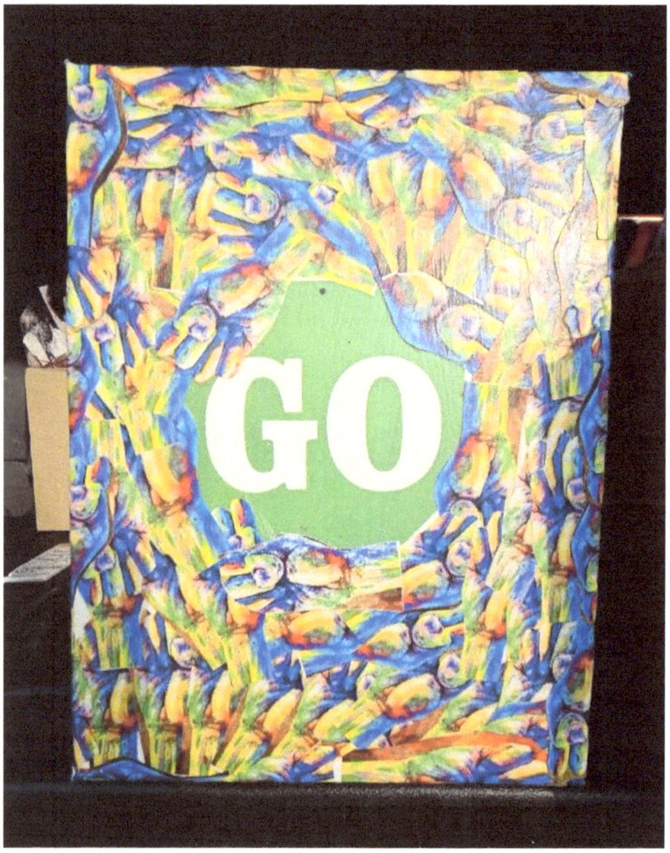

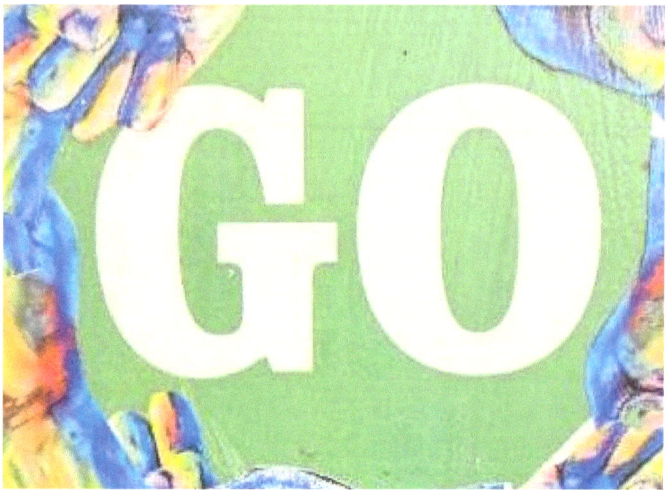

- Brooklynn Johnson

WHY BLACK HISTORY MONTH SHOULD LAST LONGER

My art is about making sure schools just don't talk about Black people during Black History Month. This should be taught all year long. I want to learn about Black people.

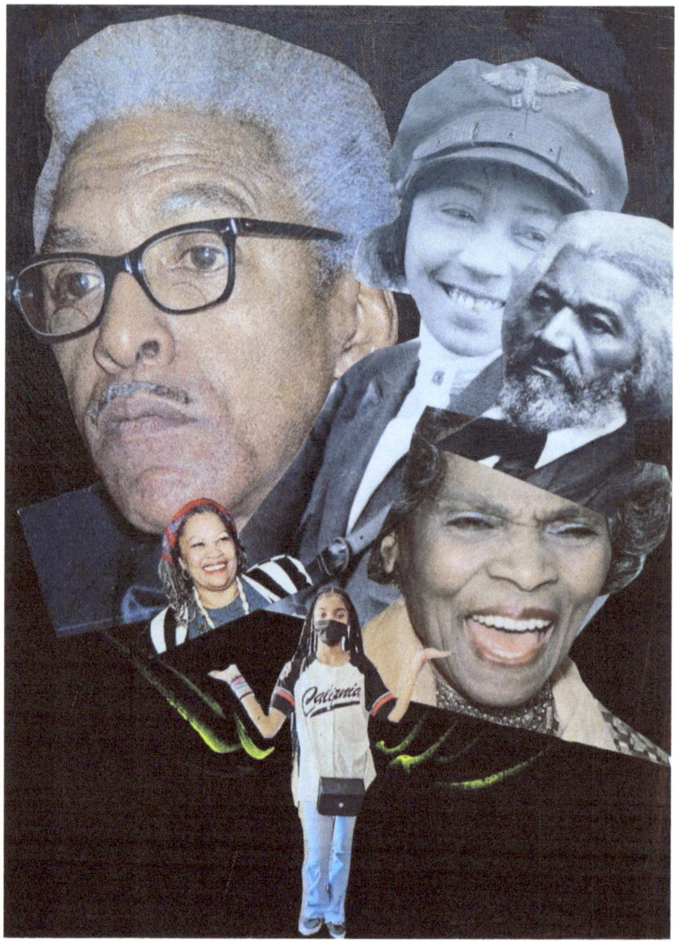

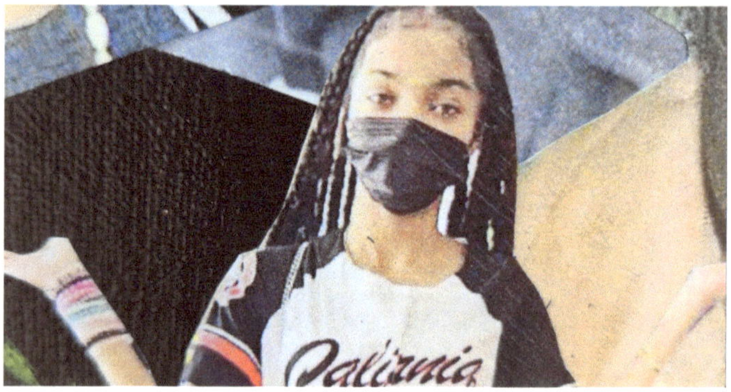

- Casey Goldwin

EMPLOYMENT DISCRIMINATION

My art is about employment discrimination against Black men and women. I researched this topic and learned how many obstacles Black people face getting a job.

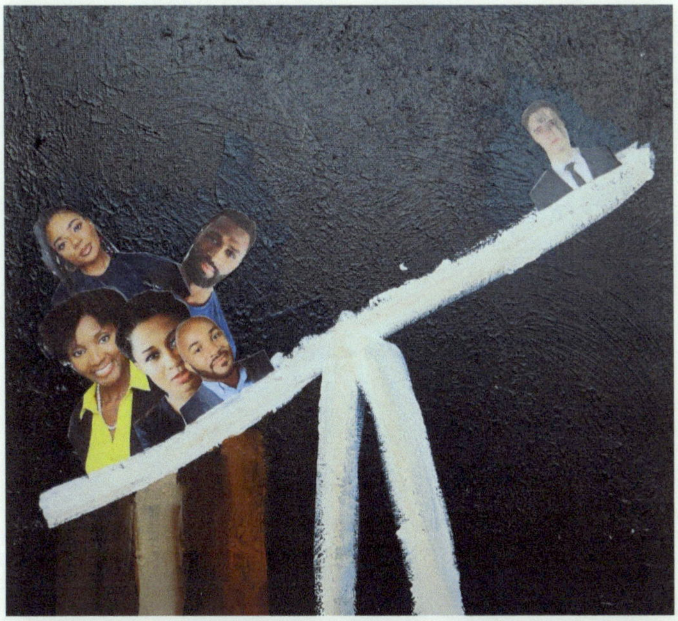

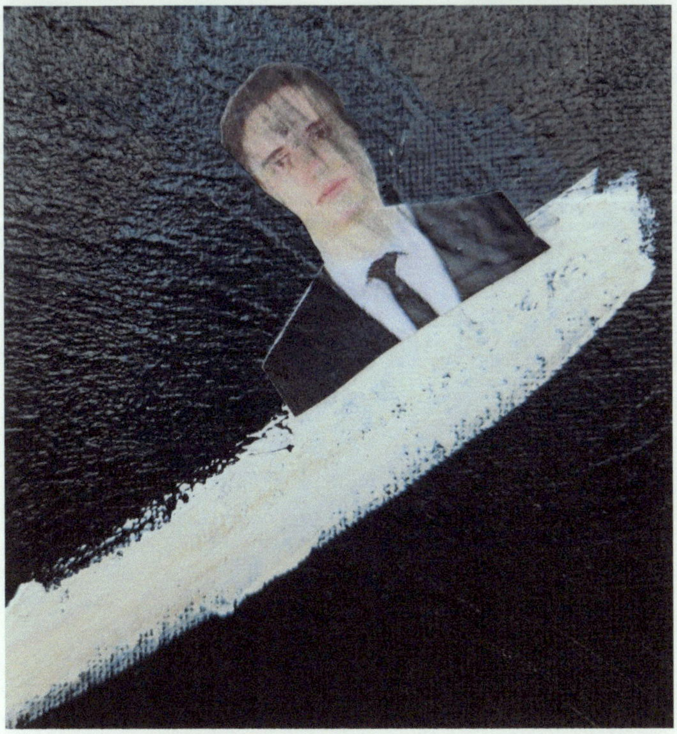

- *Kennis Talton*

WOMEN'S RIGHTS

My art is about women's rights and knowing how many struggles Black women continue to experience. Remember, our rights are HUMAN RIGHTS.

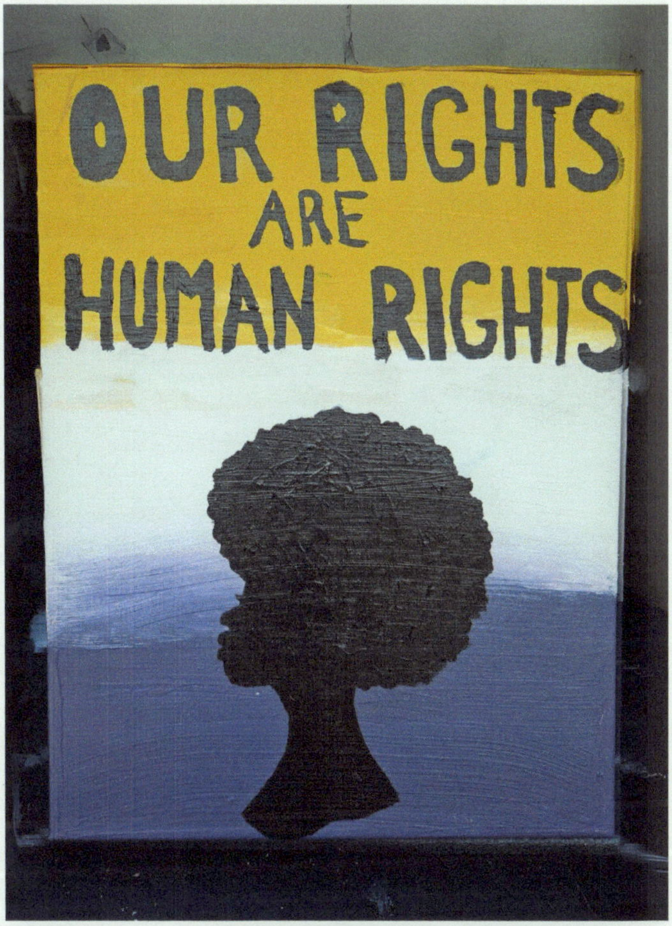

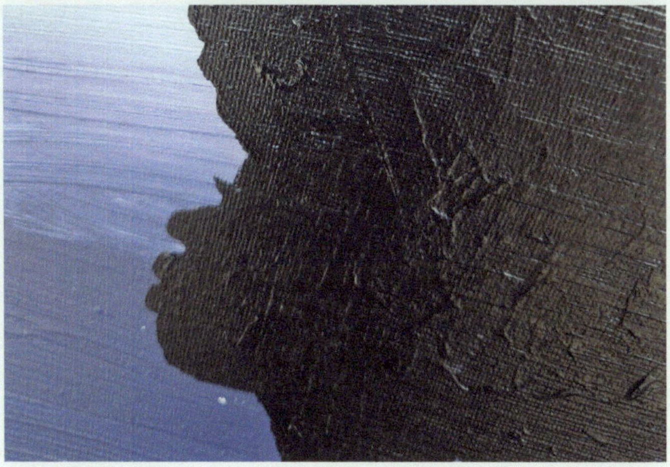

- *E'Laysia Rucker*

THE NEW NORM; BROKEN AMERICAN SCHOOLS

- Angel Cunningham

My art is about the school-to-prison pipeline. I didn't know about this before I did my research. I learned how schools are a way for kids to end up in prison. Their test scores in third grade help people decide how many prisons to build. Prisons are filled with people who have a hard time reading, writing, and people who didn't make it through school. I made prison bars over the children.

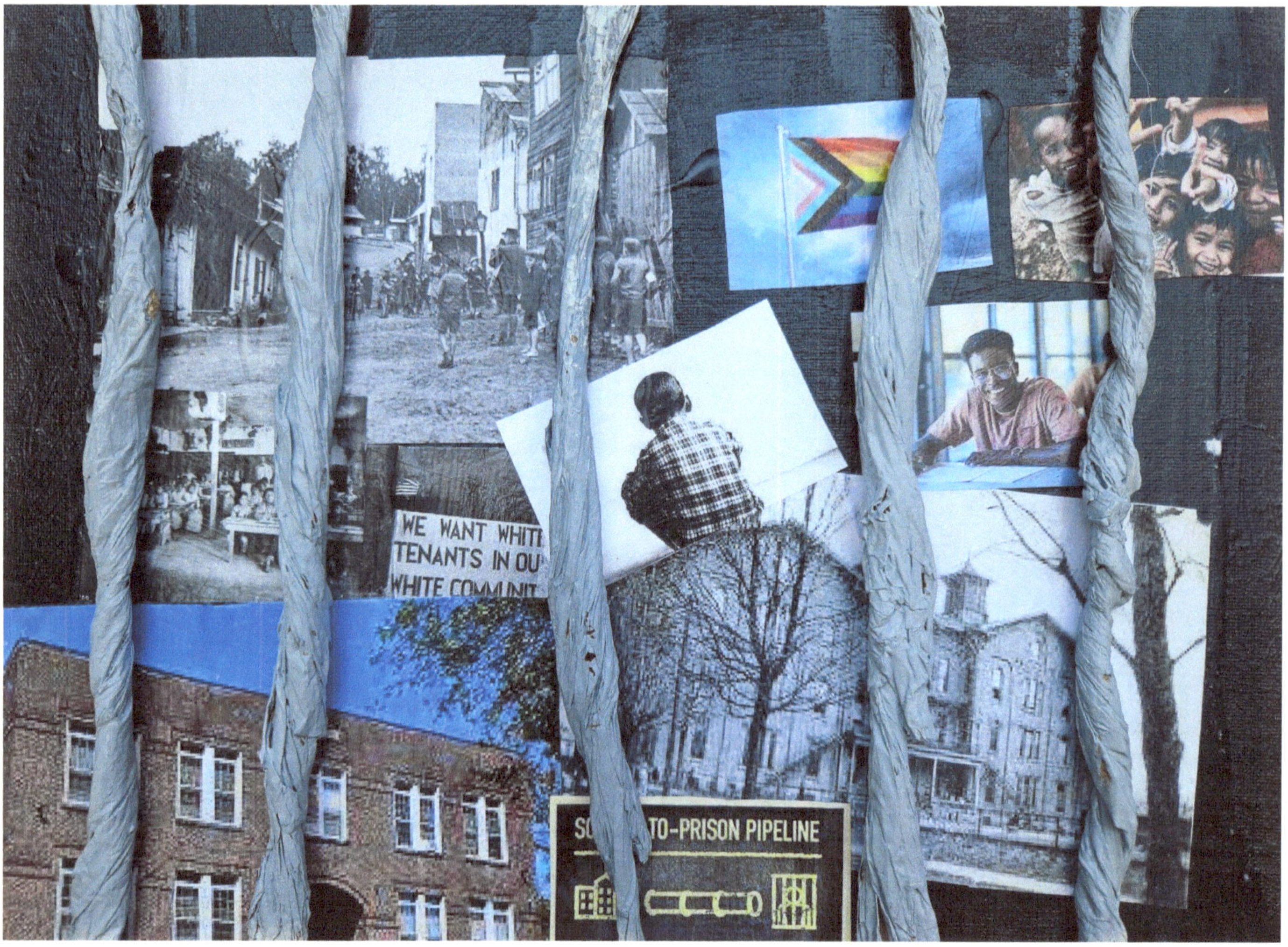

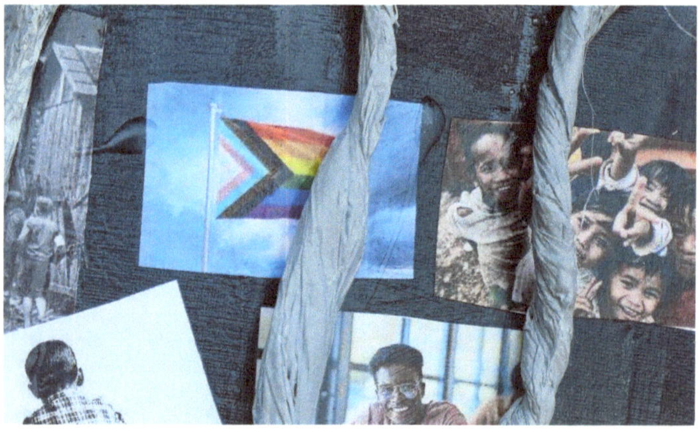

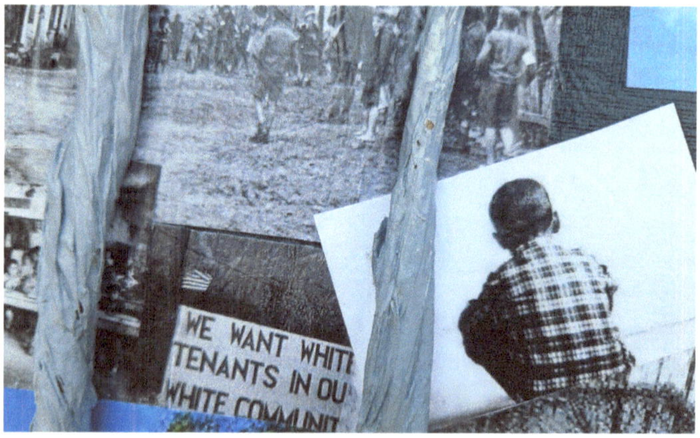

EMMETT TILL TRAGEDY

My art is a time-line starting from slavery until today. I researched a lot of things that happened in history to Black people. Racism still happens today. Hate against Black people still happens.

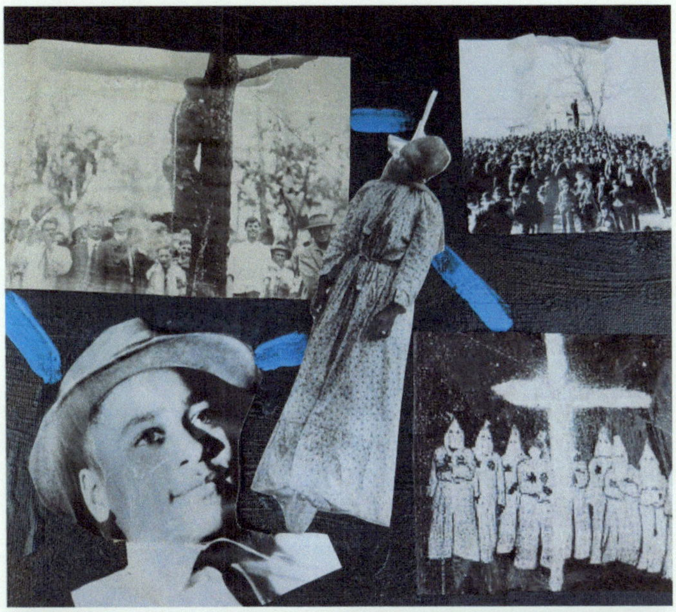

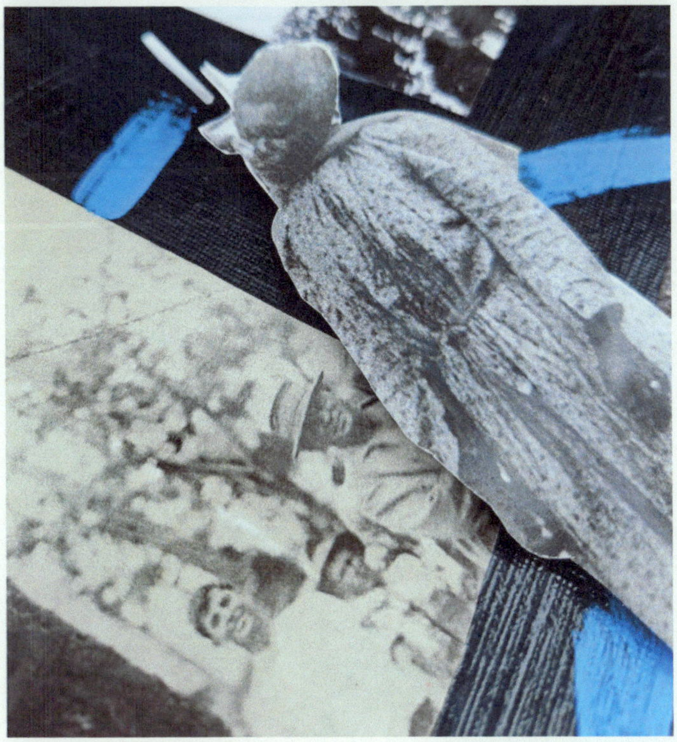

- Jayden Garrett

DIFFERENCES ARE DRIVEN BY SOCIETY

Gender differences are just made up. My art is about the stereotypes about men and women. There shouldn't be colors that go with someone's gender. Pink isn't just for girls. Blue isn't just for boys. We need to change the way we think. Girls and boys can do the same things. They don't have to do certain jobs or act certain ways.

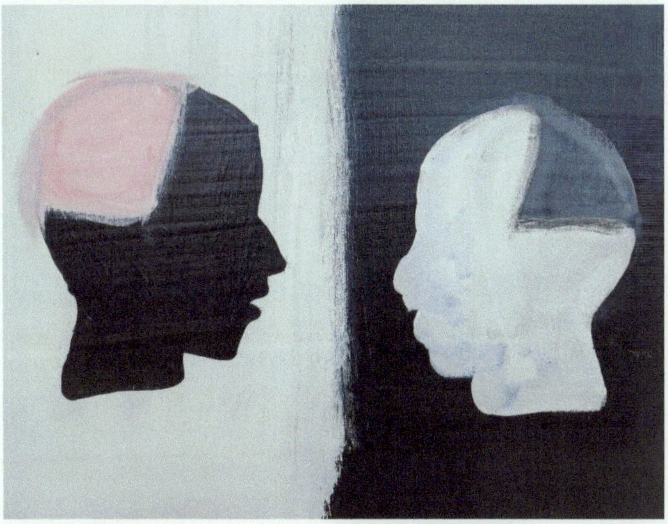

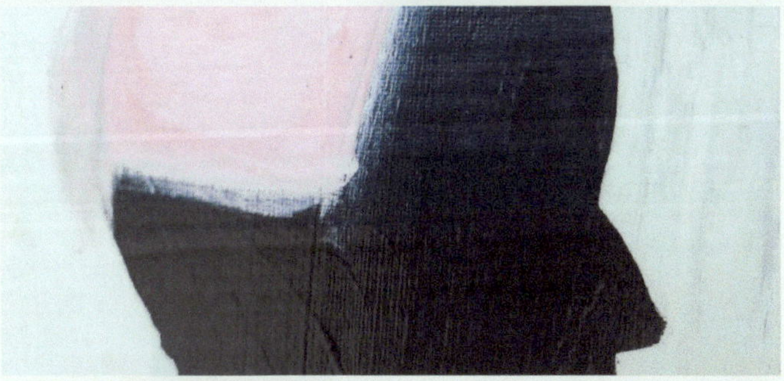

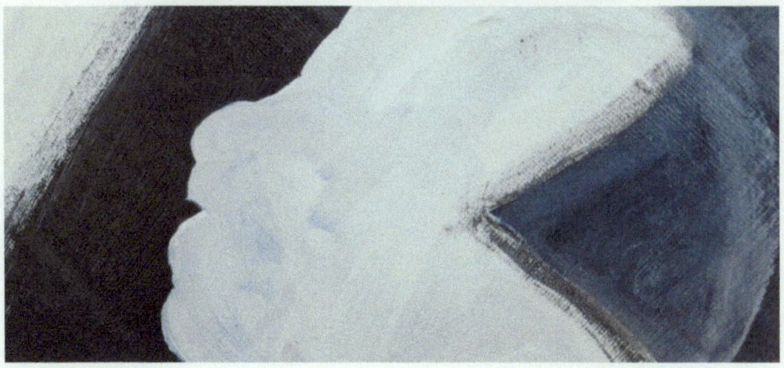

- Marquel Darby

GUN VIOLENCE

My art is about gun violence and all of the school shootings that happen. I researched how many school shootings there are in the United States. There were at least 77 school shootings this year!

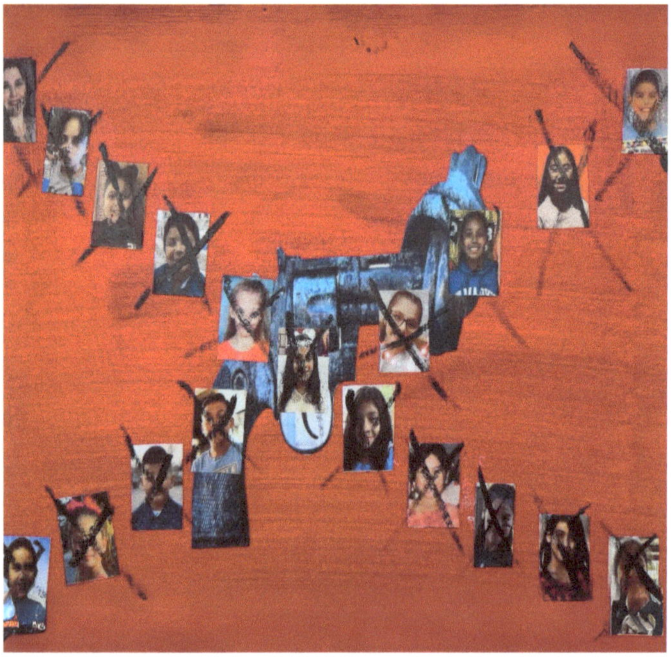

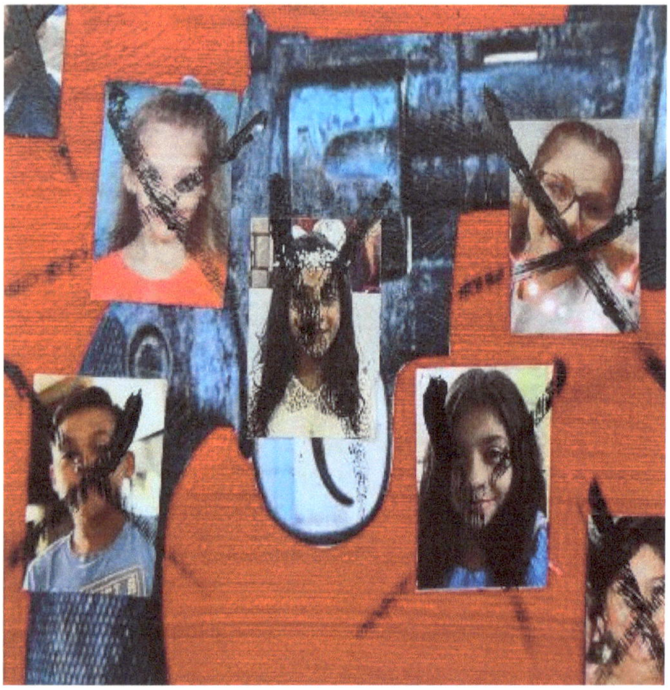

- Stephen Goldwind

BLACK LIVES MATTER

My art is about Black Lives Matter and the people who died from police killing them. I wrote a poem and mod-podged it on my art. I am raising my fist saying power to Black people.

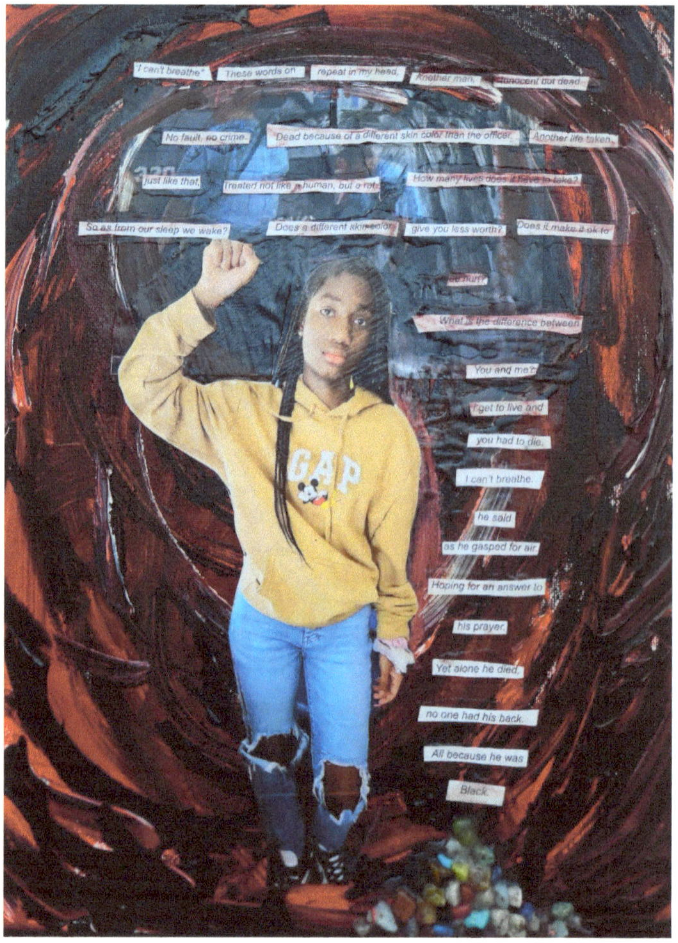

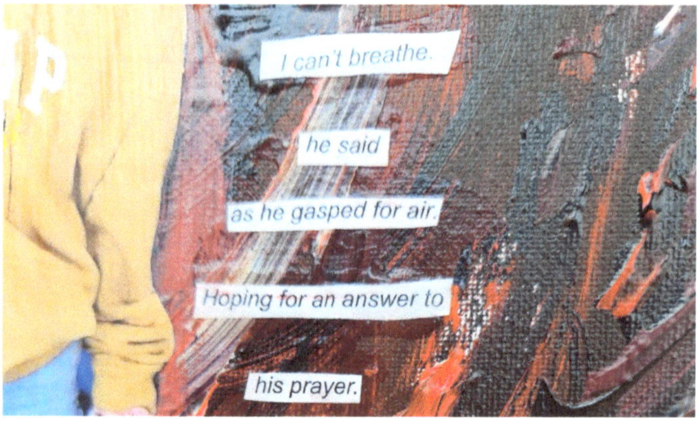

- Autumn Allen

EIGHTH GRADERS

Injustice

- Sebastian Montiel

My art is about the Tulsa Massacre and Black Wall Street. The Black community was destroyed by fire and hundreds were murdered. I made a hole in the canvas to show the mass graves White people made to hide what they did to this community.

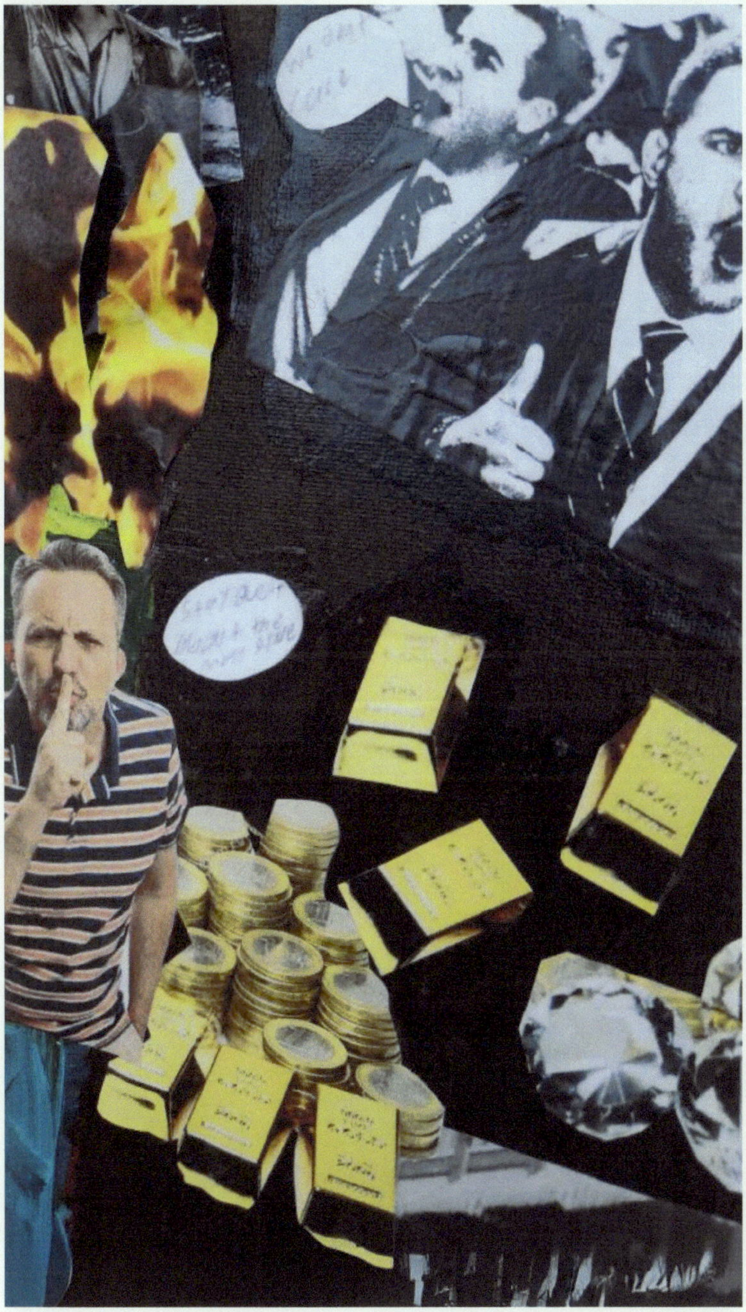

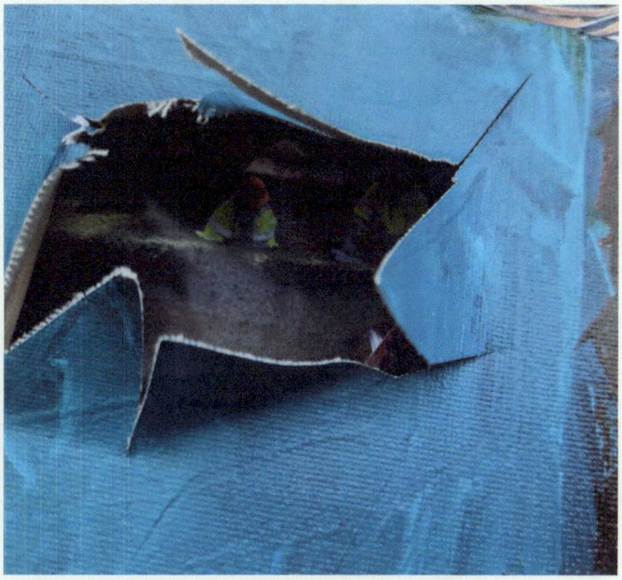

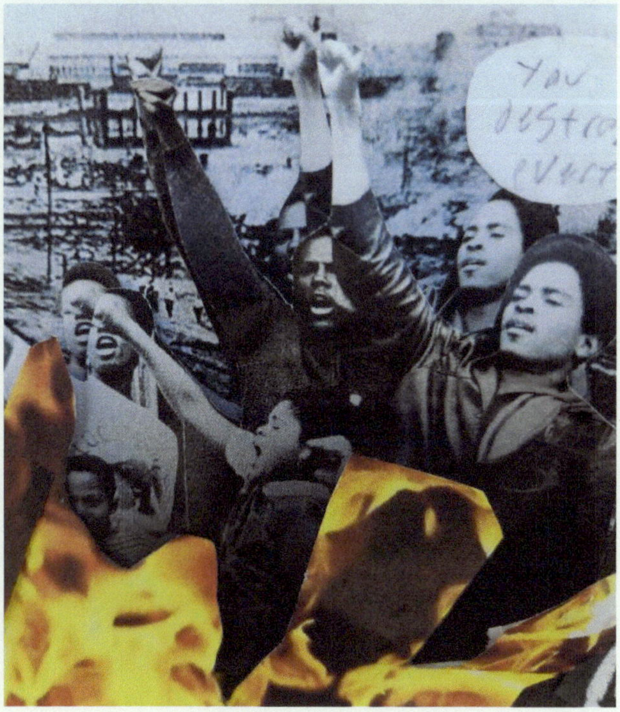

The School-to-Prison-Pipeline - *Xayden Harrell*

My are is about the school-to-prison pipeline. I never heard of this before. I did research and learned all about it. My art takes you from school to prison and shows where so many young Black men and women end up because they didn't have the same schooling experiences as most White students.

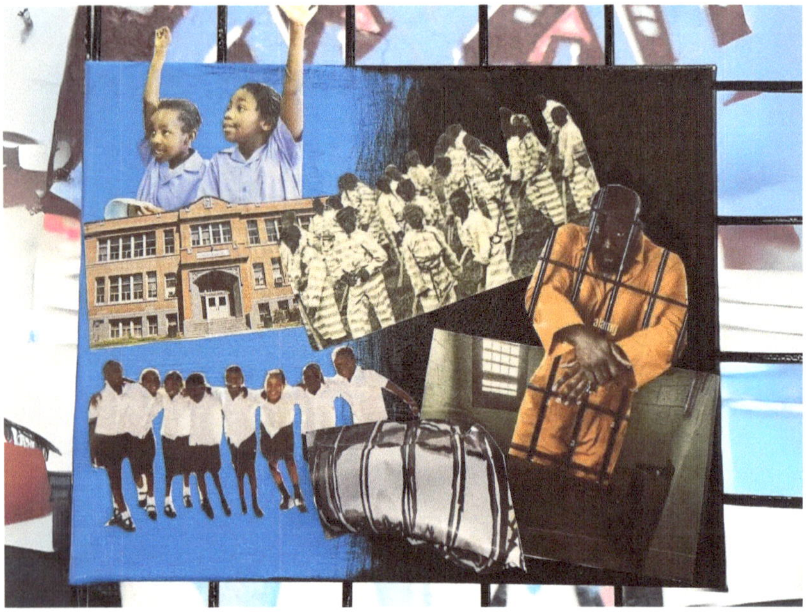

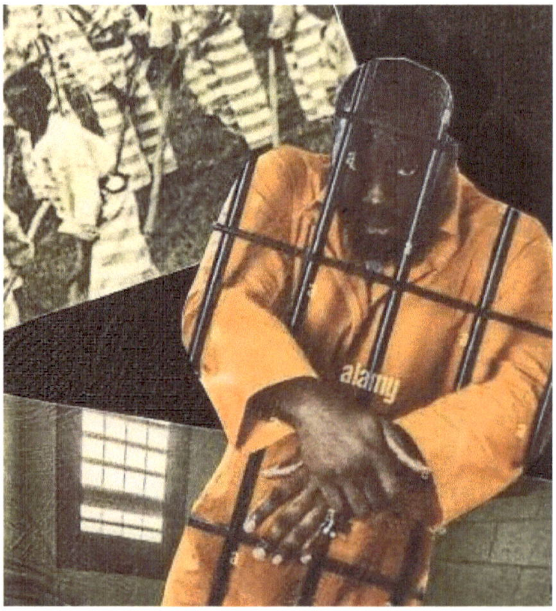

Toxic Masculinity - *Bria Johnson*

My art is about the negative messages being sent to men and women about the roles they play.

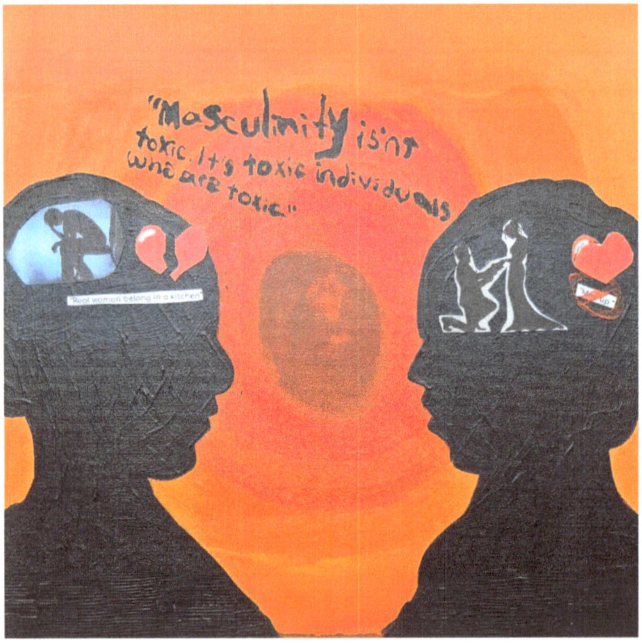

On Fire-Book Banning! - *James*

My art is about book banning. I did research. These are books that are banned from schools. I don't understand why books are being banned from us. I put flames around the books that are banned because that is part of book banning. Sometimes people set books they banned on fire!

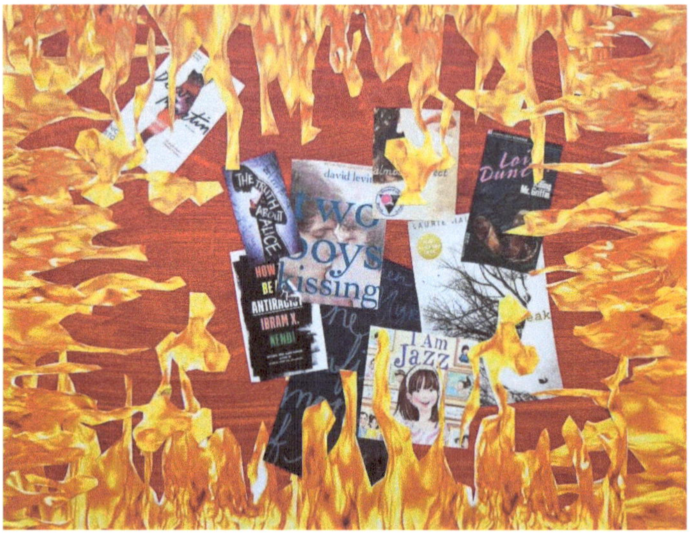

It Should Not Be a Secret! — *Hailey*

My art is about banning books. I didn't know this was a thing. I researched the thousands of books that have been banned by schools. I read a lot of those books. I made a hole in the canvas. I made it a secret room. We took a picture of me sitting reading and we put it in the secret room. I found caution tape and put it across the canvas and around the secret reading space. We should not have to hide what we read. Books should not be banned.

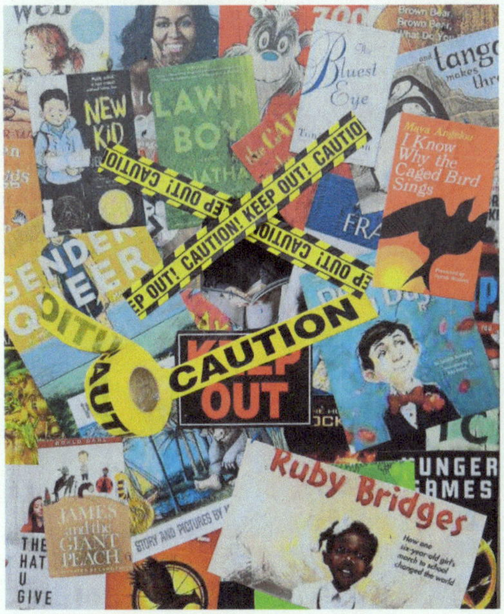

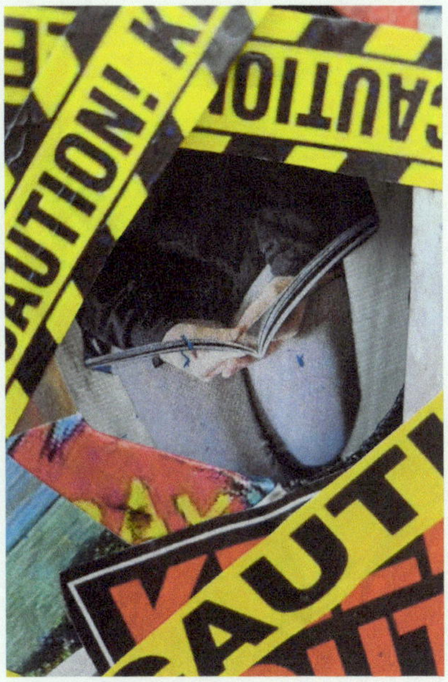

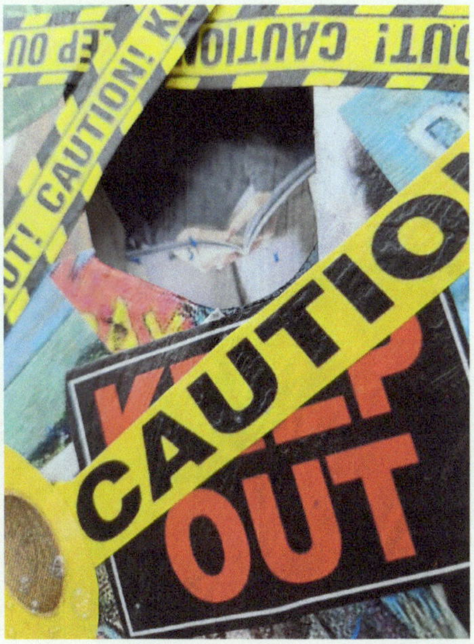

The Causes of HB 327 — *Christopher Salary Jr*

My art is about Ohio's HB327. This bill says schools cannot talk about race, real history, or about the LGBTQ community. They call this divisive. This bill is erasing our history. We need to learn about these things. I made a hand in the fist to show power to the people. It's in African American flag colors. I also put a rainbow on the left side to show we need to care about people who are in the LGBTQ community.

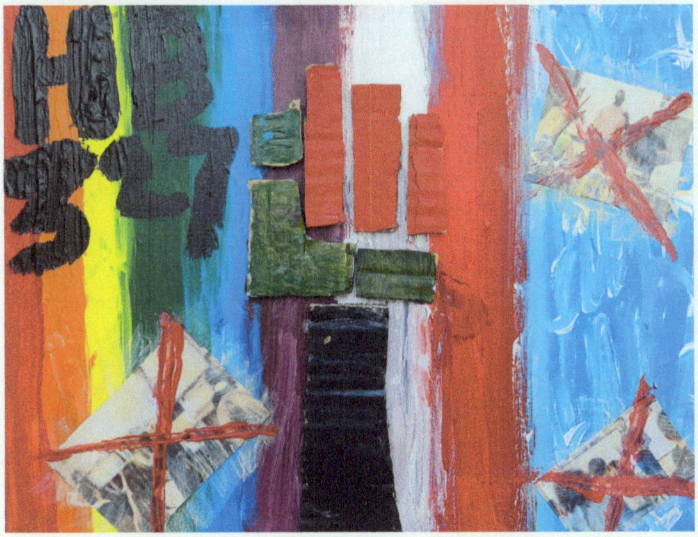

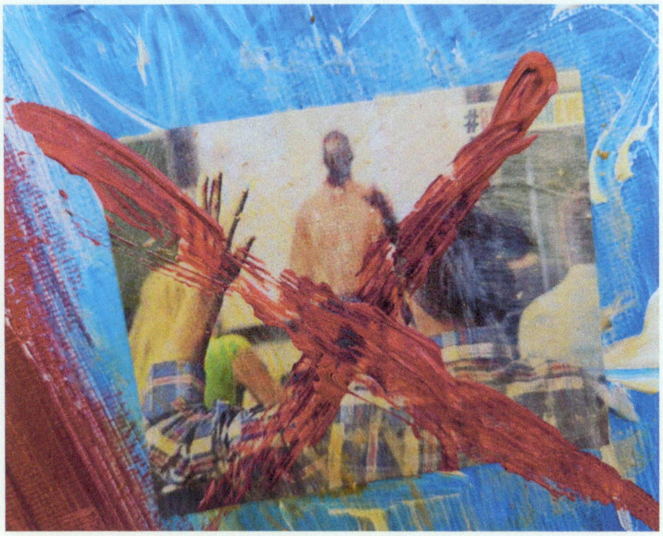

A Refugee Problem - *Azaryah Paulk*

My art is about the way refugees are treated in this country. We do not treat them fairly. They are just as important as American citizens. We need to support them through this difficult time.

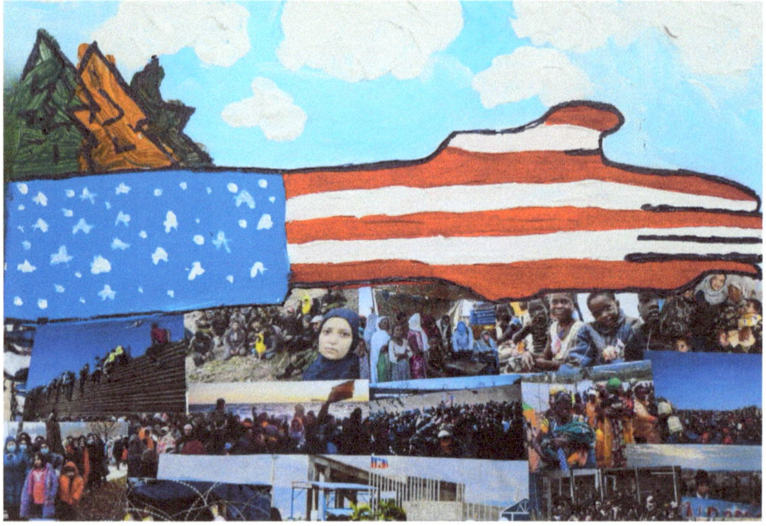

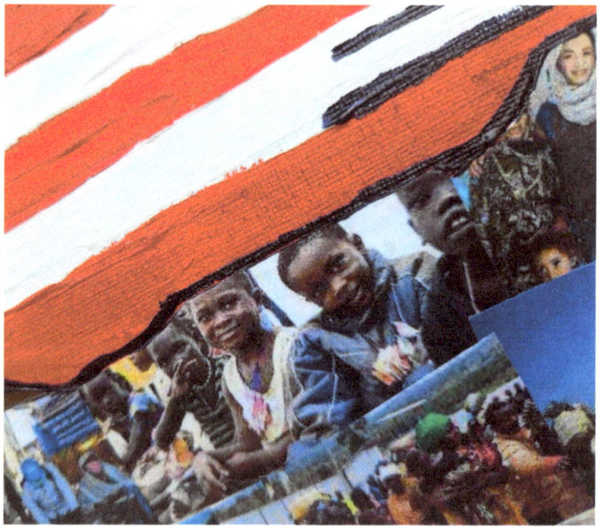

Differences vs. Disabilities - *Eric Calhoun*

My art is about understanding the power of words like learning "disabilities" versus "learning differences." I did my research and learned how students who receive special education services feel when they are told they cannot do something because they are unable or have a disability. There is nothing wrong with having a learning difference. It's not that someone is not able to read, they may read differently. It's not that students can't learn. They just learn differently. Bad things have been said to students who have learning differences. I painted the one canvas red to show anger when someone is told they can't do something because they are not able. I painted the other one blue because that is my favorite color and this is a good thing to see students as learning differently and seeing their strengths.

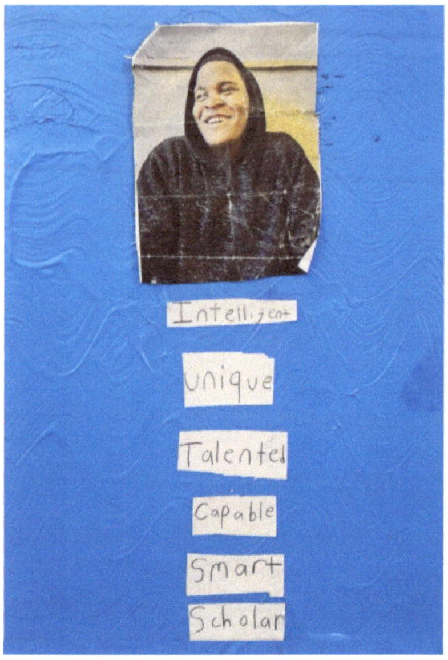

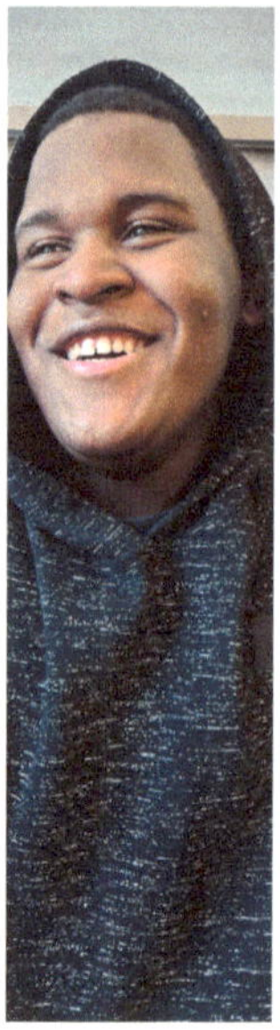

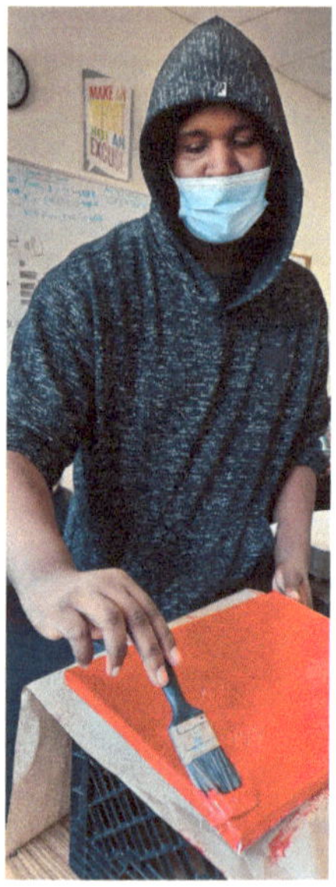

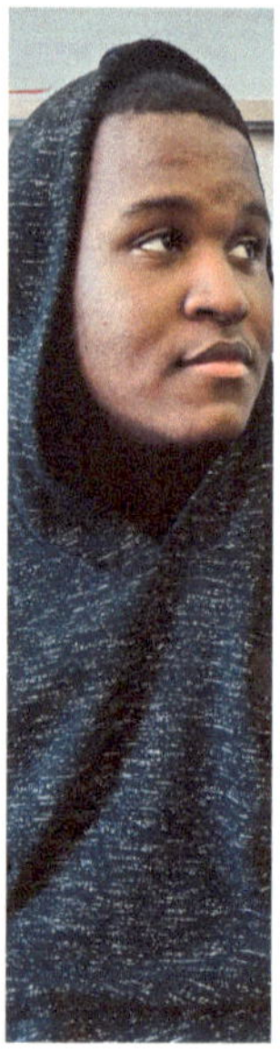

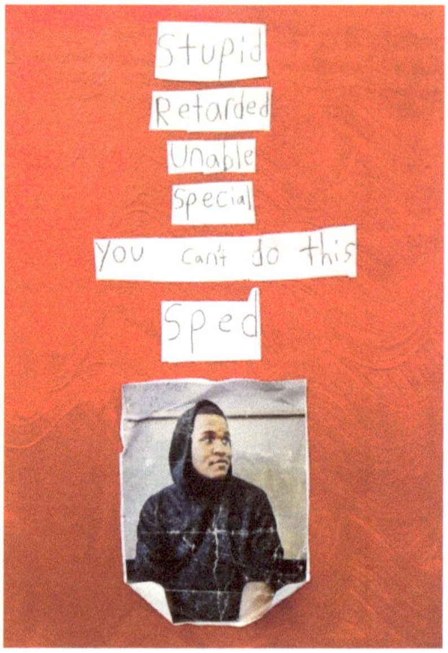

Why We Need More Black Teachers - *Taron Bell*

My art is about needing more Black teachers in school. I found an article about this during my research. I cut up the article and modpodged it to the canvas. Then, I found pictures of White teachers because they are over 90% of the teachers in schools. I made it an exclamation mark because this needs to change. It needs to change now!

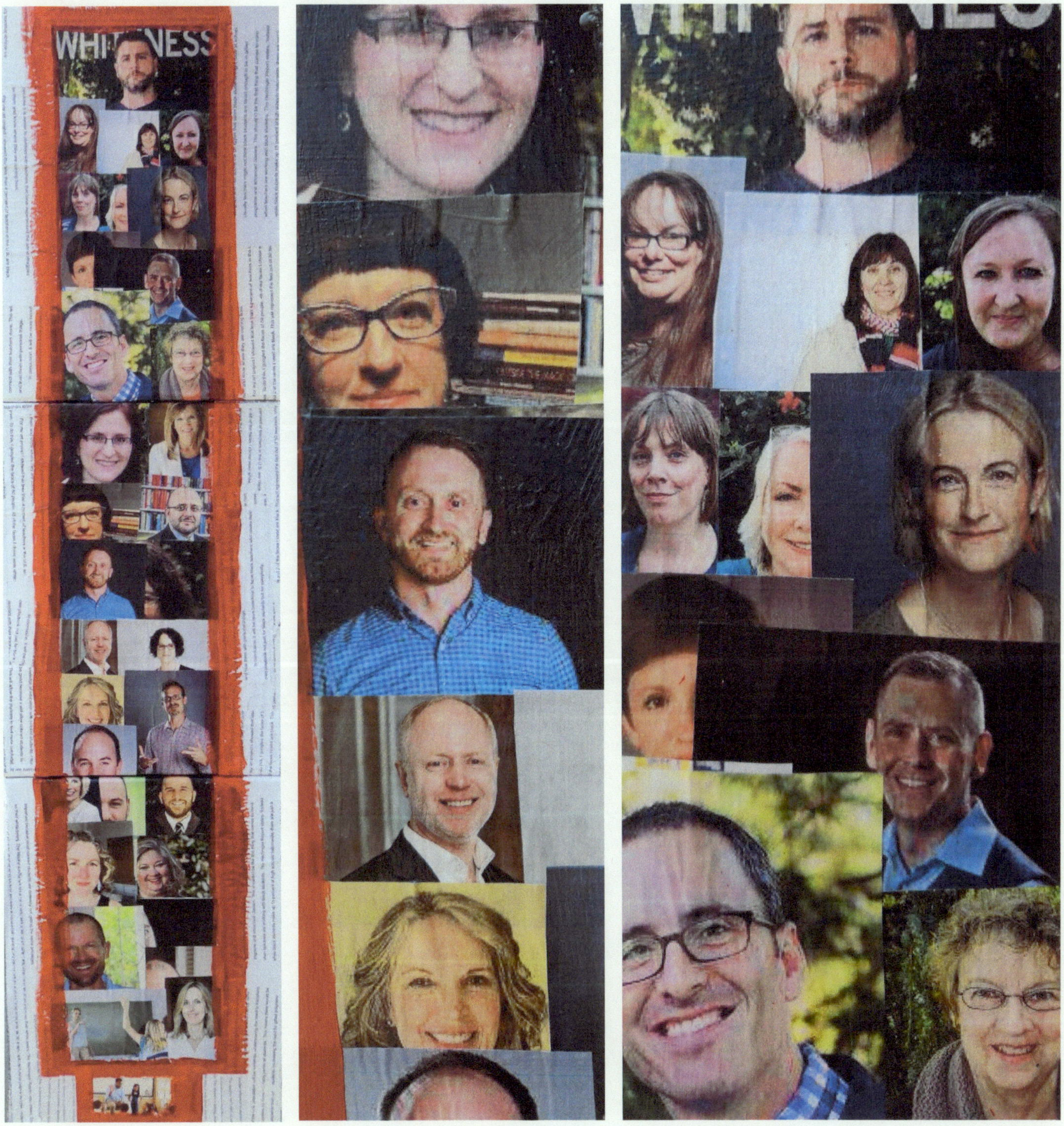

Money Talks - *Ce Ce*

My art is about how money talks. Politicians allow money to talk so that's how decisions are made. The more money you have, the more power you have. Stop telling people you are helping people when you are more interested in keeping the money for yourself.

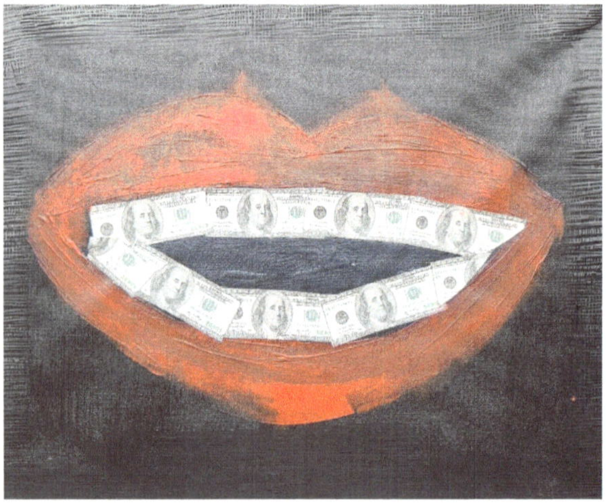

Black Wall Street - *Sincere Davis*

My art is about Black Wall Street. I didn't know about this before I did my research. I didn't learn this in school. I found pictures of the Tulsa massacre. I learned about the wealth of Black people who created Black Wall Street. I painted the background black, red, and green to represent the African American flag colors. I found pictures from the fires. I burnt the edges of the photos and put cardboard behind the photos to make them pop out at you. We need to see this.

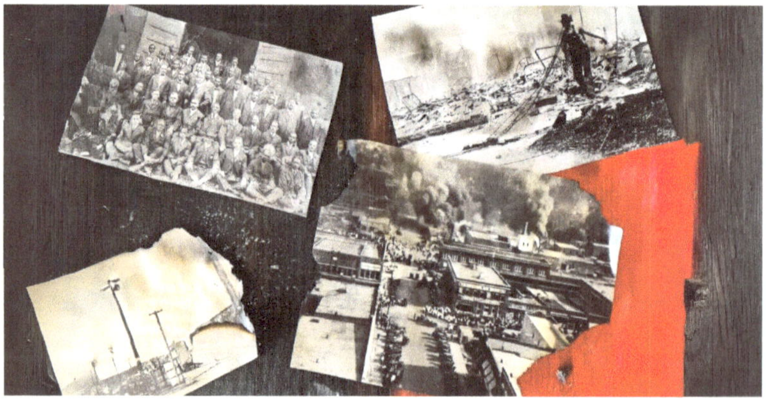

Harlem Cultural Festival Unity Art Piece - *Zion Hicks*

My art is about the Harlem Cultural Festival. It took place between 1967 and 1969. It was held in Harlem to celebrate Black people and Black music. I never learned about this in school.

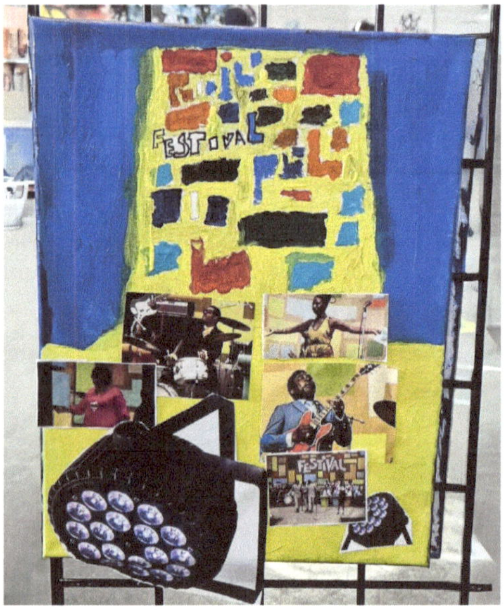

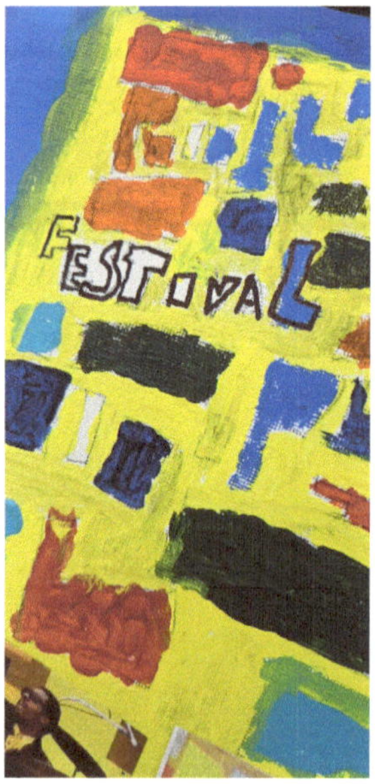

Black Lives Do Matter - *Jayden Pollard*

My art is about Black Lives Matter. I did research on this topic and learned about the Black power symbol. I also painted yellow on the canvas to represent gold. This movement is valuable.

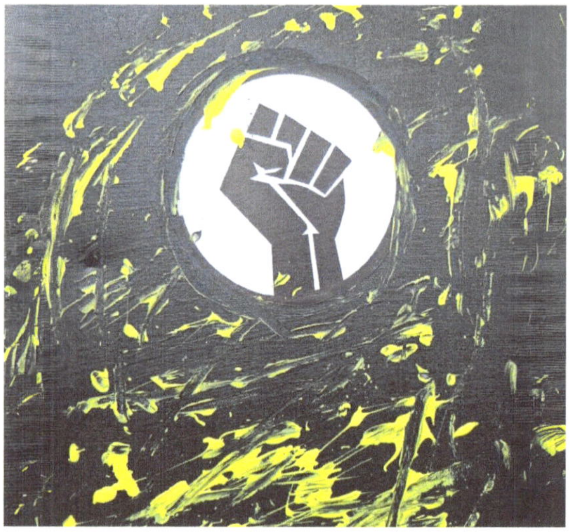

Body Shaming

- Samiya Hughes

My art is about the way young people look at their bodies and what society thinks is beautiful. We should look at everyone as beautiful. We all come in different shapes and sizes. Don't shame people for their bodies. They are beautiful.

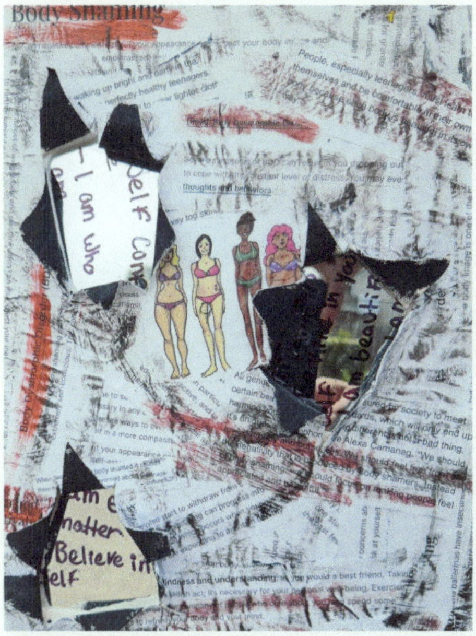

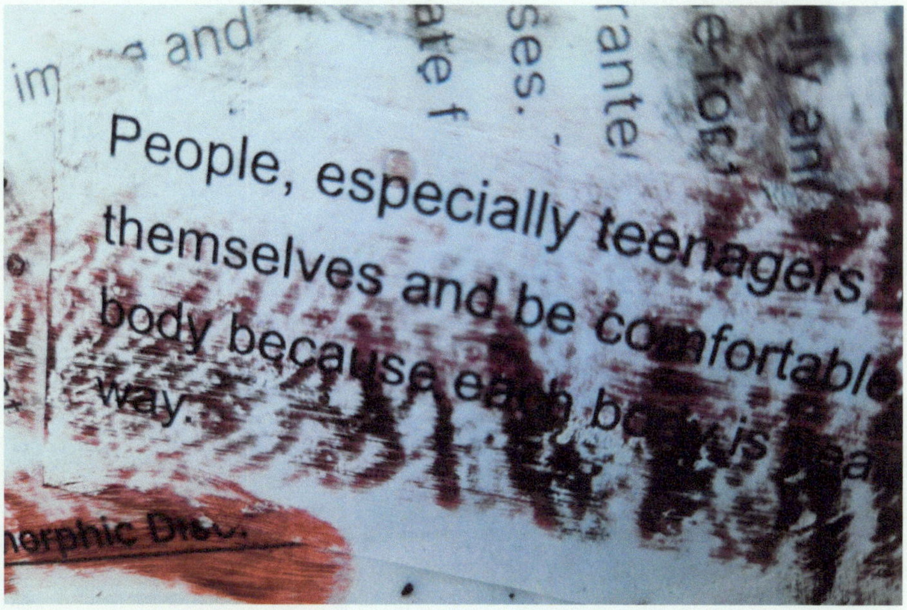

Women's Rights

- Madison Cox

My art is about women's rights. I learned a lot in my research. People need to know what is going on. Black women make less money and Black girls have more discipline in schools. We need to do something about this. I put the fist about power in the middle of a silhouette of a young Black woman.

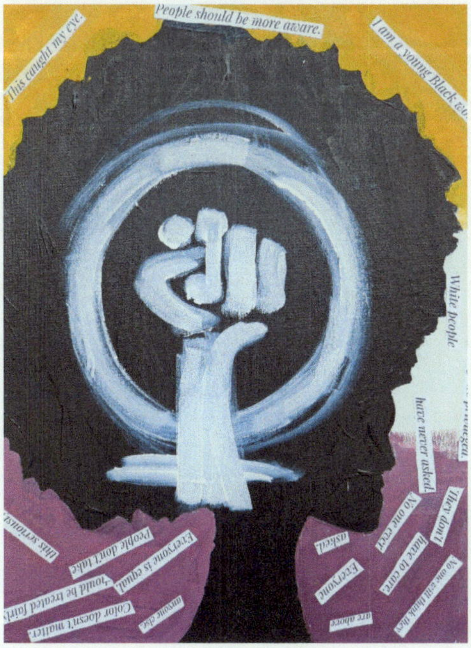

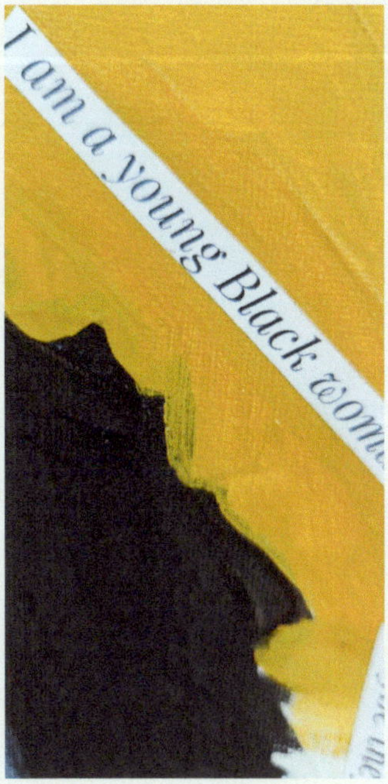

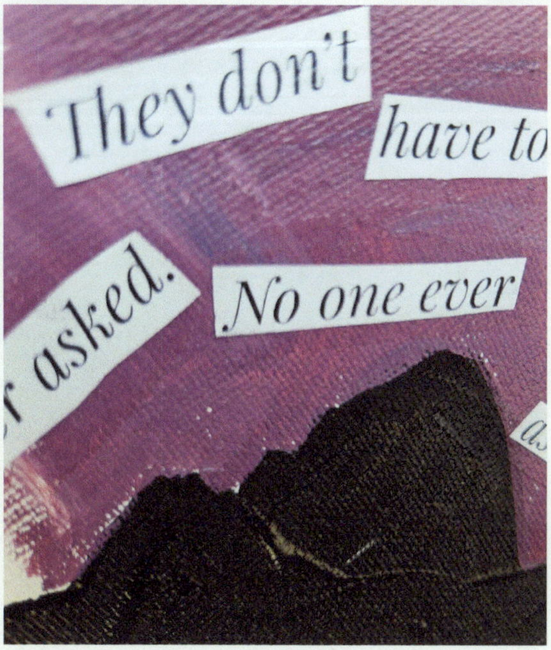

Time

- Jayden Johnson

My art is about the idea that we have not learned about any of these Black people in school. I made a watch because all of these people made a difference. We need to learn about this from the start of school, which is 8 in the morning. That's why the clock is set at 8. This should be learned every day.

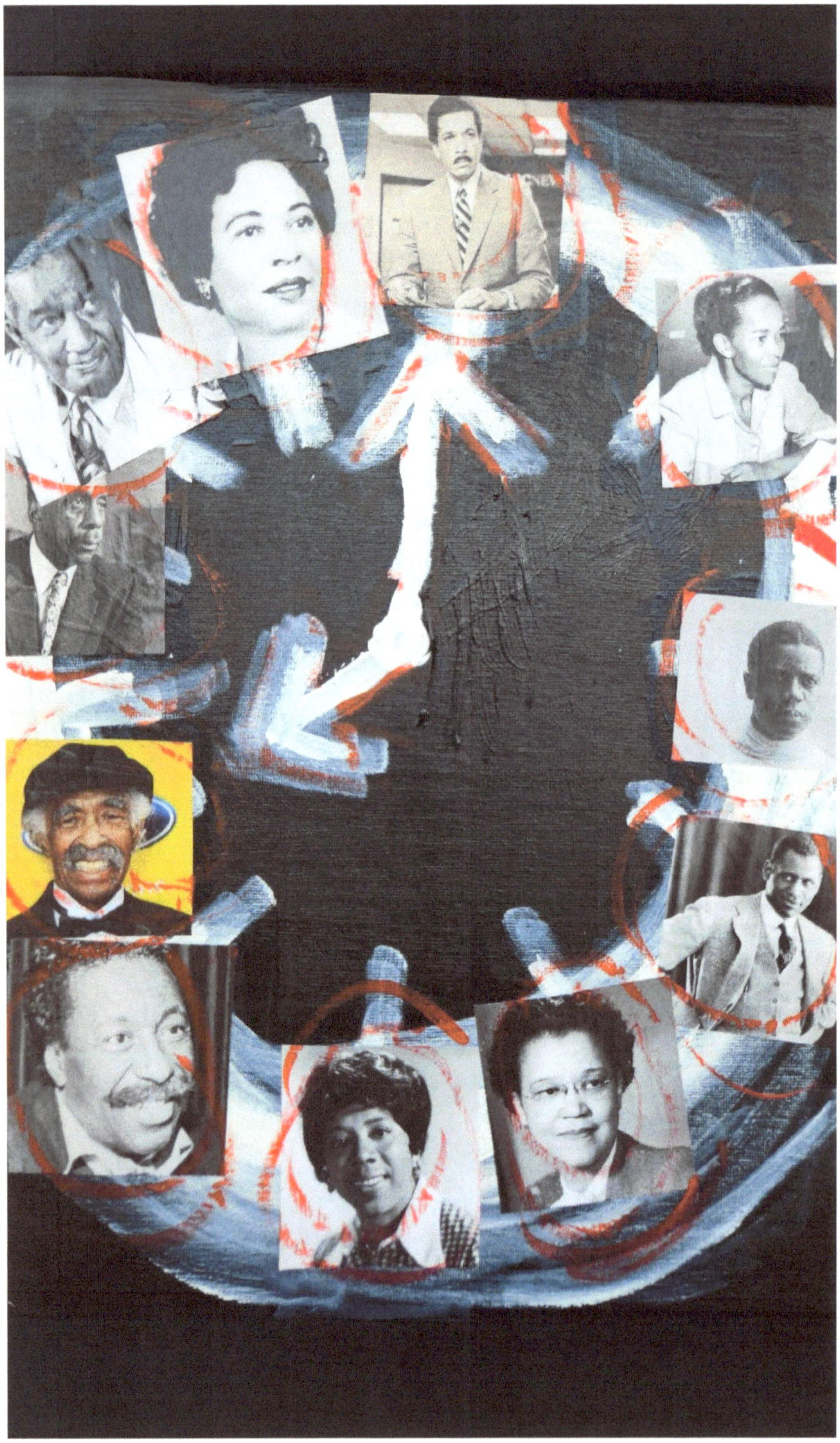

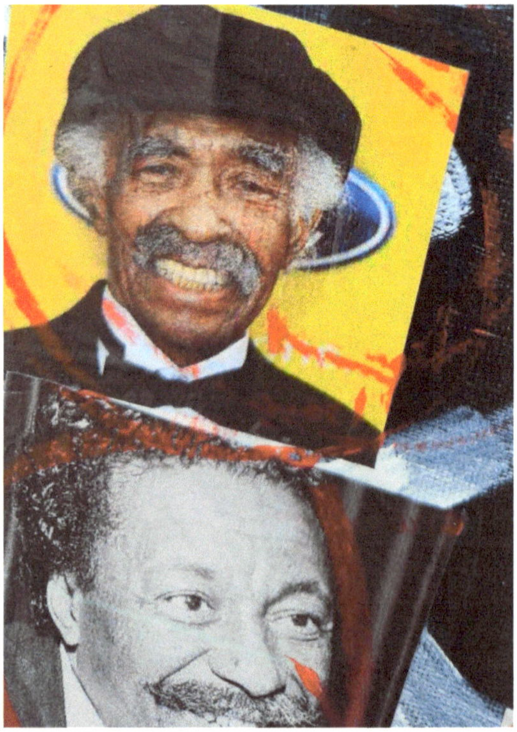

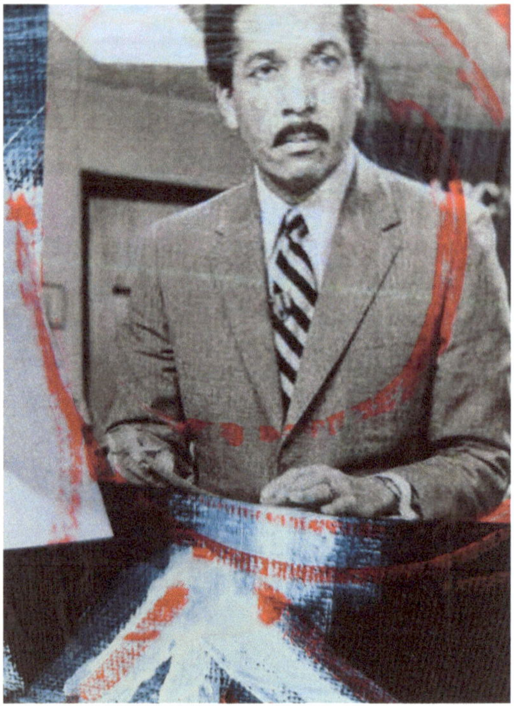

Black Dolls v. White Dolls: Children Choose the White Dolls - *Diamond Watson*

My art is about the experiment where Black children were asked about who is the bad doll, who is the doll you play with, and other questions about which doll they wanted. I was sad to see Black children choose the White doll when they asked who was the nice doll. And when they asked who was the bad doll, they chose the Black doll. They called the Black doll ugly. I want Black children to feel good about who they are. We need to learn good things about Black people in school.

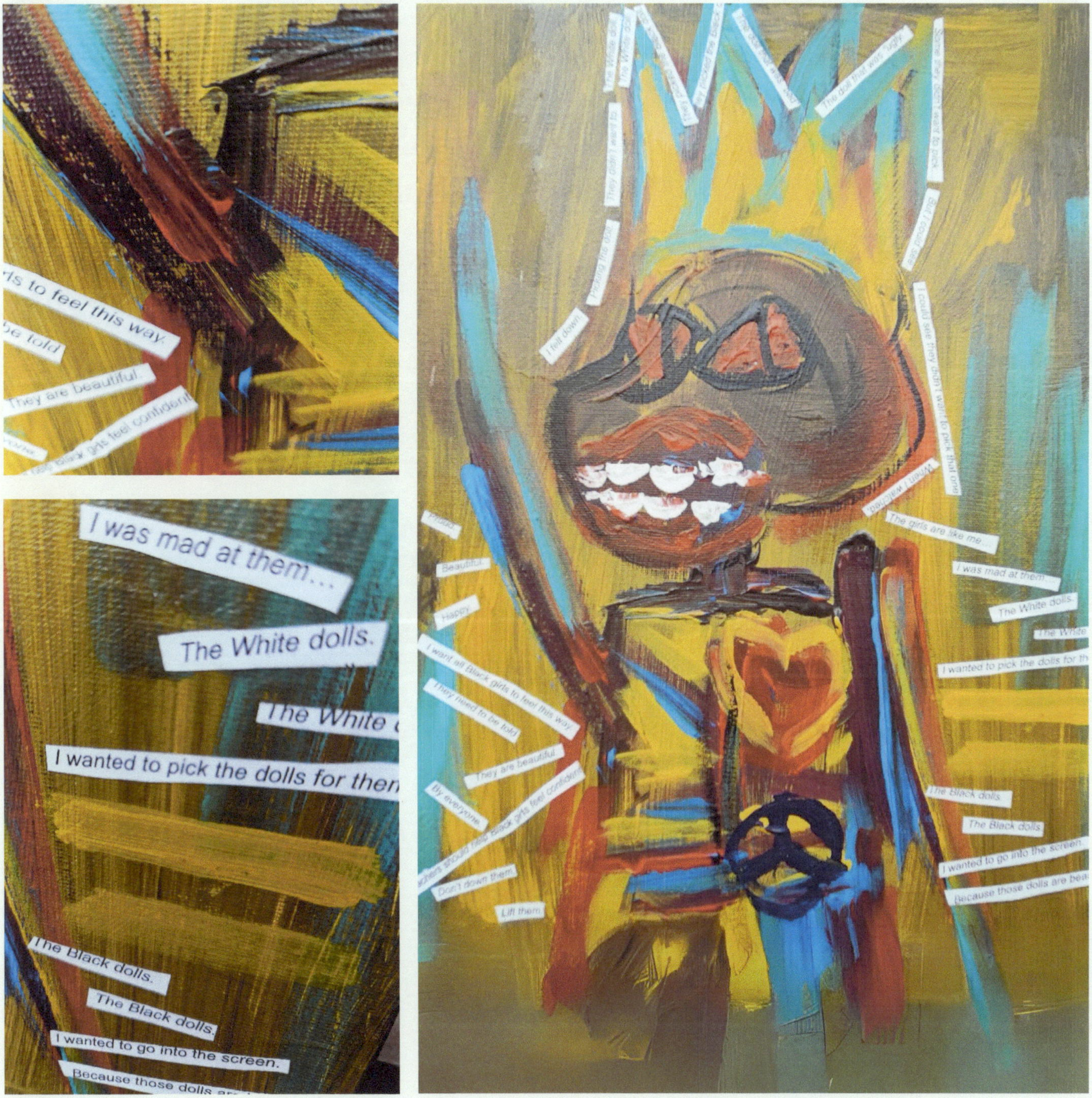

Fighting for Rights

- Beautiful Walker

My art is about the power women have and how often they are held on a string and the puppetmaster, society, decides what women can and cannot become. I did my research on gender roles and gender norms. I learned about how women are treated in this country, especially Black women. The black lines are the stereotypes and negative beliefs about women...the laws...the rules...the beliefs that society has for women. We cannot be controlled.

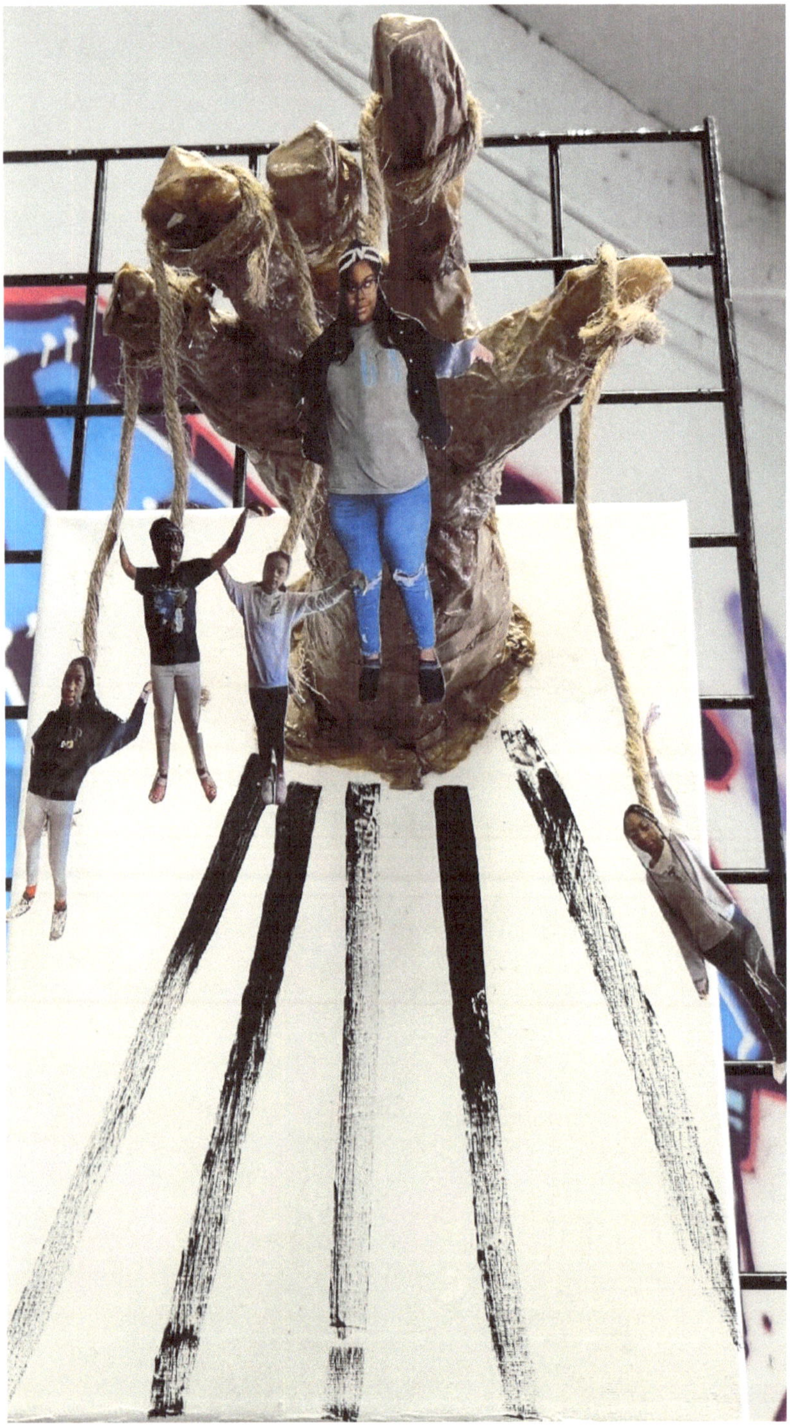

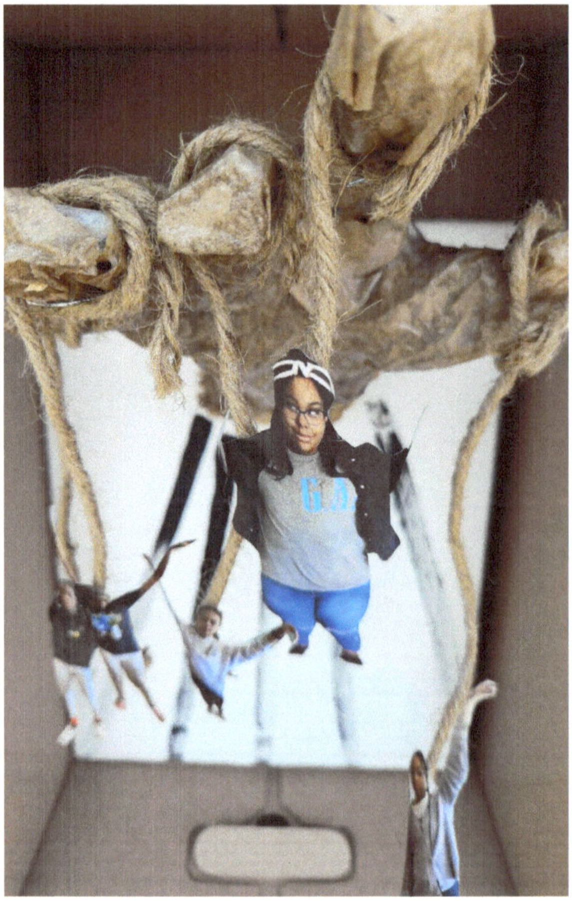

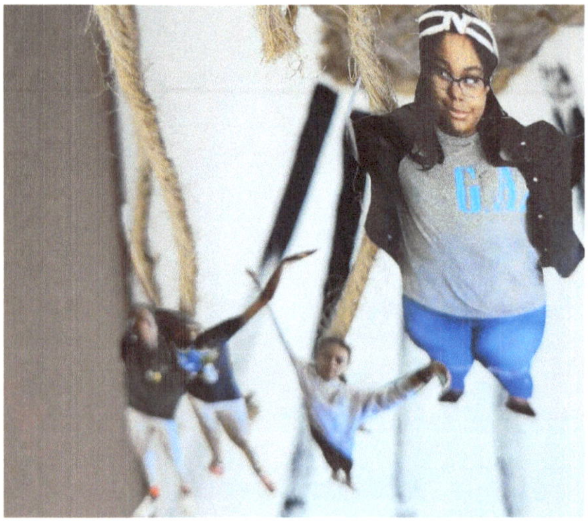

Injustice to Boys

- Kelvontae Hardaway

My art is about the injustice to boys because we are told not to cry and not to share or show our emotions. I did research and learned how often this happens to boys. It's okay for boys to show they are angry, but anything else is considered bad for boys. I painted prison bars blue because blue is usually thought of as a boy's color. It's like being in prison when you are told you cannot cry or be afraid or show your emotions. I am breaking through the prison bars and smiling in my other canvas. I am showing that I can be me. I can be all of me and share my emotions. It's okay to cry. It's okay to be scared. It's okay to be nurturing.

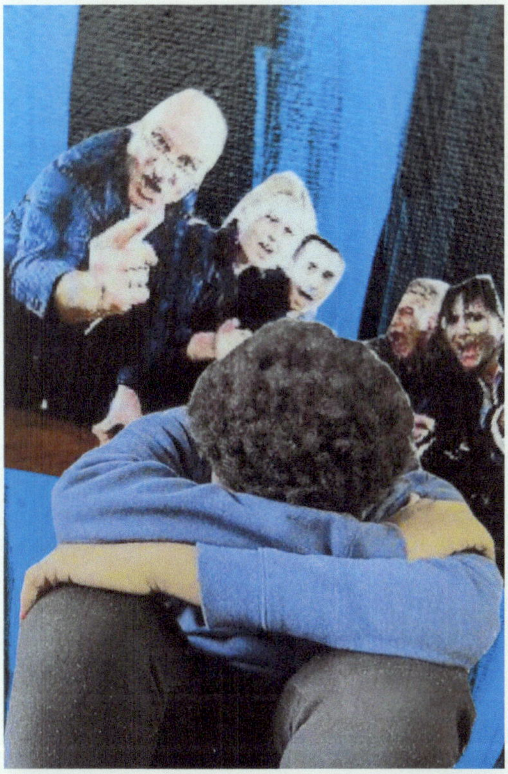

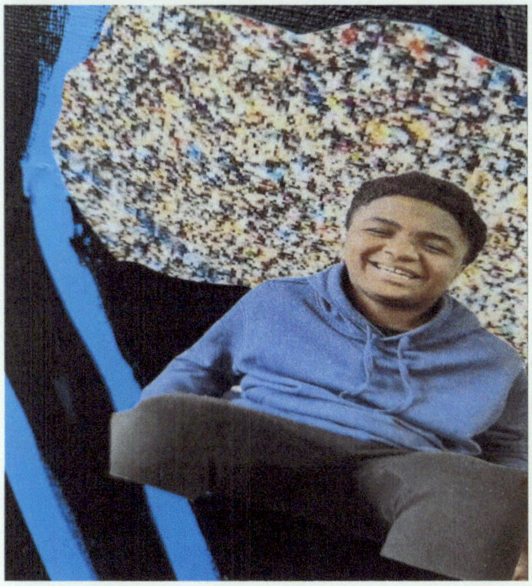

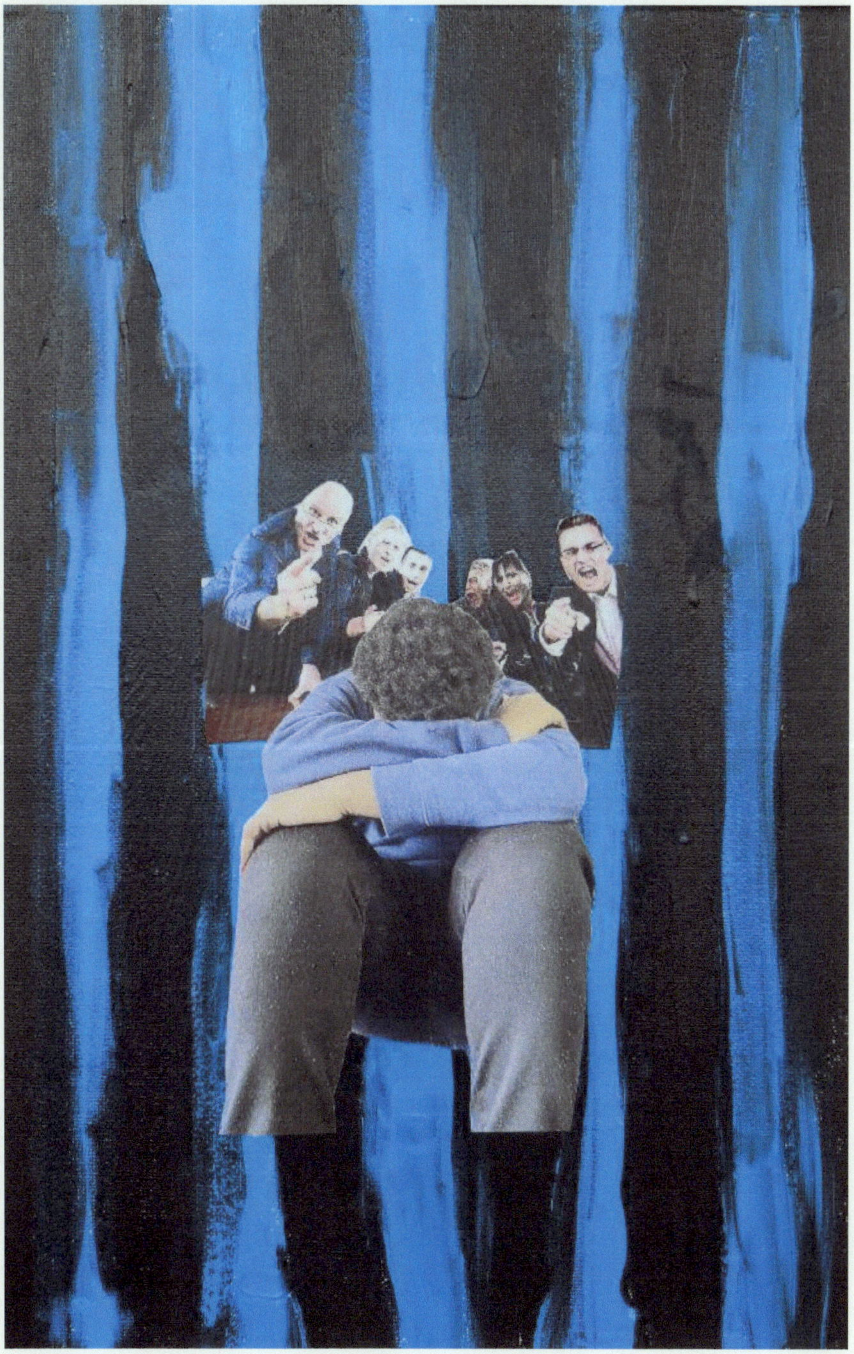

The Mind of a Child - *Richard Treadwell*

My art is about things I heard about being Black. This stays with me.

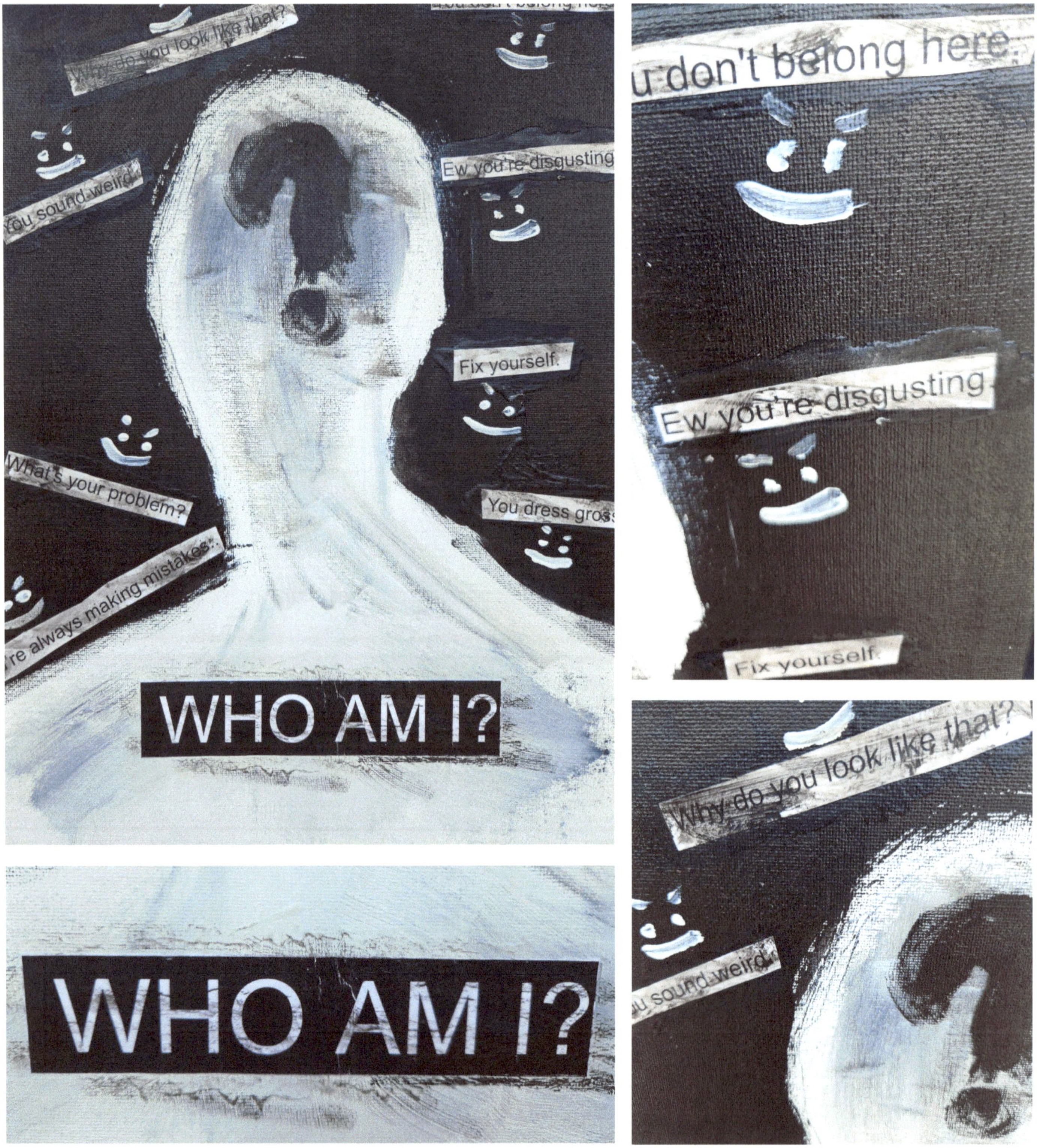

Blue-Eyed Project — *Chinja Scott*

My art is about the brown-eyed blue-eyed experiment. I never even heard of this before I researched it. I saw how the kids turned against each other just because a teacher told the kids that one group was better than the other. I also learned about Ruby Bridges and what she went through as a child.

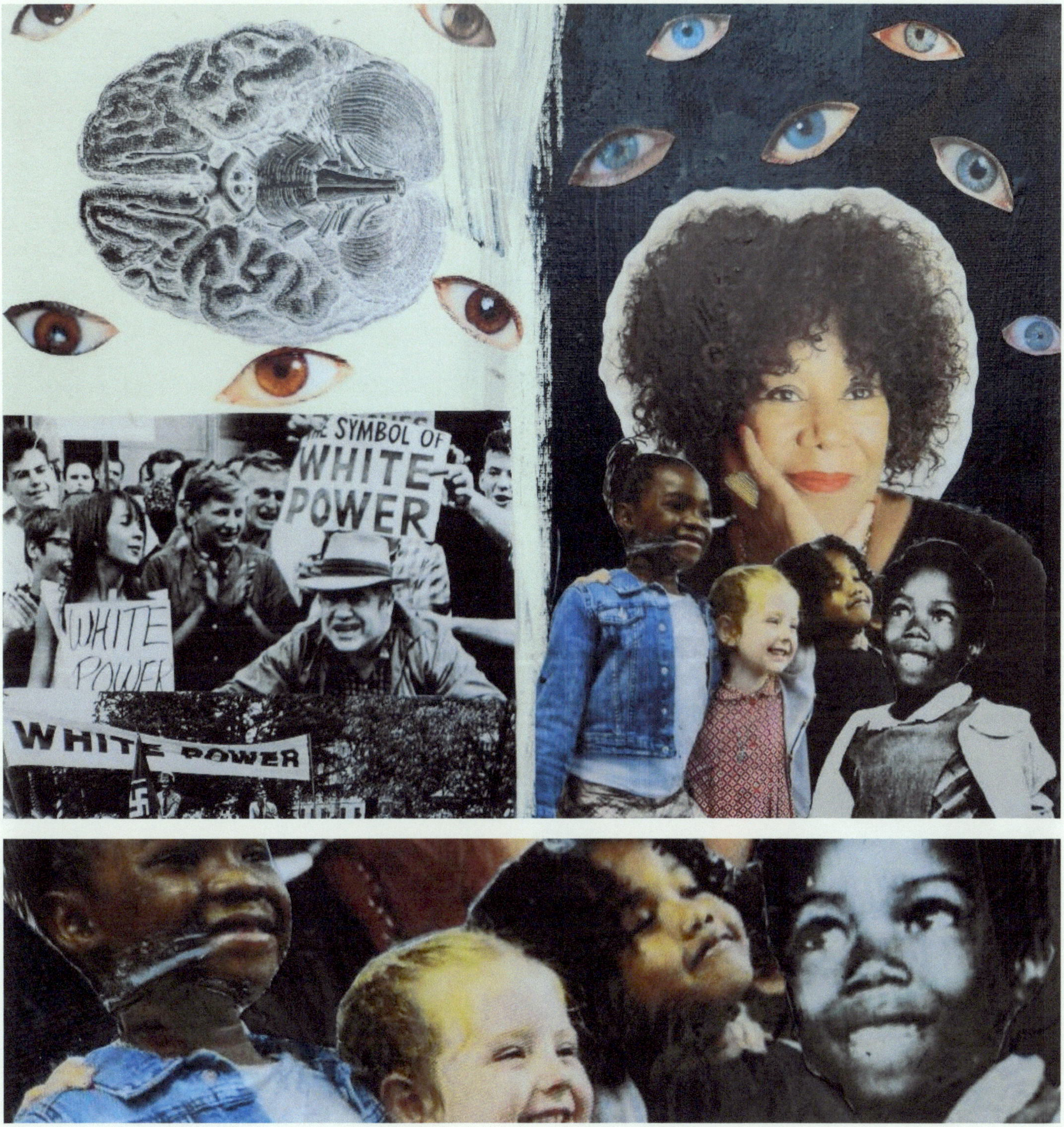

The Problem and Solution to Gun Violence - *Jaidyn Wise*

My art is about gun violence. There are too many guns in this country. I did my research and learned about how much violence there is…how many school shootings happen…that we have more guns than people…and you don't need a permit or training to own a gun in Ohio. I found an image with a tied up gun so it doesn't shoot. That's what I want. I want guns to go away. I don't want gun violence.

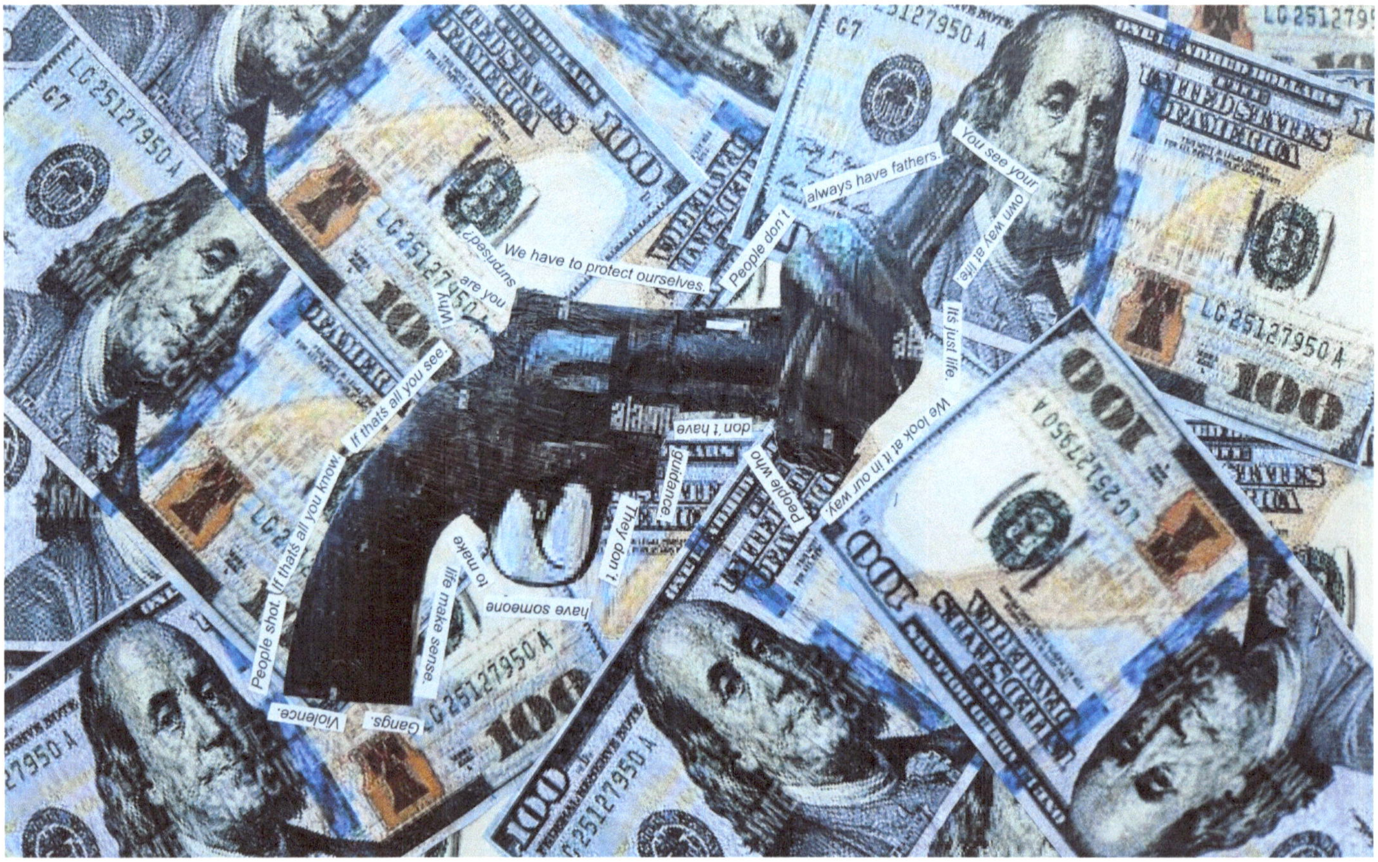

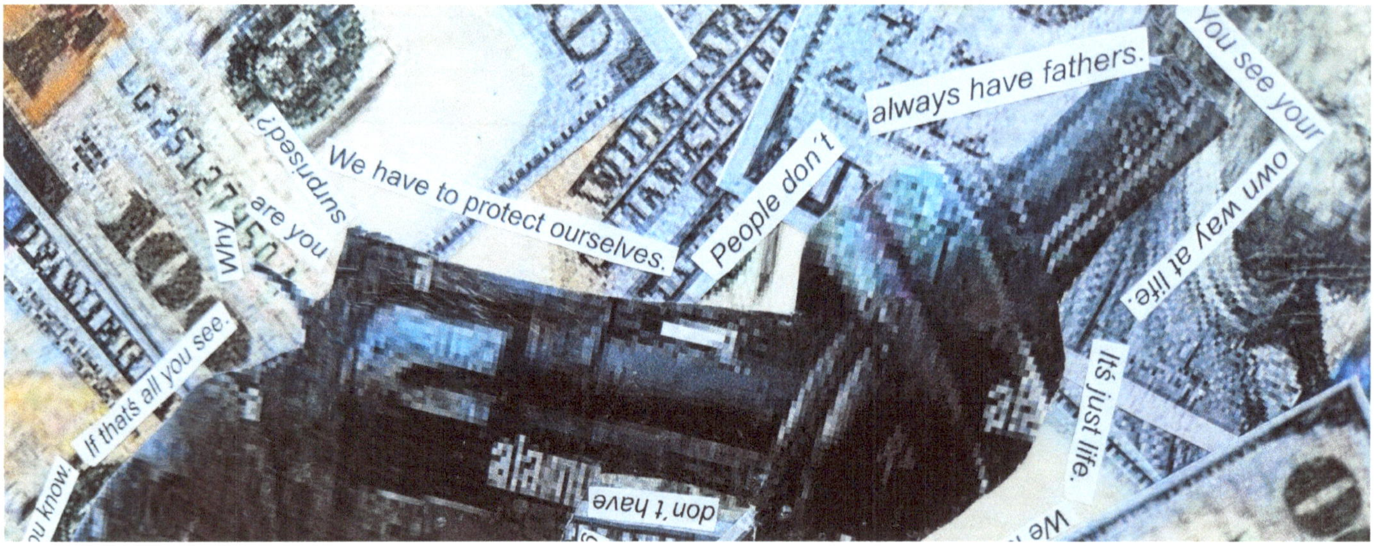

Reality

- Laquoia Patterson

My art is about mental health and depression.

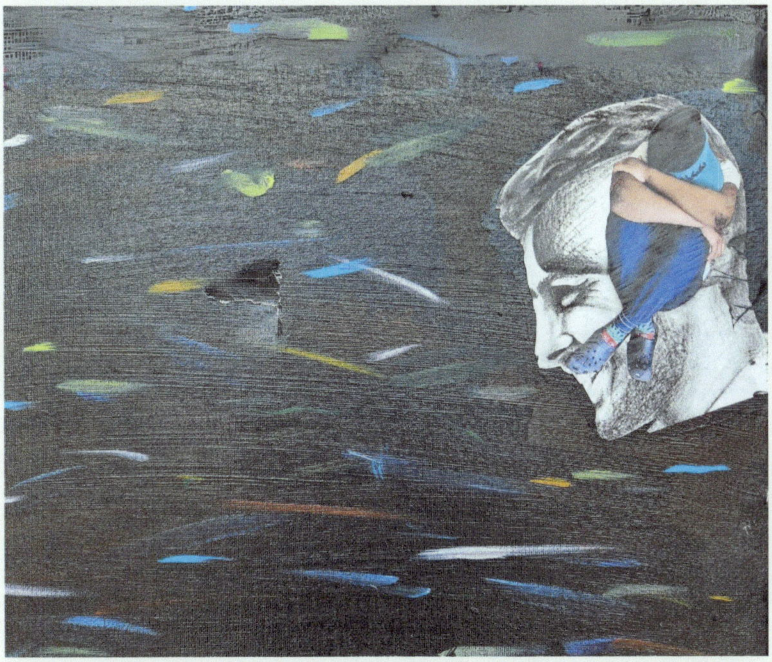

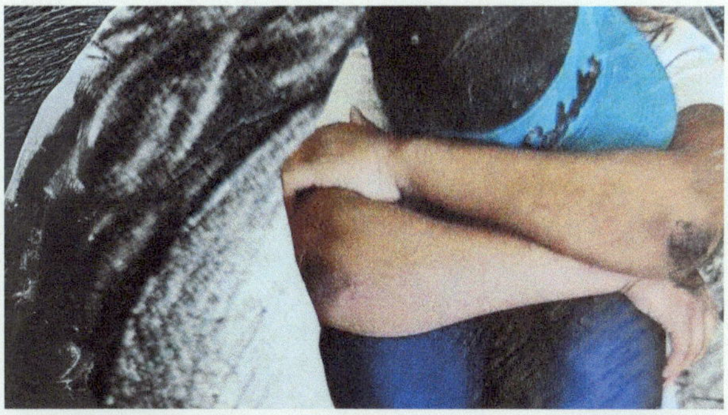

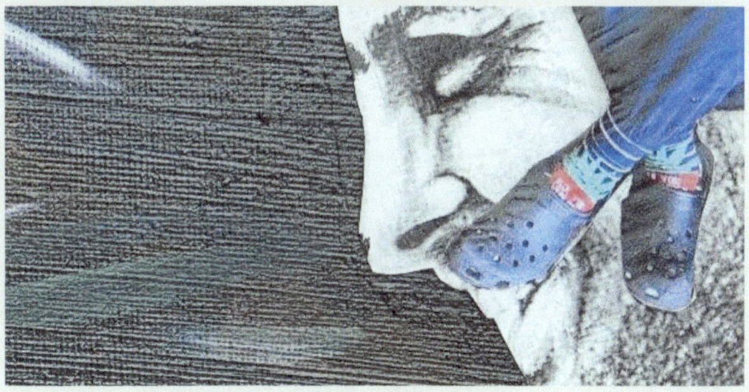

Dream Popper

- Phillip A Lane

My art is about Ohio's House Bill 327. I did research on this topic. There are people who are trying to make it so we can't talk about race, racism, real history, sexuality, sexism, and things that we want to talk about. This is not okay.

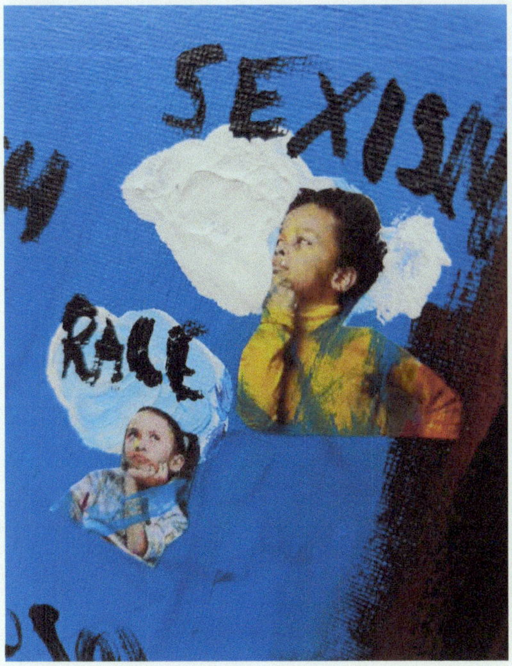

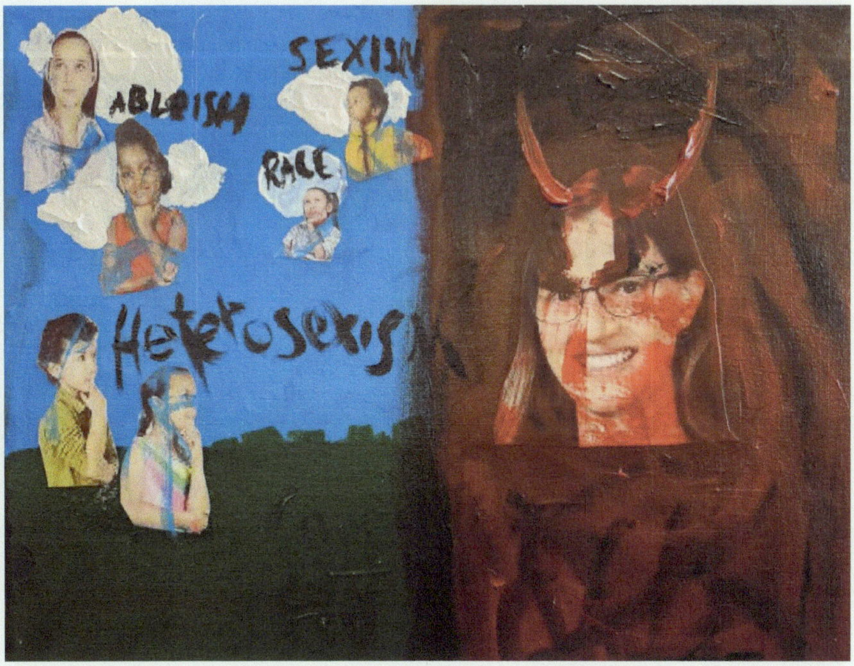

Equal (Neighbor) Hoods

- Marquis Hicks

My art is about redlining. I never heard of this or learned this in school. I did my research and learned all about it. Banks and cities colored neighborhood maps according to the number of Black people in those areas. Depending on where you lived, you might not get a loan or start a business or get a place to live or have good schools because too many Black people lived there. I had no idea this happened.

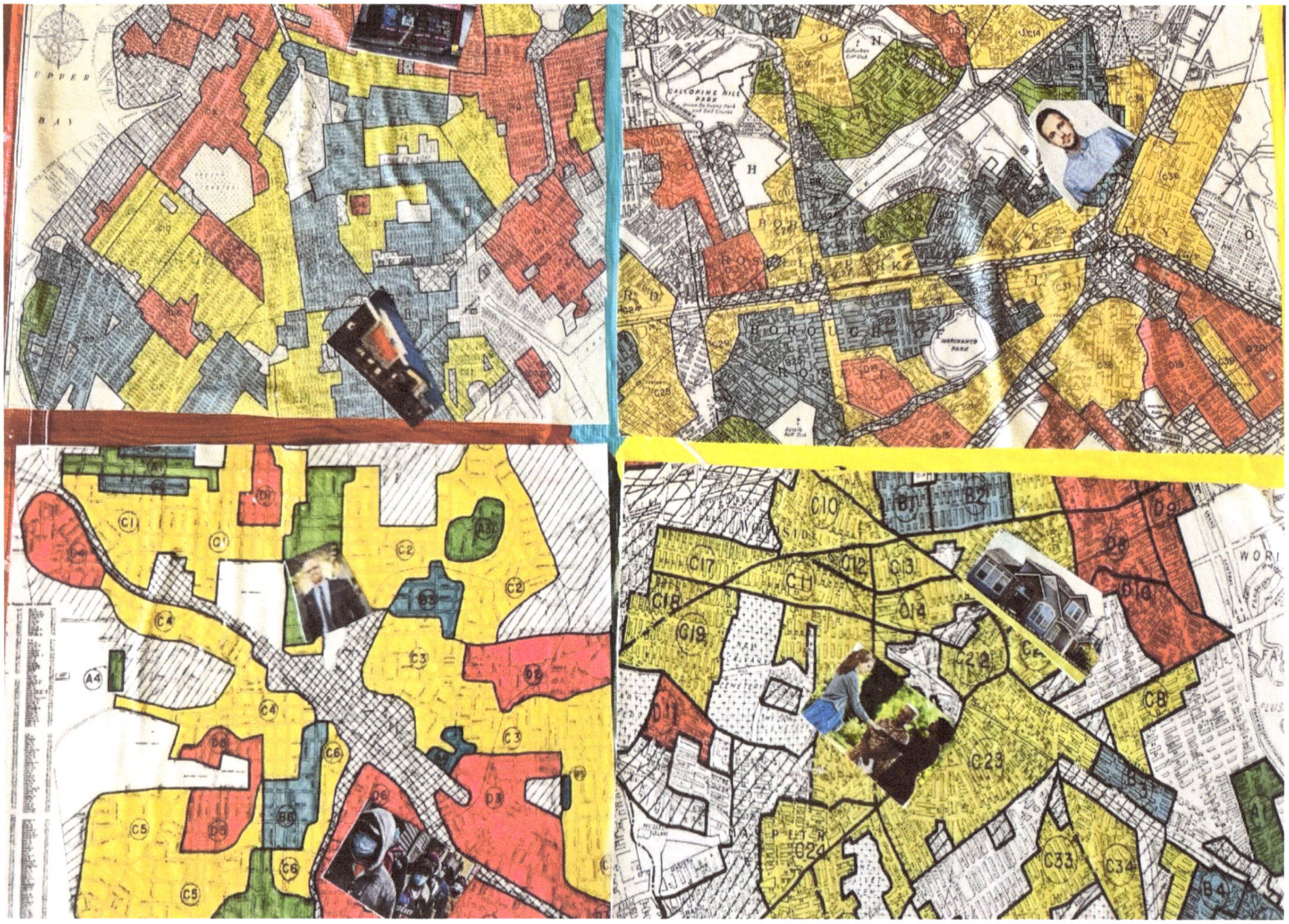

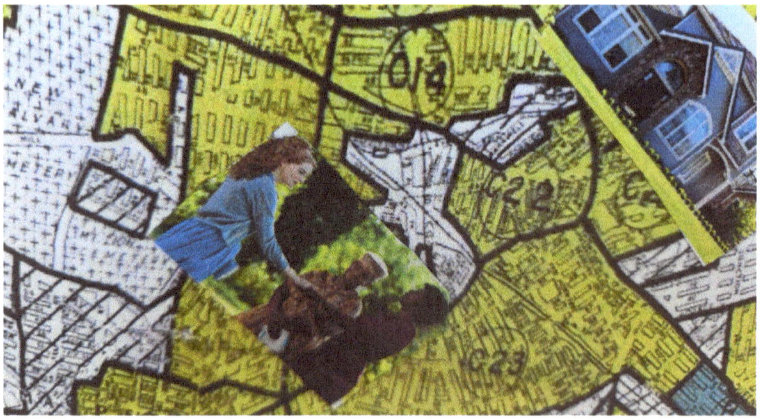

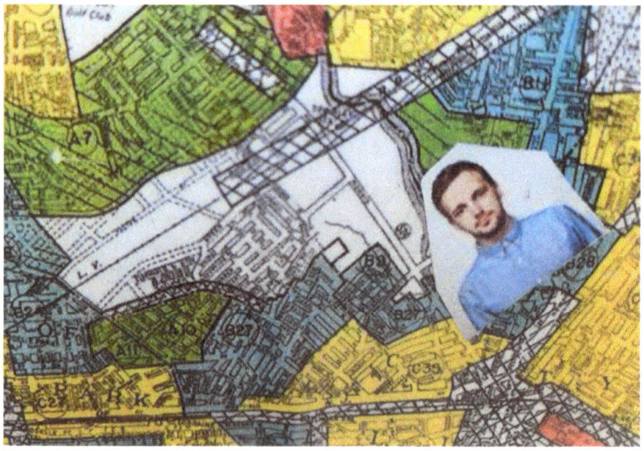

Art for Resistance Through Change Pop Up

AKRON ART MUSEUM

December 2022

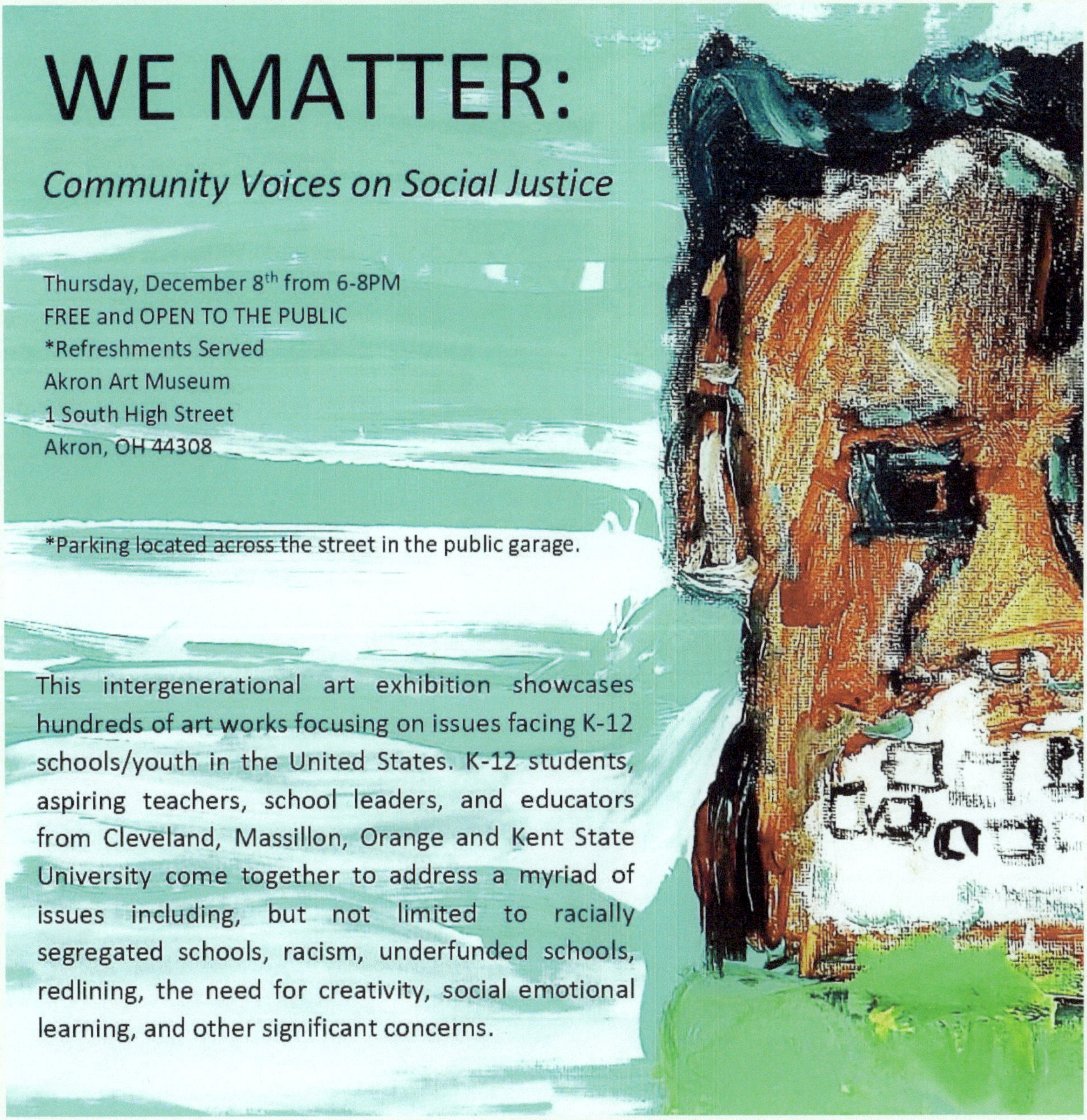

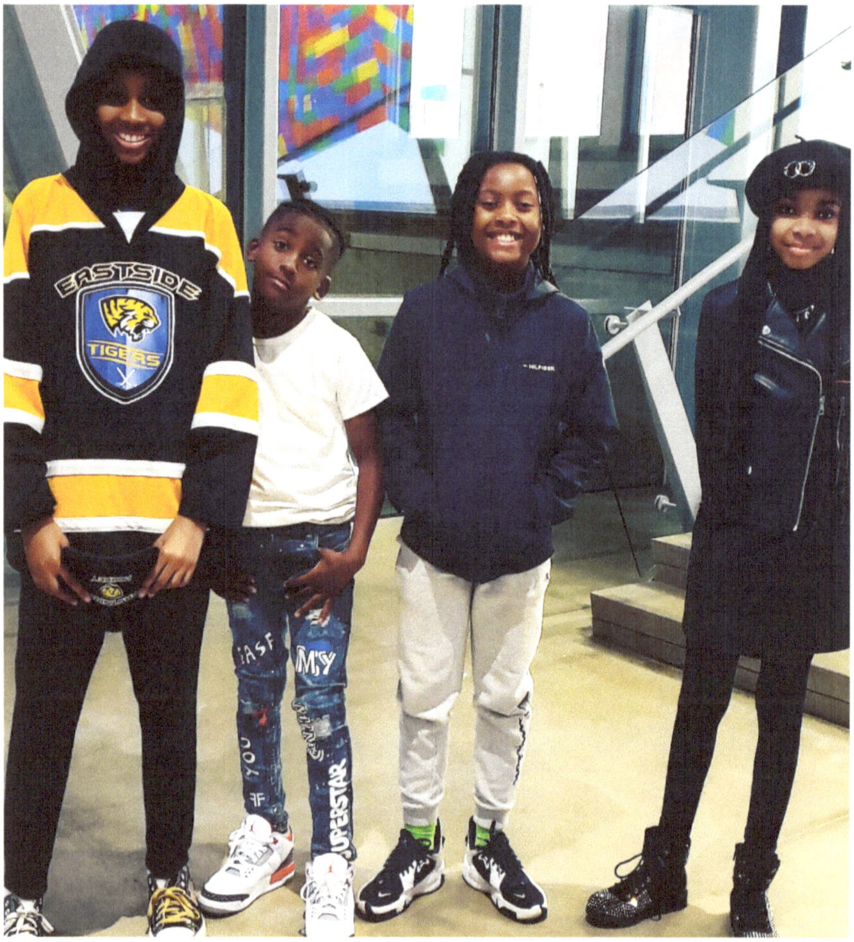
EASTSIDE
TIGERS
SUPERSTAR

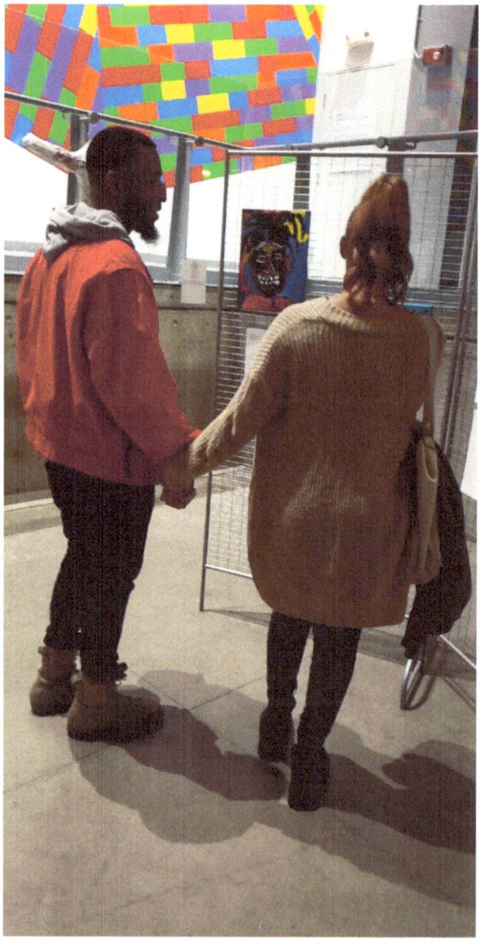

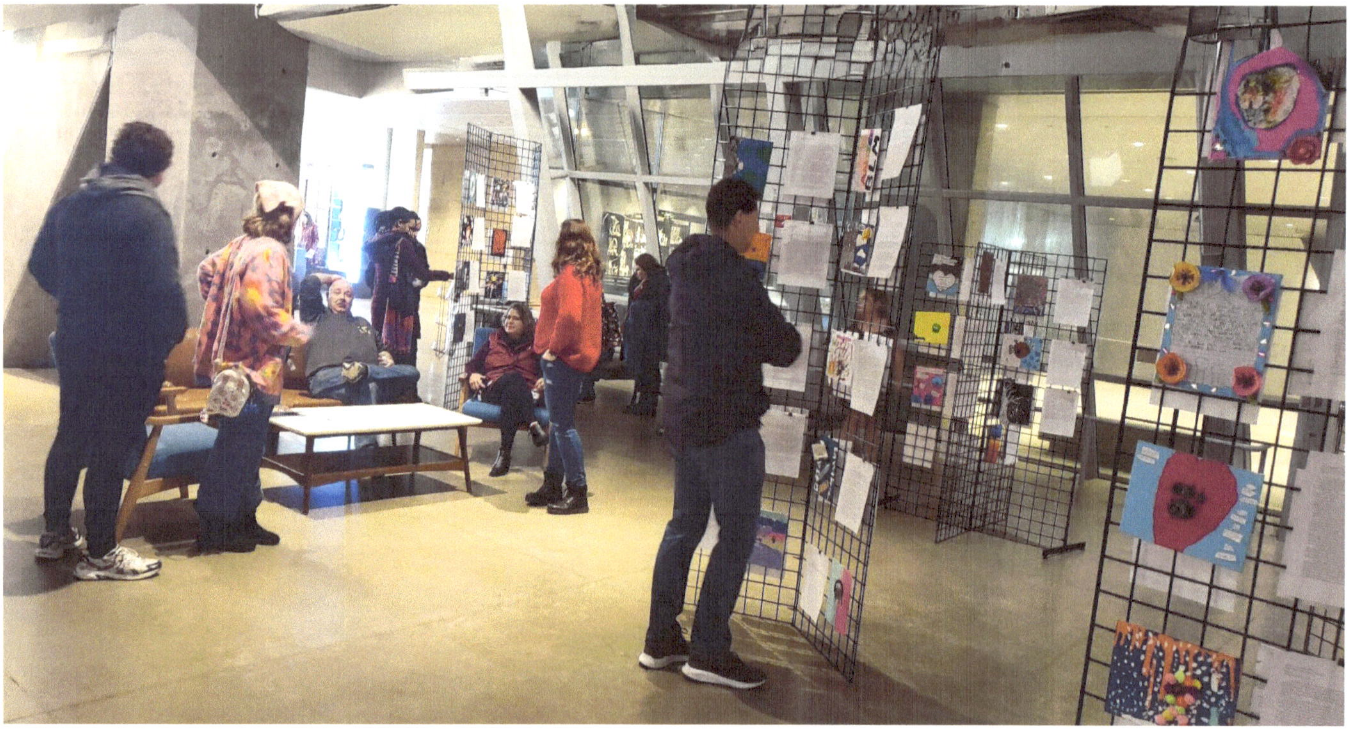

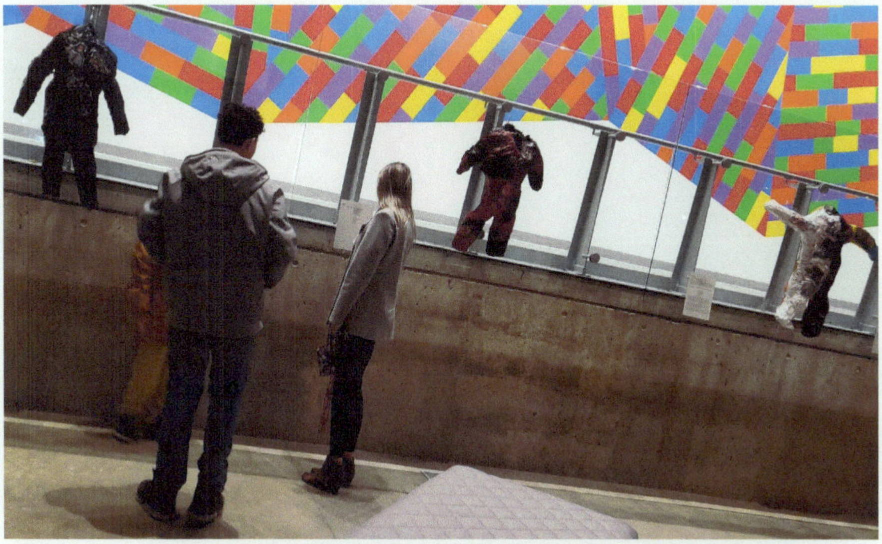

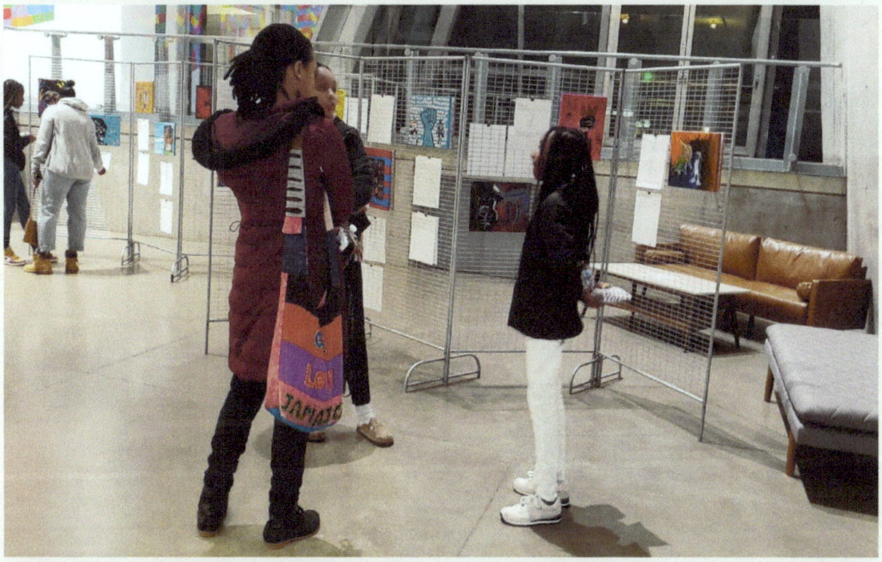

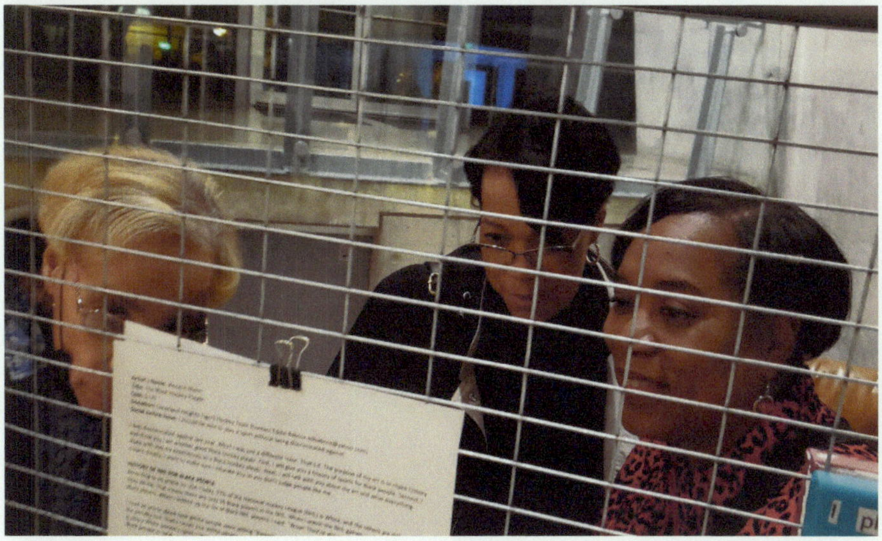

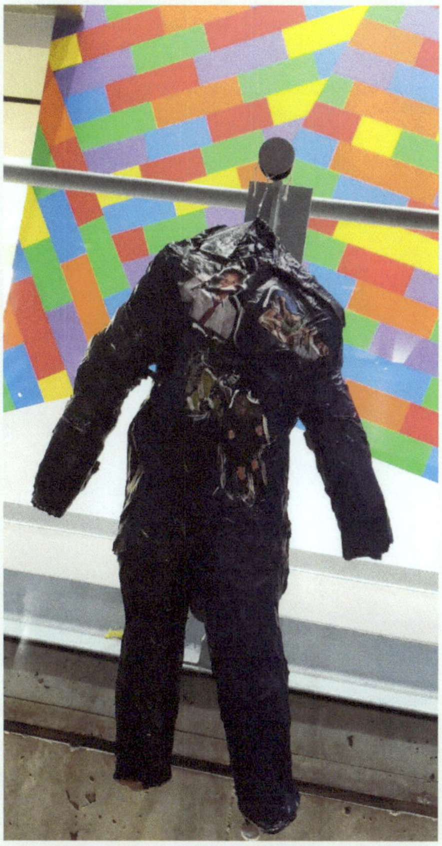

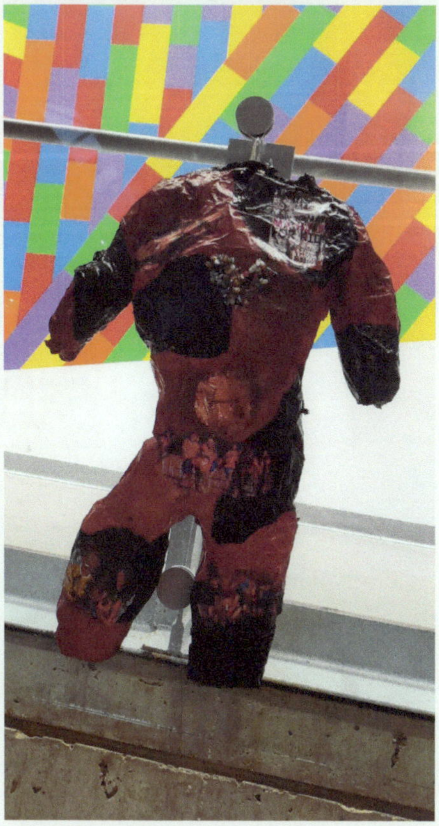

OUR VOICES MATTER:

Summit Artspace Exhibition:
A Community Based Social Justice Art Exhibition

January - March 2023

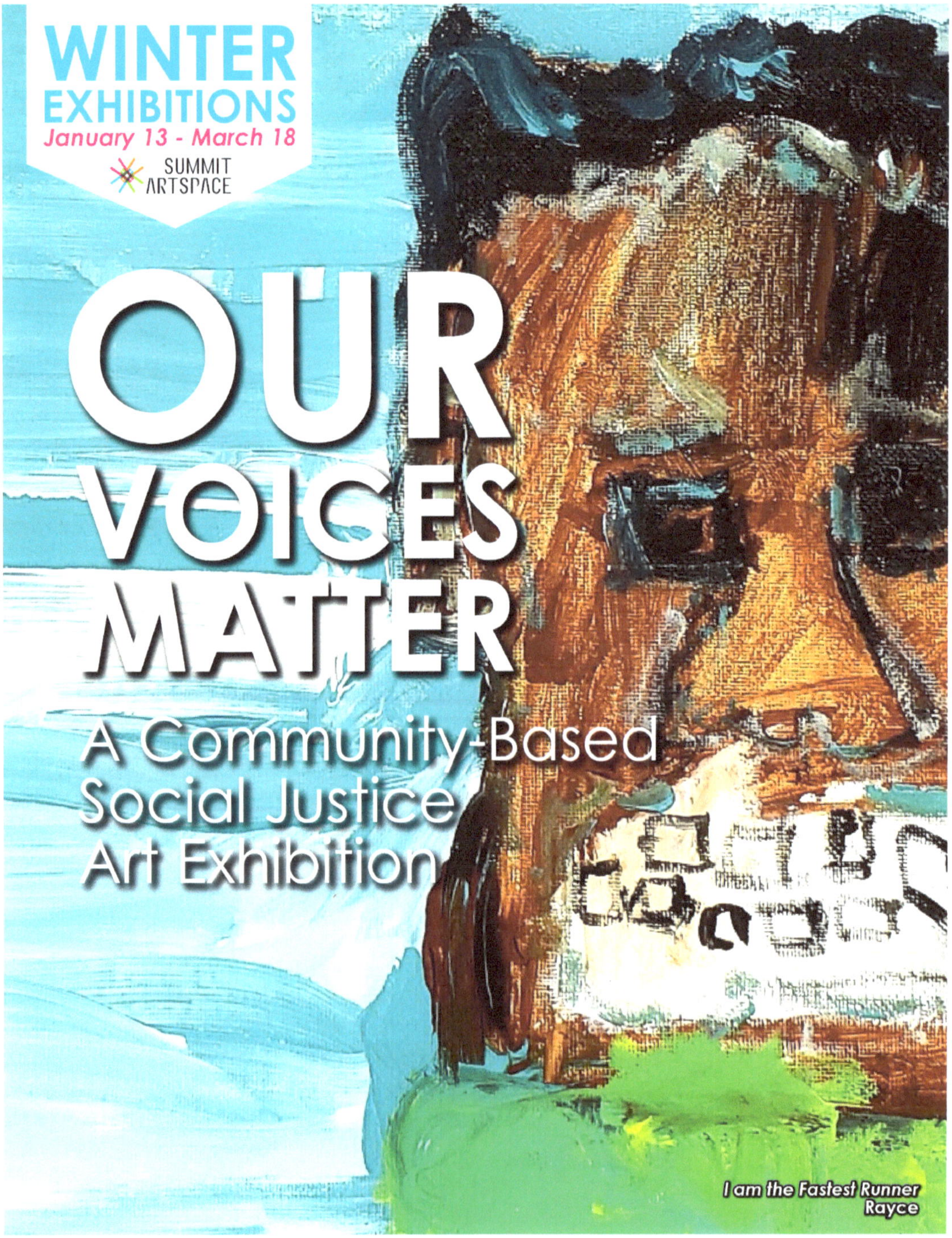

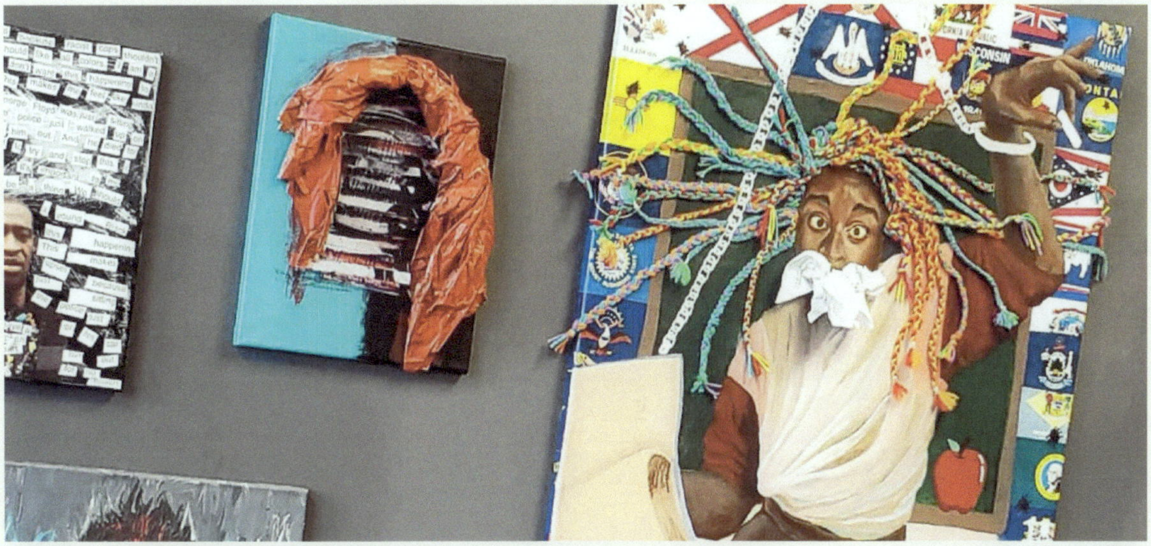

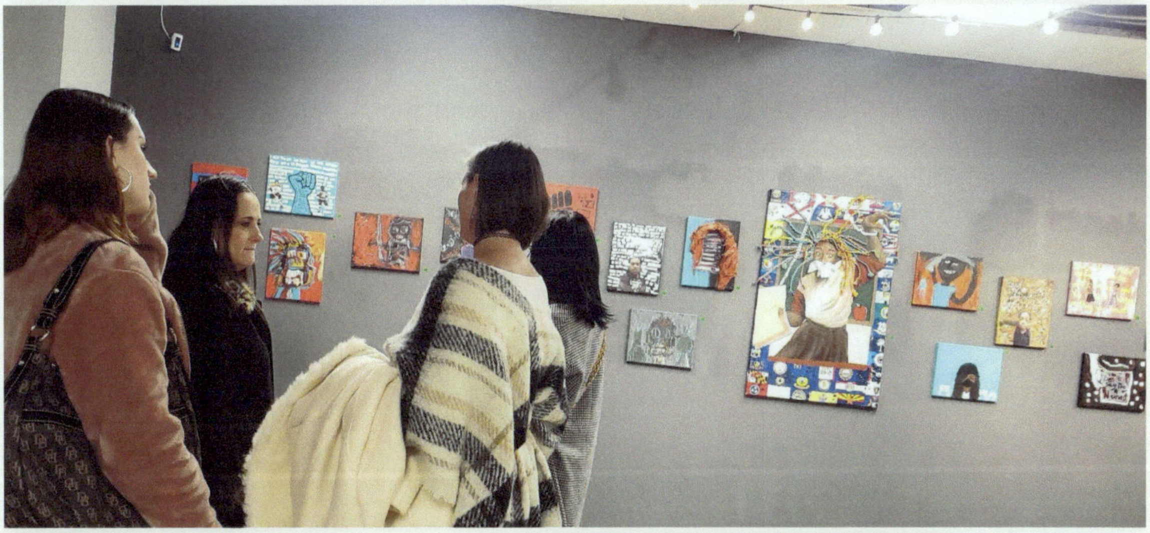

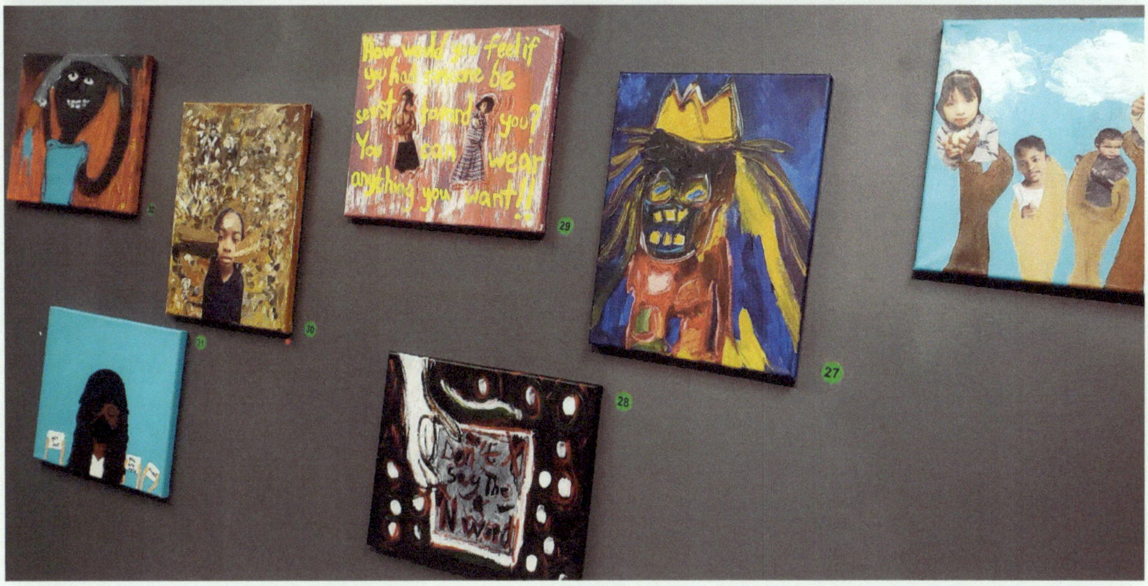
How would you feel if you had someone be sexist toward you? You can wear anything you want!!
Don't Say The N-Word
27
28
29

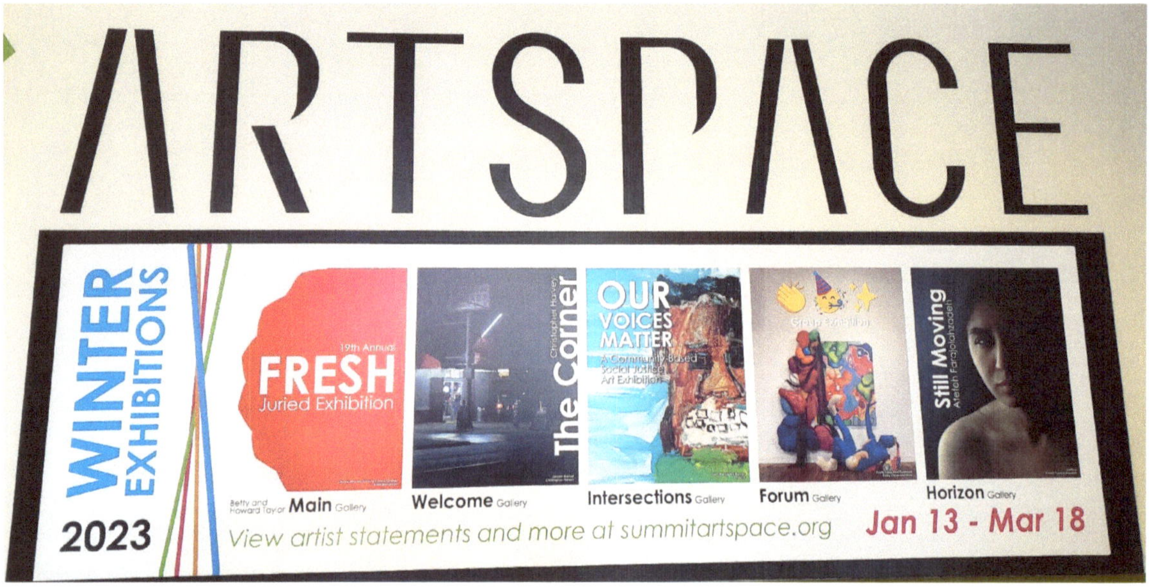
ARTSPACE
WINTER EXHIBITIONS
2023
19th Annual
FRESH
Juried Exhibition
Betty and Howard Taylor Main Gallery
The Corner
Christopher Harvey
Welcome Gallery
OUR VOICES MATTER
A Community-Based Social Justice Art Exhibition
Intersections Gallery
Forum Gallery
Still Moving
Horizon Gallery
View artist statements and more at summitartspace.org
Jan 13 - Mar 18

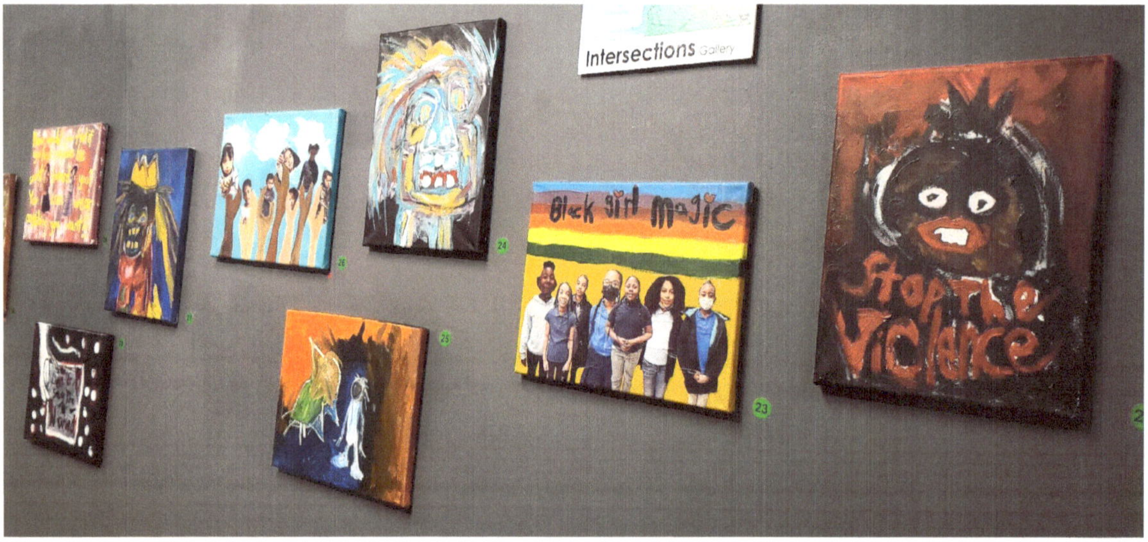
Intersections Gallery
Stop The Violence

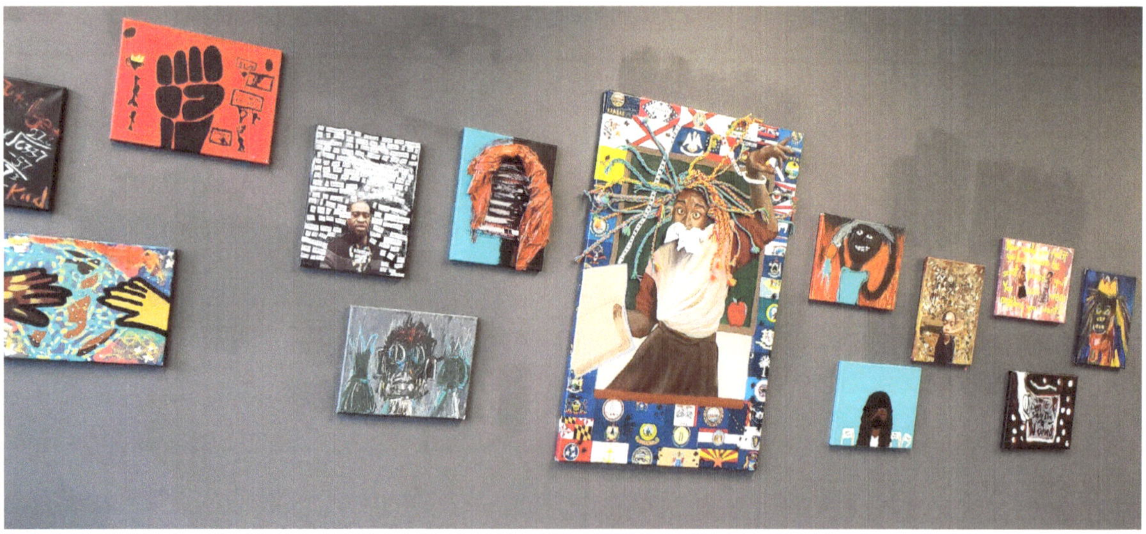

Speakezie Art Exhibition

March 2023

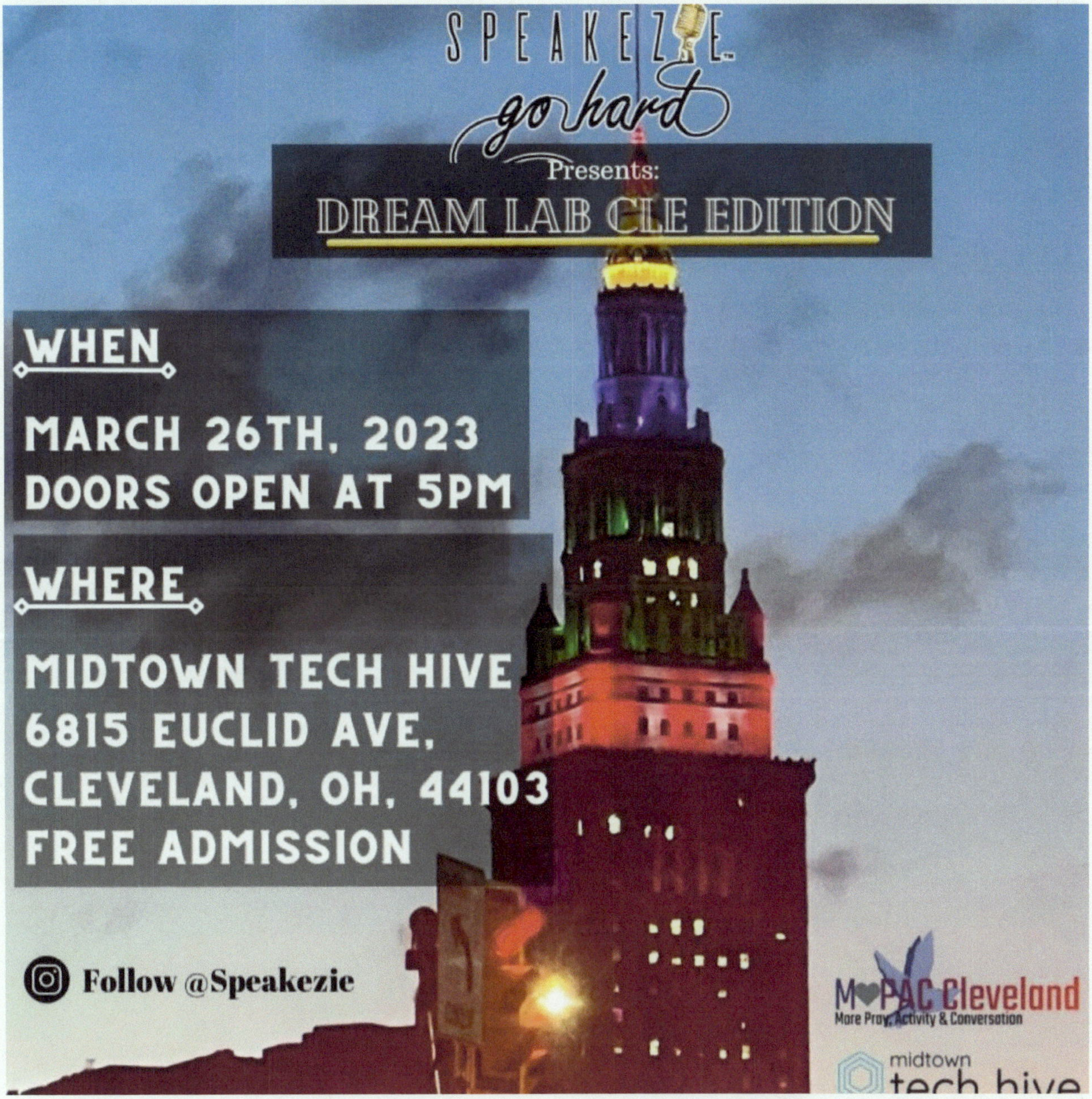

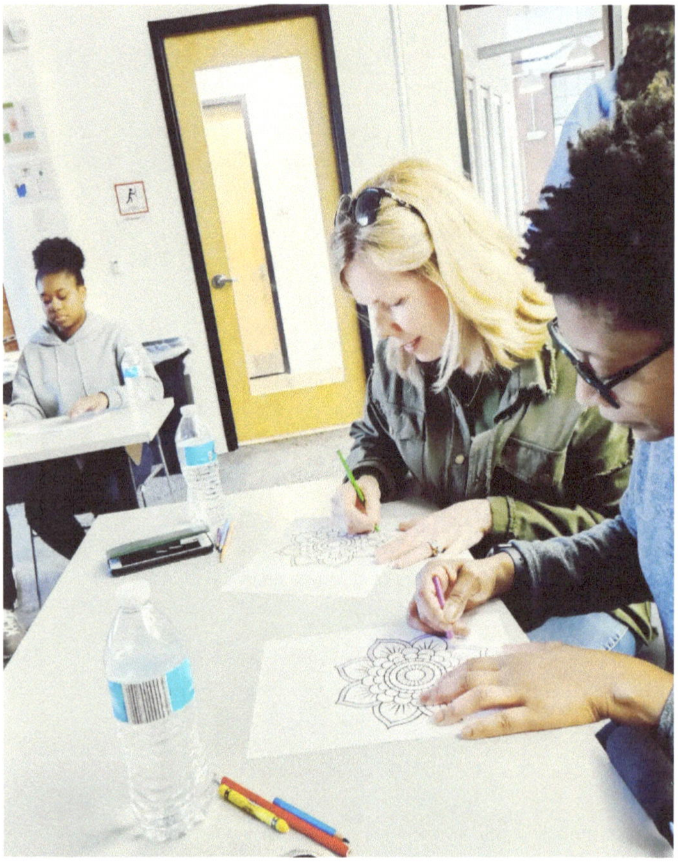

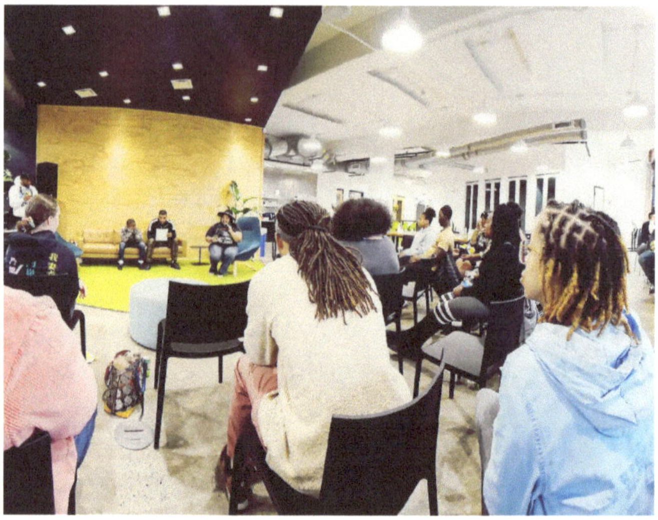

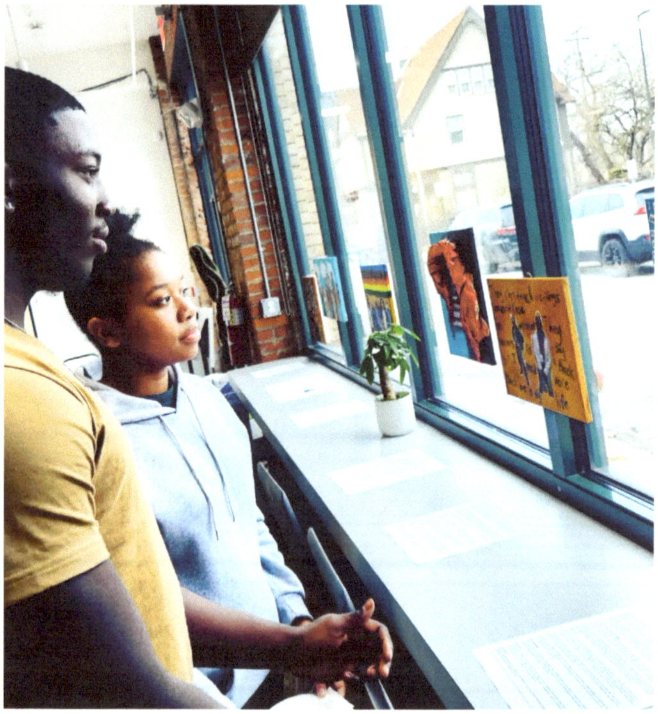

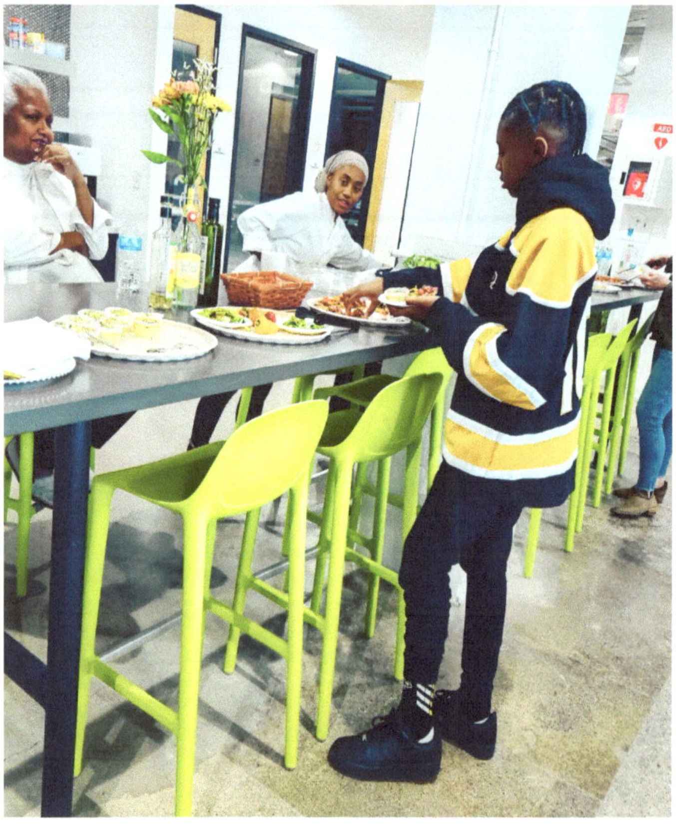

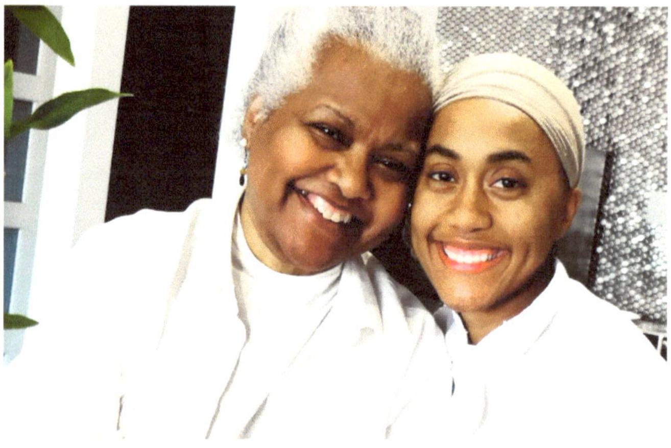

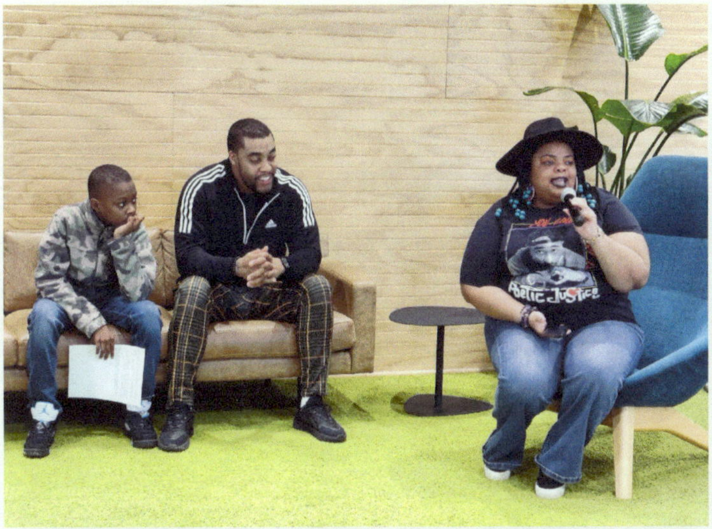

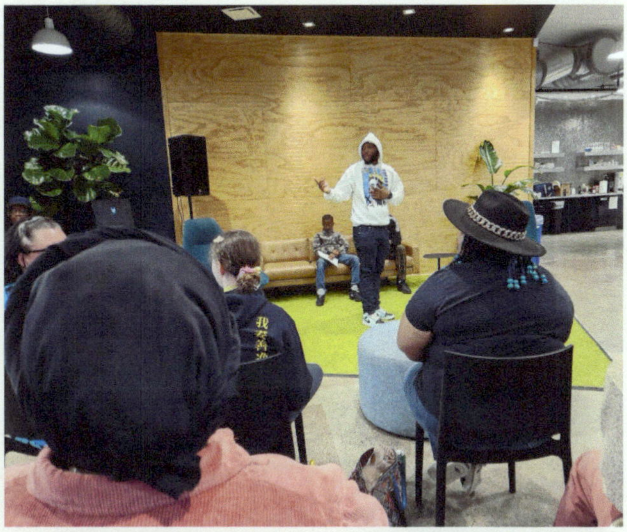

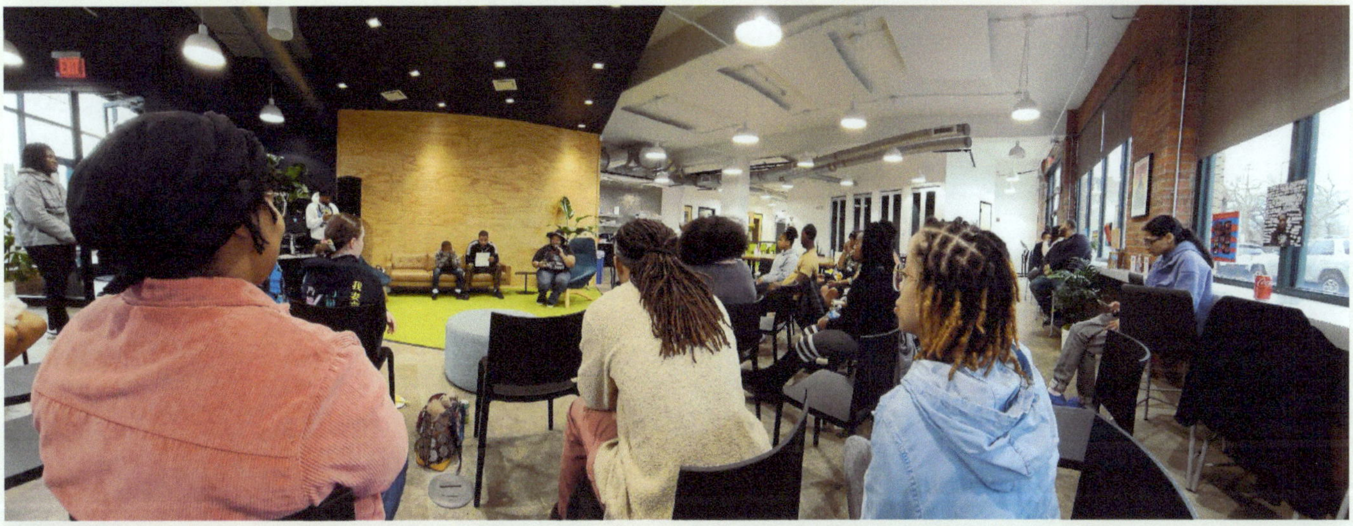

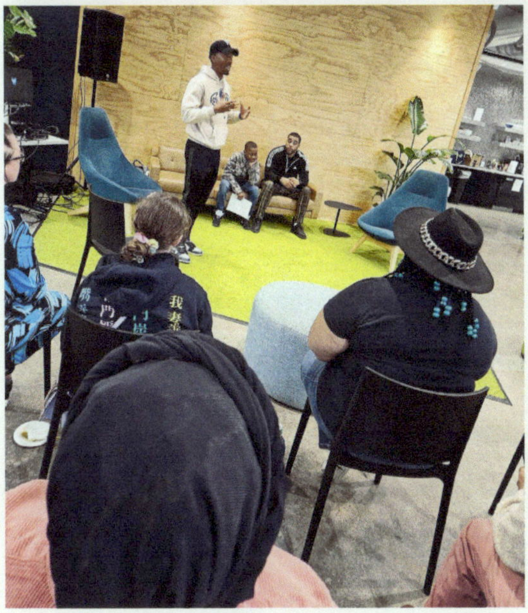

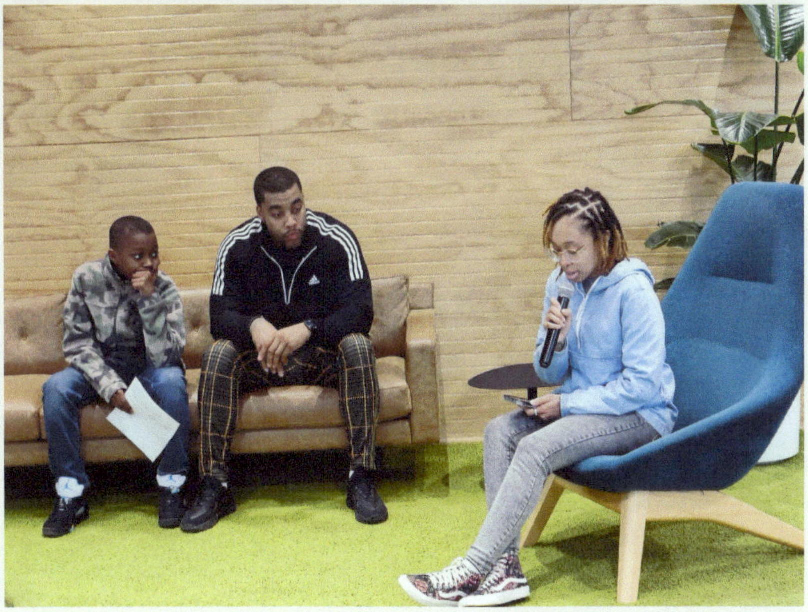

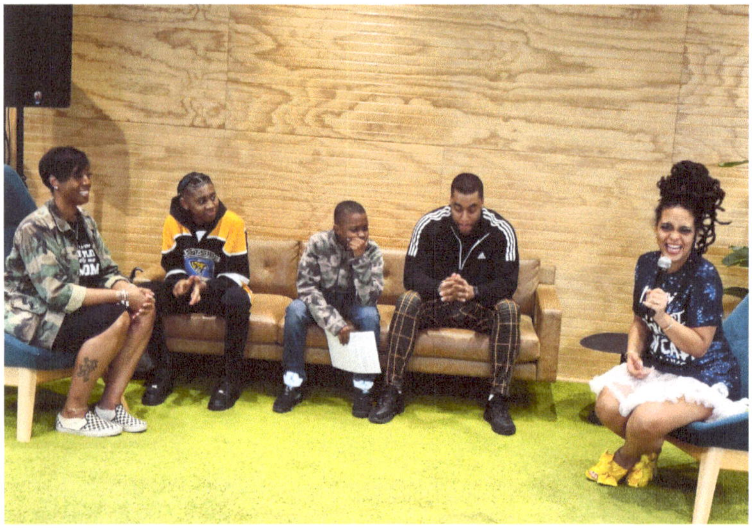

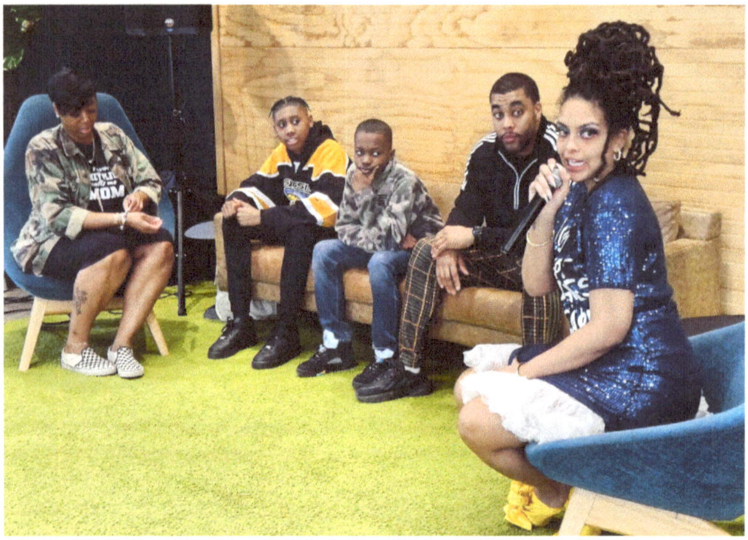
MOM

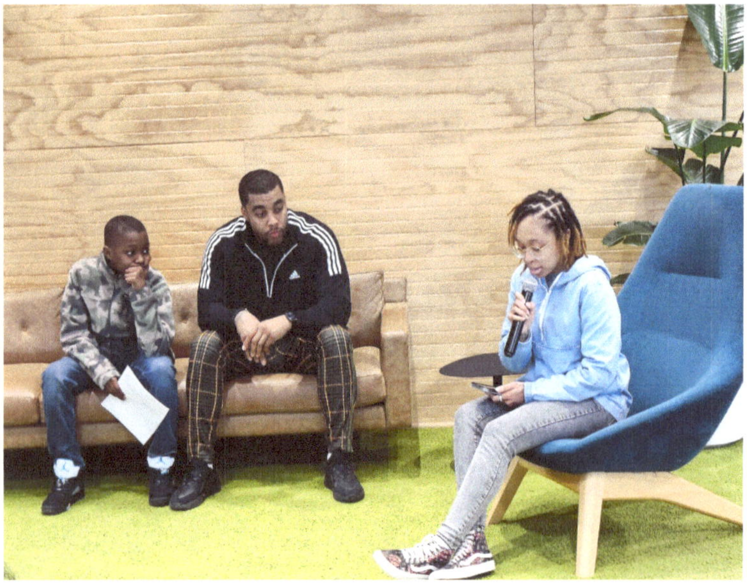

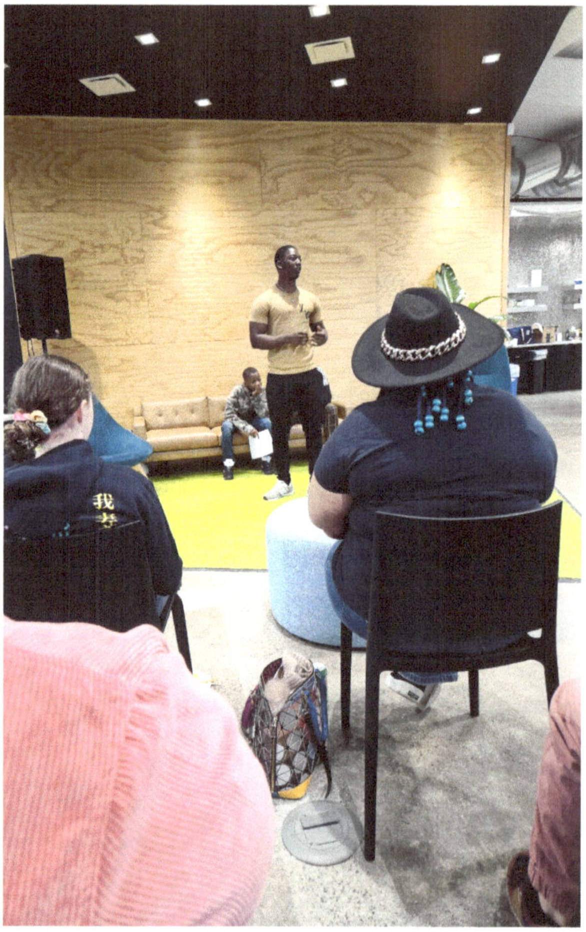

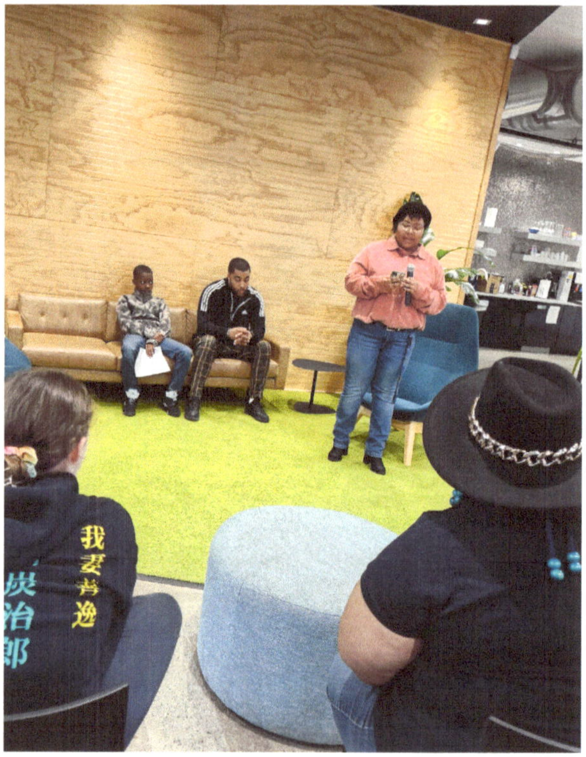
我妻善逸
炭治郎

HUMAN HEART STUDIOS

Art Exhibition

May 2023

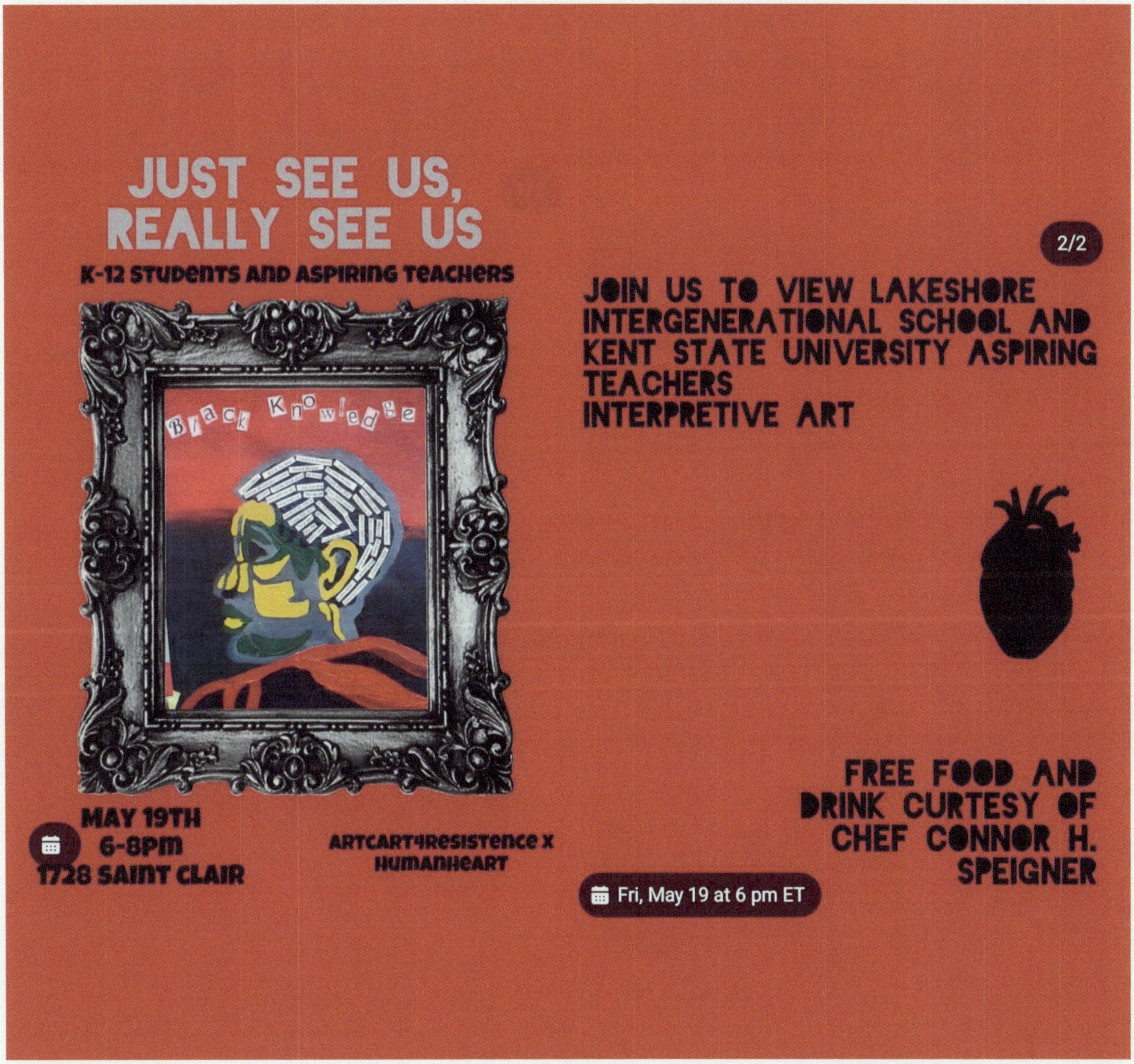

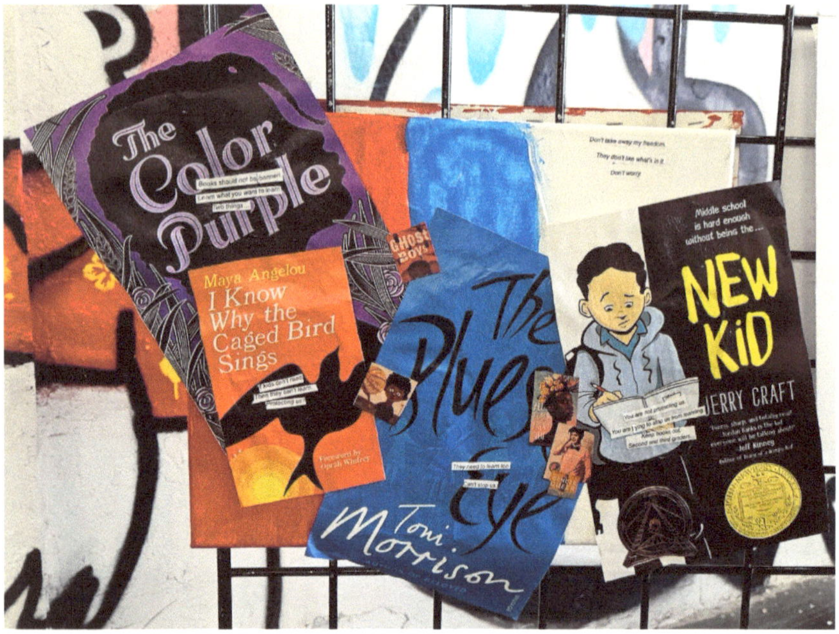
The Color Purple
Maya Angelou
I Know Why the Caged Bird Sings
The Bluest Eye
Toni Morrison
Middle school is hard enough without being the...
NEW KiD
JERRY CRAFT

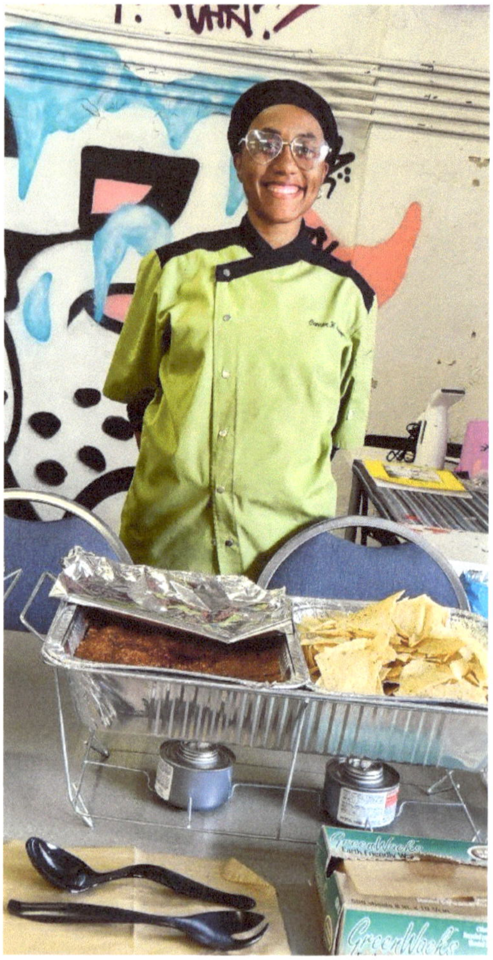

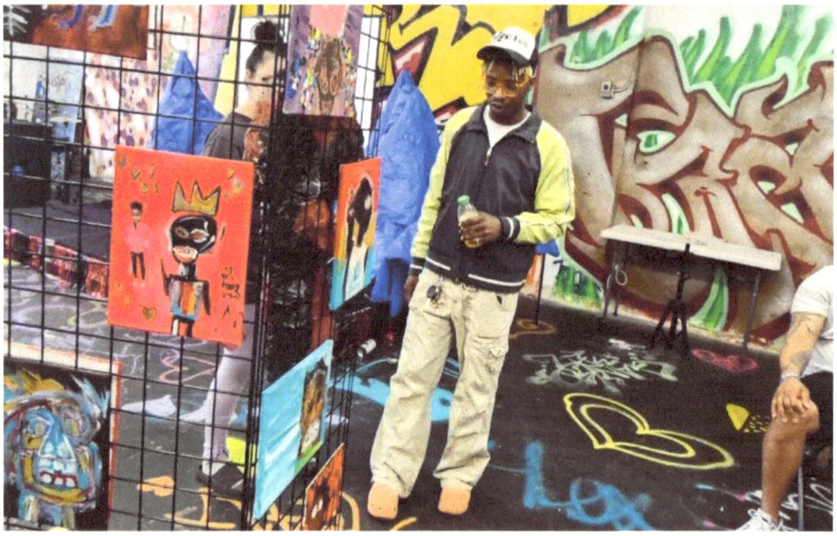

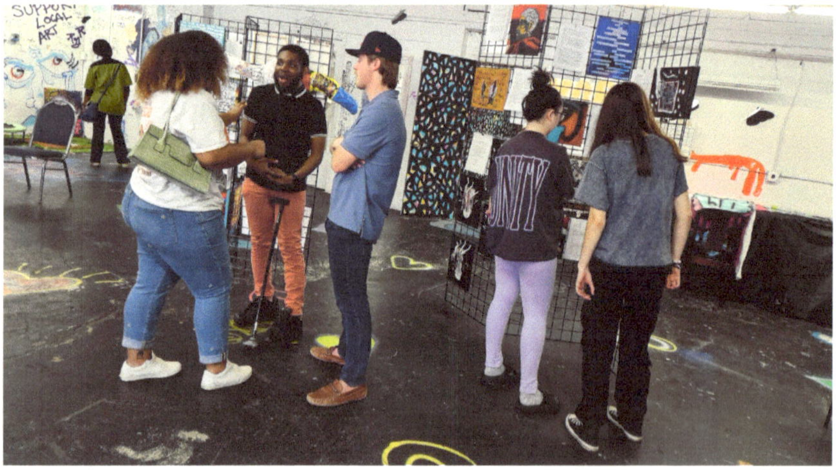

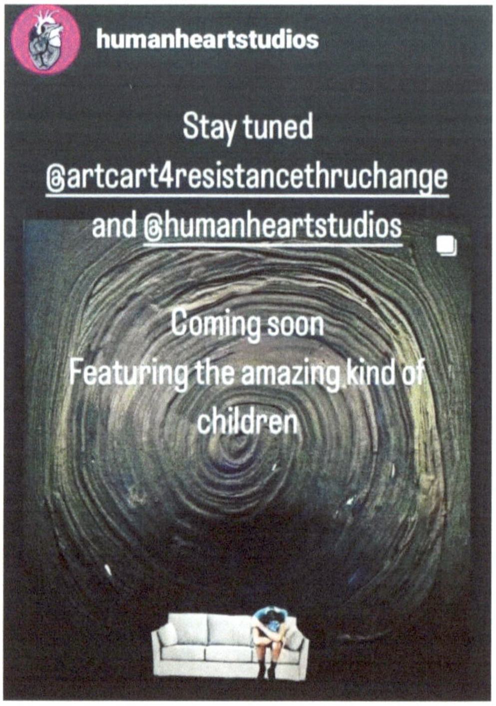
humanheartstudios
Stay tuned
@artcart4resistancethruchange
and @humanheartstudios
Coming soon
Featuring the amazing kind of
children

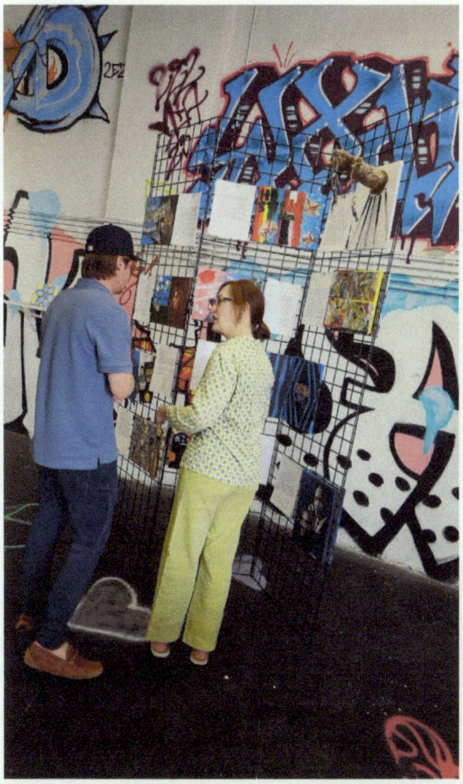

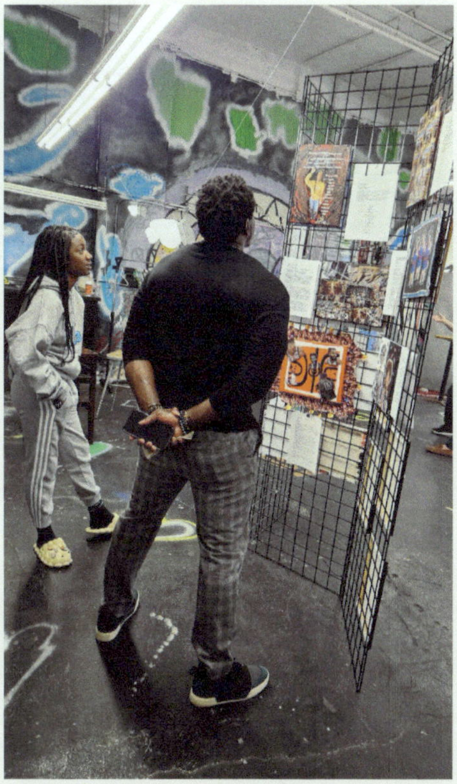

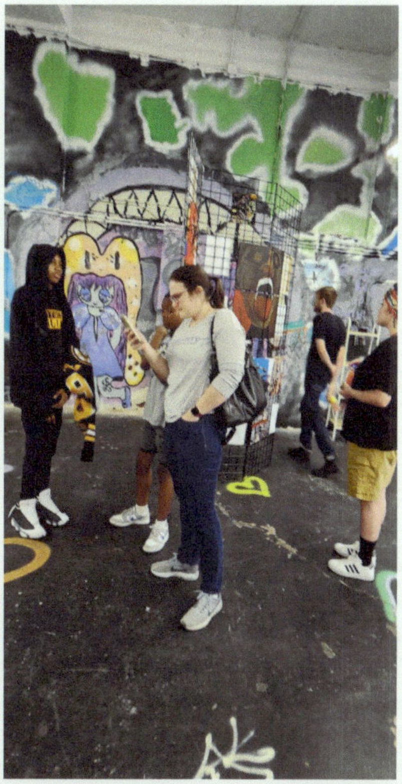

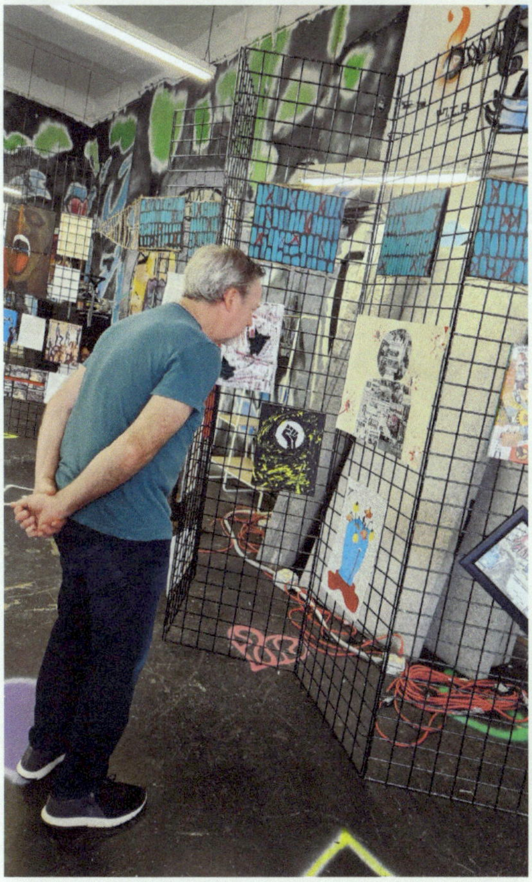

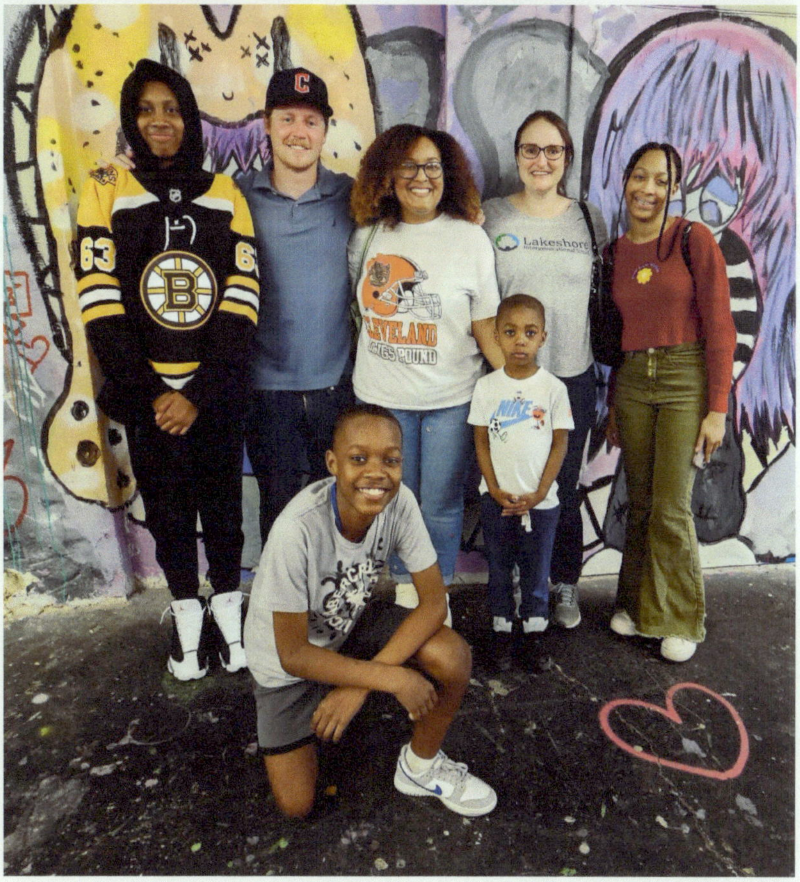
Lakeshore
NIKE

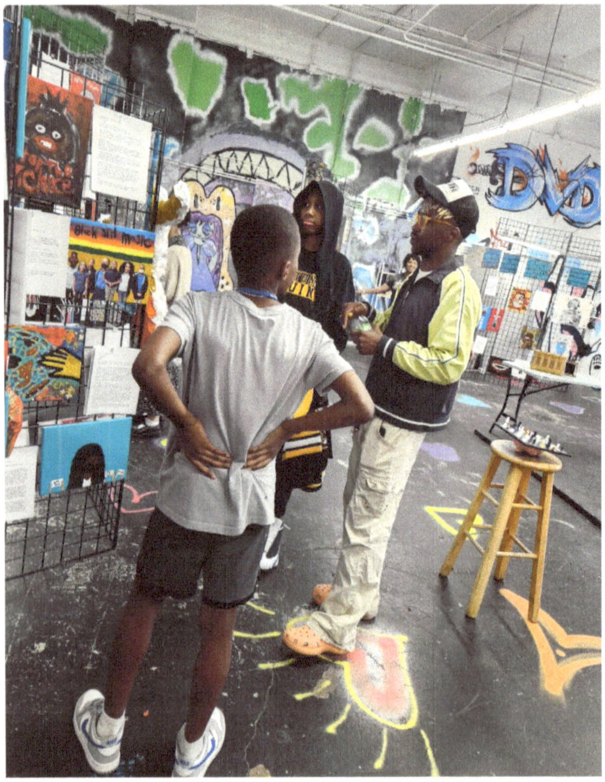

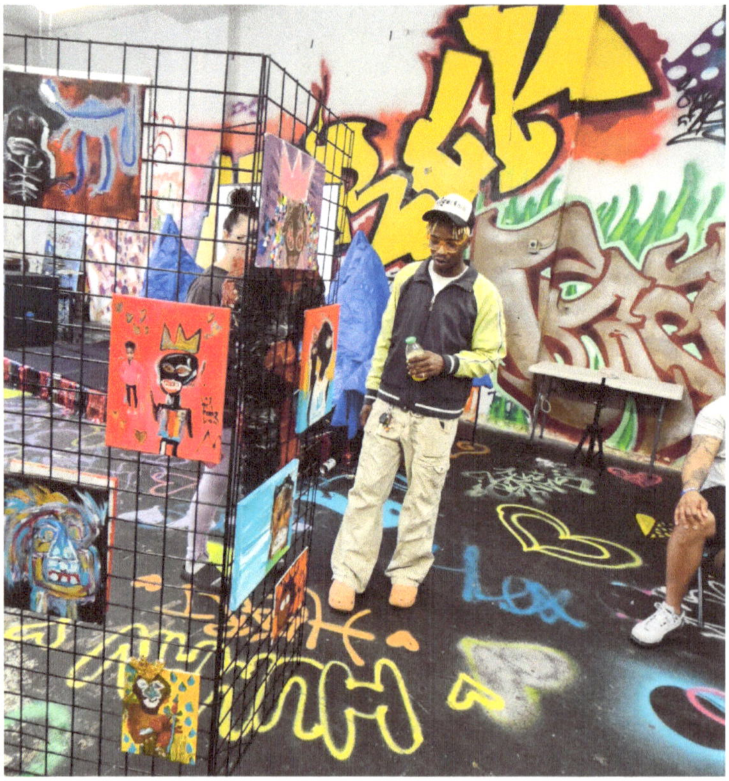

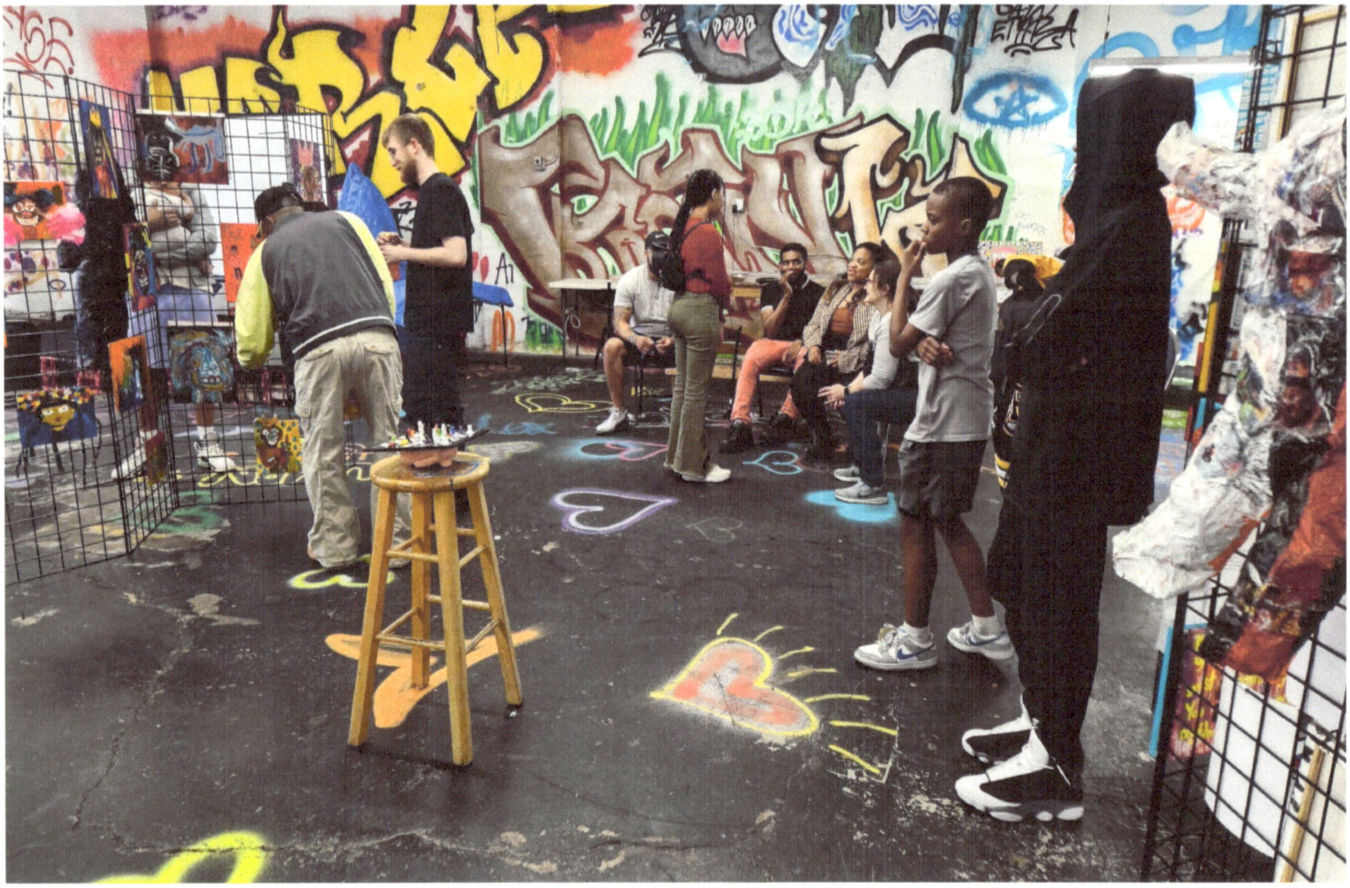

RADIO INVITATION

for Young Artists to Speak on Cleveland's WOVU 95.9 FM

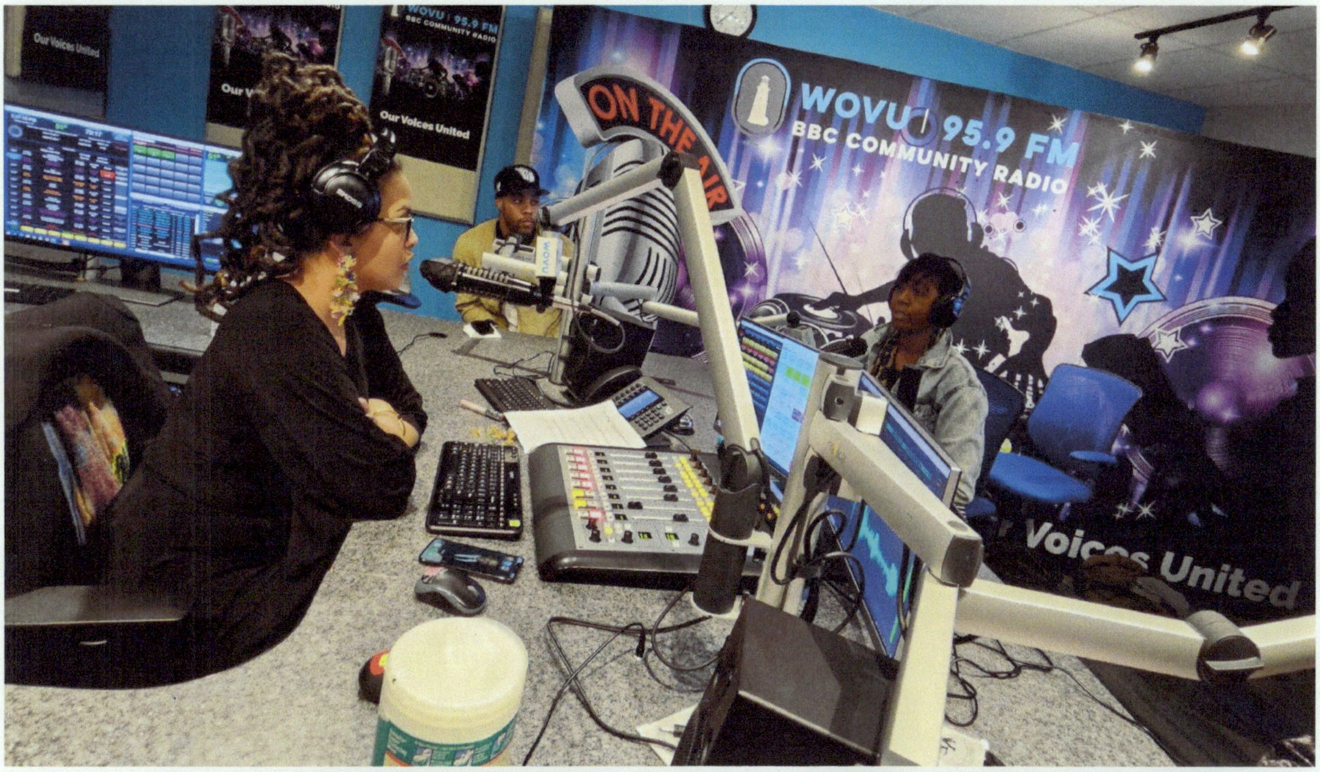

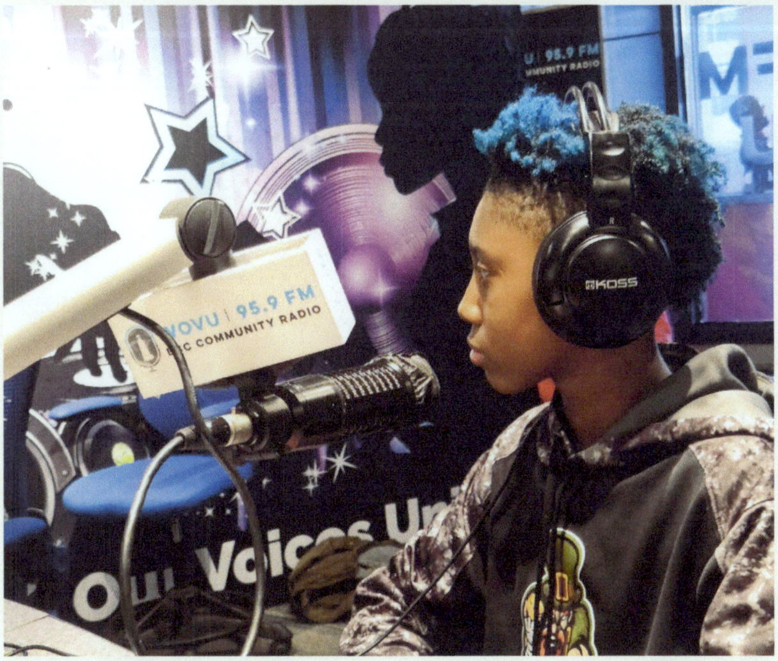

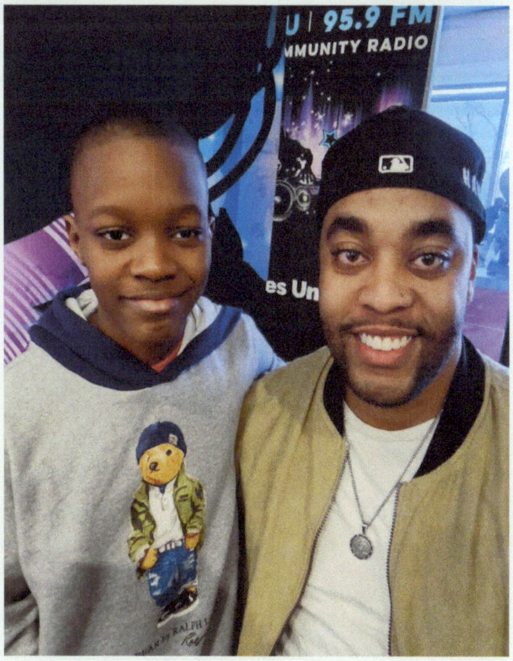

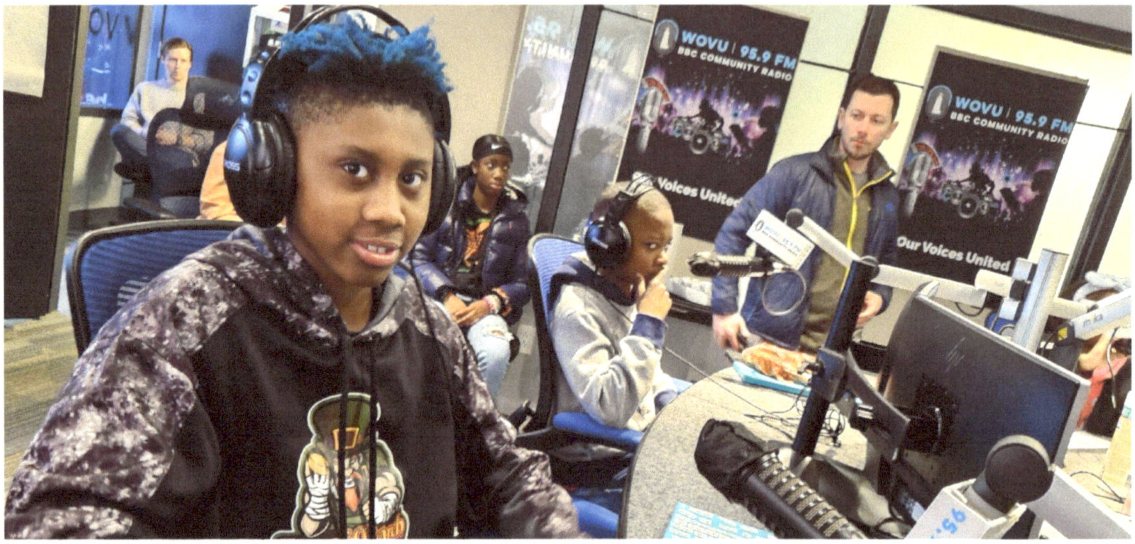
WOVU | 95.9 FM
BBC COMMUNITY RADIO
Our Voices United

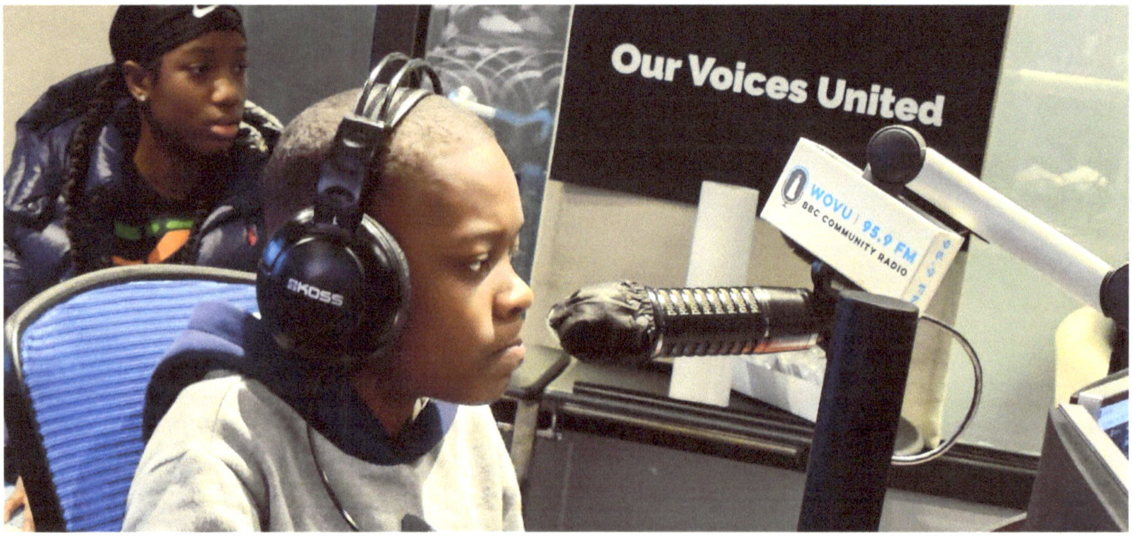
Our Voices United
WOVU | 95.9 FM
BBC COMMUNITY RADIO
KOSS

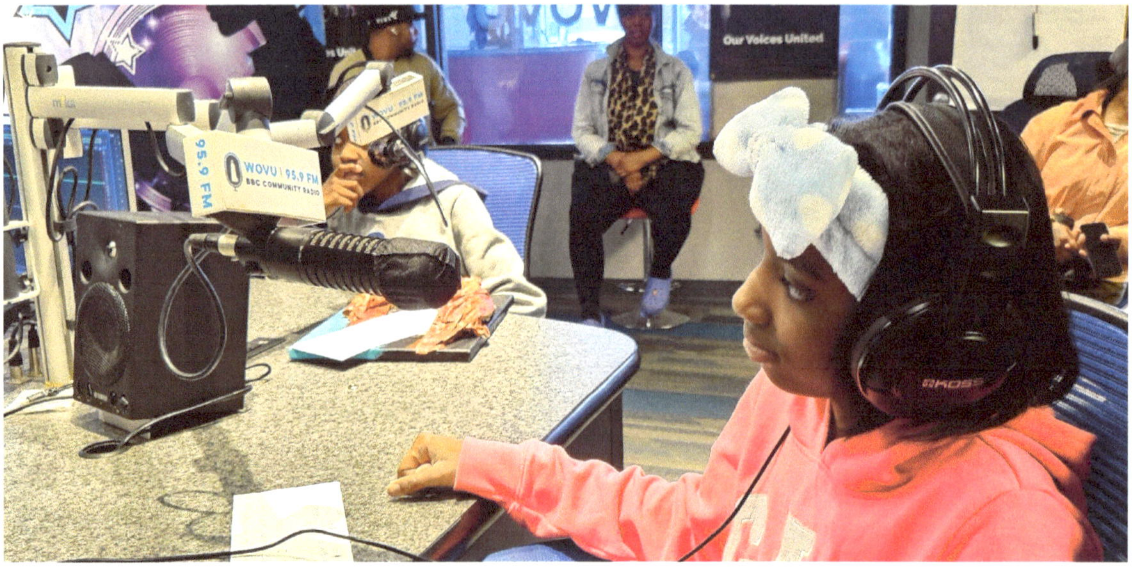
Our Voices United
WOVU | 95.9 FM
BBC COMMUNITY RADIO
KOSS

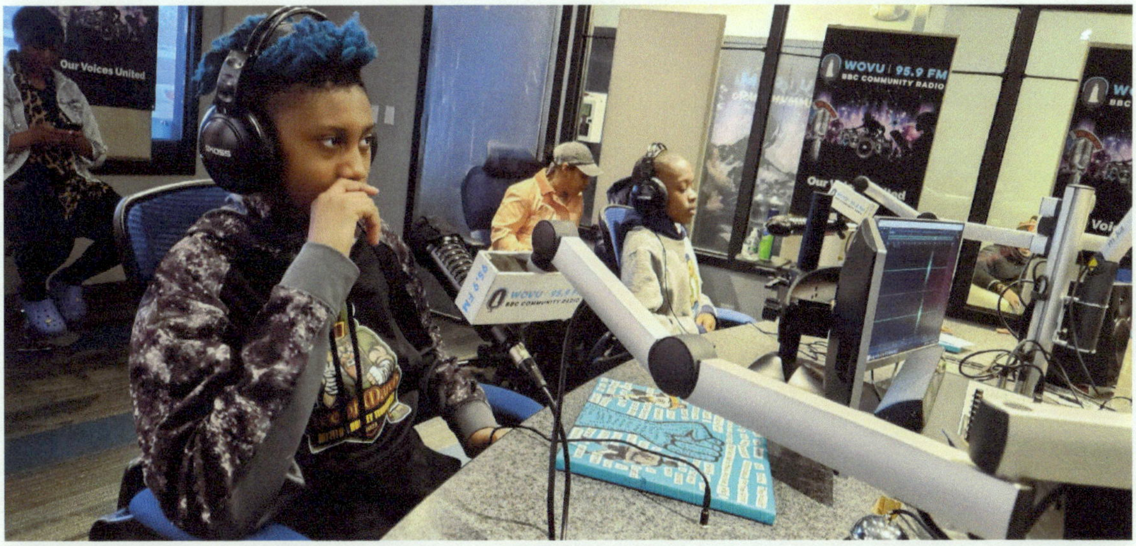
Our Voices United
WOVU | 95.9 FM
BBC COMMUNITY RADIO

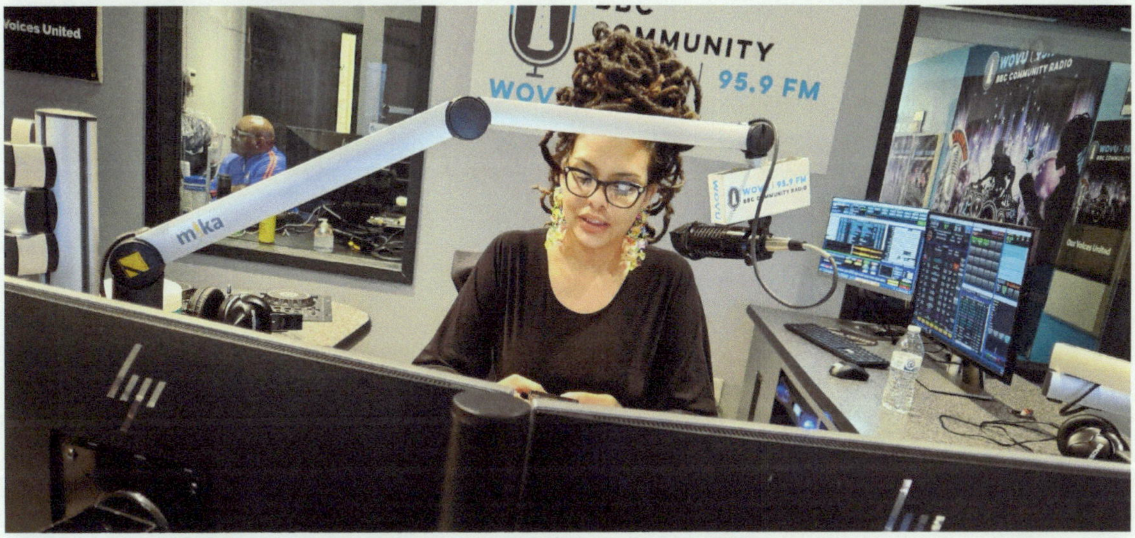
95.9 FM
BBC COMMUNITY RADIO
Our Voices United

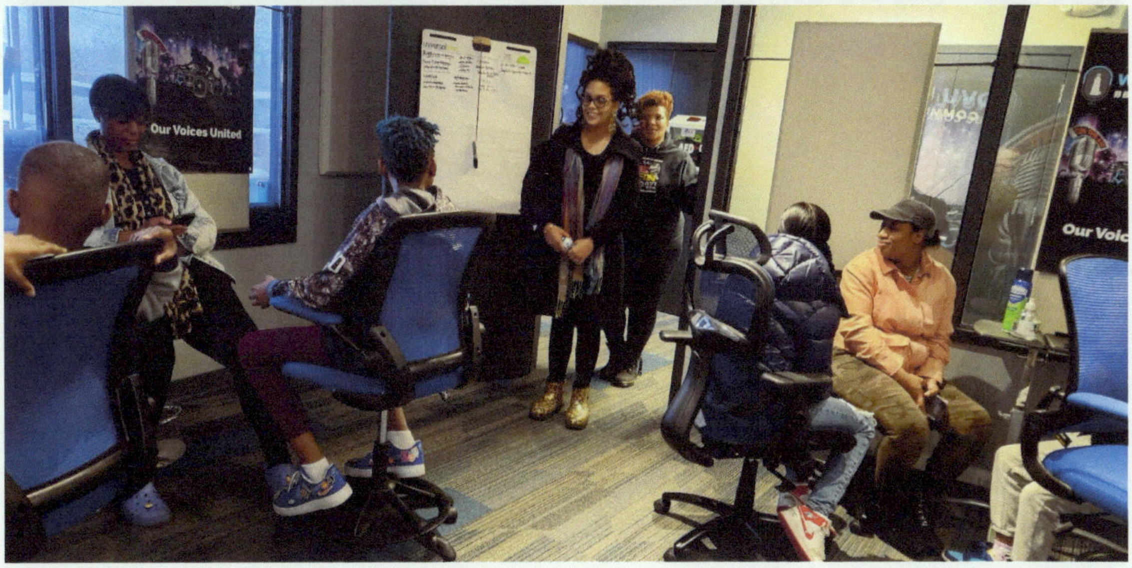
Our Voices United

TESTIMONIALS

"Keep breaking barriers, making change, being bold, standing tall and using your voice to empower yourselves and each other."

"You all have done such an amazing job! Every piece catches the eye with so many colors and shapes and dimensions, and on top of that they're emotive and thought-provoking. Thank you for sharing with us."

"This exhibition was great. I hope my son makes art as good as you kids one day. You all have very bright futures ahead. You guys will all be successful."

"The artwork was beautiful. The amount of creativity and level of detail was impressive. Art has changed a lot since I was in school. Inspirational."

"To me this exhibit gave me a deeper look at how my students view life and being black in America! I am so proud of all the pieces of art!

"I was impressed with how much the kids shared about their feelings and were able to translate those feelings and opinions into art. That grabbed my attention. They should do more of it."

"I was amazed at the writing and artwork of this project. The writing was very clear and vulnerable and I feel like I met each one of you through your voices and artwork."

"This exhibition was beautifully put together. It's nice to see the youth care about what's happening around them and want to make a new change about where they are going next. I'm excited to see where they go next in school and life."

"I am beyond blown away by all of your talent! You all show so much emotion in your pieces. It is moving. I can't wait to see everyone progress in their art careers."

"Everything looks great! There was a day or two where I had a bit of doubt regarding us getting everything finished but we got it done! Thanks for all of your help Christa."

"This exhibition was the first in a long time for me to experience. I enjoyed my evening to the fullest. Lets keep empowering our youth to be the best they can be at all times. Positivity is an upward bound, so lets keep striving."

"Great Artwork. Enjoyed Every piece."

"I am so amazed by the art that the kids have done. Everyone's statement was so powerful. Great job everyone."

"I am so honored and inspired. I hope all the students are proud of themselves. Soooo Good! We wanna see more ART."

"Wonderful Art. Keep up the good work."

"I was very amazed at the art that was displayed today at this event. Thank you for having us. Chris, I appreciate it alot, it means a lot also. Thank you for having me speak on stage."

"The students were amazing. I really love that they had a chance to be vocal in this kind of environment. Speakezie is something that is needed for our youth. Hopefully we'll be back for another one. Thanks Christa"

"I love the show! Keep up the great work! Keep at your dreams you are always heard!"

"Absolutely amazing. Everyone expressed themselves through their art with lots of emotion. I'm very proud of all these young talented adults."

Bad Racket Studio Collaboration

"Voices Matter" Podcast on Spotify

ART FOR RESISTANCE THROUGH CHANGE

Connect with Us

on Instagram

@ArtCart4ResistanceThruChange

@ARTCART4RESISTANCETHRUCHANGE

SCAN QR with your smartphone

www.ingramcontent.com/pod-product-compliance
Ingram Content Group UK Ltd.
Pitfield, Milton Keynes, MK11 3LW, UK
UKHW060039010826
14090UKWH00041B/285

* 9 7 9 8 9 8 9 4 7 4 4 1 7 *